SOUL MATES
Journey
— TO —
HEAVEN

DiAnnie shocks her fiancé, without notifying Thomas of
her arrival to their home One year of continuously
communicating online

THOMAS 'N DIANNIE

BALBOA.PRESS
A DIVISION OF HAY HOUSE

Balboa Press books may be ordered through booksellers or by contacting:

Balboa Press
A Division of Hay House
1663 Liberty Drive
Bloomington, IN 47403
www.balboapress.com
844-682-1282

Because of the dynamic nature of the Internet, any web addresses or links contained in this book may have changed since publication and may no longer be valid. The views expressed in this work are solely those of the author and do not necessarily reflect the views of the publisher, and the publisher hereby disclaims any responsibility for them.

The author of this book does not dispense medical advice or prescribe the use of any technique as a form of treatment for physical, emotional, or medical problems without the advice of a physician, either directly or indirectly. The intent of the author is only to offer information of a general nature to help you in your quest for emotional and spiritual well-being. In the event you use any of the information in this book for yourself, which is your constitutional right, the author and the publisher assume no responsibility for your actions.

Any people depicted in stock imagery provided by Getty Images are models,
and such images are being used for illustrative purposes only.
Certain stock imagery © Getty Images.

Scripture quotations marked KJV are from the Holy Bible, King James Version (Authorized Version). First published in 1611. Quoted from the KJV Classic Reference Bible, Copyright © 1983 by The Zondervan Corporation.

Print information available on the last page.

ISBN: 978-1-9822-7519-8 (sc)
ISBN: 978-1-9822-7520-4 (e)

Balboa Press rev. date: 09/30/2021

CONTENTS

DEDICATION

Our soul's journey walking through this life together, granted through God's grace, everything matters. "On earth, as it is in heaven." This series of manuscripts is a dedication of God's love that is obtainable.

INTRODUCTION

They walked into each other's dreams, and God's love was revealed through this romantic dimension of love. After a year of continuous messaging, emailing, and telephone calls, DiAnnie and Thomas finally come together for the first time.

Thomas and DiAnnie's first communication was on 15 February 2018 on a Christian free dating website. Thomas was praying at the time, feeling that his soulmate was in heaven waiting for him. DiAnnie tired of dating immature men, was drawn to Thomas's profile on this Christian dating site. DiAnnie tapped Thomas on the shoulder with the most extremely long email of introduction. On the same website, Thomas was taking a Bible testing quiz, which he enjoyed.

For many years, Thomas has been approached by other ladies with just one line, leading to them wanting money sent to them. Thomas instantly had his supernatural spiritual feeling, "God, are you kidding me?"

DiAnnie and her mother, Anna, supernaturally prayed for this love that DiAnnie would find with Thomas. James 1:27. *Pure religion and undefiled before God and the Father is this. To visit the fatherless and widows in their affliction and to keep himself unspotted from the world.*

Thomas living alone for many years, kept himself unspotted from the world and dreaming of a love he had never experienced, and their romance together has only strengthened through their communication.

From that time forward, Thomas and DiAnnie have written two books prior to this one. "Introductory series, "Soulmates Journey to Heaven" and "Soulmate's Journey to Heaven" published within the month "Series 1, Soulmates Journey to Heaven"

With all of its twists and turns, this ongoing romance of the most romantic love would like nothing more than to share this with others. I am mostly concern with the heart and the inner part of a person, you are a unique person, and I appreciate you as you are.

True enjoyment is when you have someone that pours out their heart to you. I realize that our being together isn't just by accident.

Ecclesiastes 4: 9-12. *Two are better than one; because they have a good reward for their labor. For if they fall, the one will lift up his fellow; but woe to him that is alone when he falls, for he has no other to help him up. Again, if to lie together, they have heat; but how can one be warm alone? And if one prevails against them, two shall withstand them; and a threefold cord is not quickly broken.*

The Holy Spirit is the strength of the cord in God's love for marriage without one harsh word. As stated in the Lord's prayer. "On earth, as it is in heaven."

Not only does Thomas and DiAnnie have many things in common and complement each other spiritually, continuously learning about one another and teaching and changing through their daily communication. DiAnnie has a mother who is a widow. DiAnnie being fatherless at the age of 14 years young. Unfortunately, DiAnnie and her mother, Anna, are the only family they have. DiAnnie has been caring for her mother, who suffers from depression. And the first thing, DiAnnie's mother said without knowing Thomas. "Respect him." A mother's intuition very early on in their relationship still astounds Thomas, one year since they first met online.

DiAnnie being fatherless and Anna being a widow allows Thomas to show Anna the love he never had the opportunity to show his mother. Thomas never realizes that he could have demonstrated his mother more love, although Thomas loved his mother to pieces. And until you miss a mother's love, you may never understand. Thomas is looking forward to showing unconditional love with reverence and lovingkindness to the fatherless and a widow. God has blessed Thomas, DiAnnie, and Anna with a prayer so miraculously brought them together in so many ways, very difficult for Thomas to comprehend or understand at times.

God's love is revealed through another dimension of these manuscripts that have been written down continuously and daily. It is a beautiful dream that you have, and when you wake up, it disappears, or you come to the understanding that it was only a dream.

The miracles and the love are revealed through a dimension of God's love that cannot be explained, imagined, or understood. All the languages in the world, deeper than all the oceans, and as far as the eye can see, and the mind cannot understand, does not even scratch the surface of the love God has for his children.

The devil continuously prowls around Thomas and DiAnnie with the power of persuasion and lies, trying to destroy this union from coming together, and Satan is going out of his way. Although the devil trembles at the holiest highest name, "Jesus Christ." Thomas, DiAnnie, and Anna are all devout Christians and have danced with the devil before. Although the devil is very cunning powerful, baffling, lies, destroys and will kill one of God's children without hesitation.

Thomas and DiAnnie devote their lives to God and service, through spiritual discernment to help others, not-for-profit or prestige, proceeds donated. God willing, God's love revealed slowly will help many hundreds of thousands of others get to heaven, informing the world of this love so miraculously given through the grace of God.

Thomas and DiAnnie, through their prayers, unshakable faith, have strengthened this love so tightly bound together that neither of them can break this love if they tried. Their hearts have been bonded before they were born. God's love matches their souls; they consume each other's thoughts with this love through prayer, giving God thanks continuously. As you will read, the miracle of them coming together happens supernaturally.

God only says this once in the Bible. John 15: 13. – *There is no love greater than this, that one should lay down his life for his friend.* Thomas's sense of humor and laughter mesmerizes DiAnnie, and Thomas will give his life for DiAnnie and her mother, Anna, in a heartbeat without hesitation. The devil works through others, thinking that DiAnnie is a romance scammer, and Thomas is very gullible. Only because it's been over one year, and they have never met until now.

And all of those souls are witnessing a miracle just by seeing DiAnnie and Thomas together. And everyone seems to be excited and overwhelmed that this beautiful Guardian Angel treasure, DiAnnie would come into this man's life with the thorns in his flesh without question. Lust and greed take; love gives. Thomas and DiAnnie know with their unshakable faith that this love cannot be purchased with all the money in the world.

Matthew 19: 6. – *Wherefore they are no more twain, but one flesh. What therefore God has joined together, let not man put asunder.* Thomas has already asked DiAnnie to marry him, and DiAnnie accepted without reservation. And this was shortly after they had just met online, and Anna, DiAnnie's mother, with her intelligent intuition, said, "respect him."

Ephesians 2: 22. – *In whom you also are built together for a habitation of God through the spirit.* Nothing happens perchance, and everything happens for a reason.

2 Corinthians 6: 1. – *We then, as workers together with God, beseech you also that you receive not the grace of God in vain.* Thomas and DiAnnie have received this love through the grace of God, and when they pray, this is acknowledging love for God and thanks for giving this romantic love freely.

CHAPTER 1

Romantic Memoirs From Heaven, January 2019

1 January 2019

DiAnnie wrote:

Hello Mr.,

I hope you are having a great and blessed day. Mine is going great, and I realized you messaged me several times. I had to take my time to read everything so imagine how much I am smiling with all the things you said, and you are surely a talkative Zorro, those that talk much are the best writers that's what people say so I can see that from you whenever you talk to me on the phone or write to me.

Glad to know that you're having a great day; mine was great; I had a busy day, so it is nice being back home and messaging you, and I will get some rest later. It's good to fast and pray because that's where our power lies as children of God. Please don't work out too much, and it is good to work out, though, but not too much; as long you keep healthy, it is okay then working out till you have poor health. Well, I know thoughts come to us sometimes, both negative and positive, and you know our God is never negative. He made everything good, so without believing Him that all is perfect is thinking from Satan. I'm glad you always realize which is good, no one is ever too big before God, and it's only those that love God that recognizes the wrong they do.

Awwe! Brian must be a hard-working person! At age 63, not sure I'm right and doing all the cleaning? God did give him a strong body, and it's just sad that his life isn't responsible at his age; I wish he realizes that, with his lifestyle, I don't think he's going to ever think about living a responsible life, also I believe the help and respect you give him couldn't be gotten from others, not much people would want to have people such as Brian around them, God always chose the rejected in society and make them people after His heart, and that's what are doing, you took a rejected man, and you are a blessing to him by providing him with a good life that he cannot get out there.

I appreciate him for making your home clean, and he must also appreciate you for being a Godly man; if not, life would've been so sad for him. I'm a hard worker and don't mind doing things at all; I'm a simple person and always ready to help others. Going to places and pushing you in the wheelchair would make people understand true Love; all I want is for people to appreciate God that He is Love, and it's all we need.

Reading about the story you sent about King David and King Saul brought tears to my eyes; it sure when a person is a God-fearing person, they can even show Love to their enemies. I wish people would read these stories and see how much God has wanted humans to love one another. We say we love God we have never seen but cannot love those on this earth with us. I realize most biblical stories are there to teach us Love from the old testament to the new testament, Jesus preaches to us about Love, so it is Love till the end. I do learn a lot from you, honey.

You're so silly, Thomas, and you think I would be bowlegged and be walking around like that? If I ever have to walk like that and was ask why I am walking that way, I'll surely tell people you made me like that... lol I guess they would think I'm crazier, right? I know we would never speak out these things outside, just kidding.

Sorry I keep making you hard. It saddens me, and I really must hurry to be with you before something crazy happens to you, and Brian asks why you are so huge in your boxer shorts? It would be me, so I don't want that. You will have all of me to yourself, which will also make me feel good having on top of me. I like all the fun you and Brian have; I know he gets to your nerves sometimes. Still, it is really funny when I am reading about what goes on there between you two, and I guess he likes being around you too. He is learning in a way because if he goes to do drugs, he would have been dead by now. He is alive because of you.

Wow, so you took off in the car and were leaving Brian there? I guess he said in his heart I'm finished! Lol, no, I guess you were very mad at him for having your credit cards go missing. Was it debit or regular credit cards? Good, you were able to get them back. When I come there, I will call him Forgetful Brian! lol hope he's not going to hate me for my hard jokes, and I'm just as silly as you two. I know that kind of look that can be like a guilty face, and sure it's like a lost child hahaha, Brian realize you're a good man. Please never change for the person you are okay with; that's why I love you and many others.

Oh sure I will be glad to be with my mother soon, we have missed each other for a few months, so it's going to be a long talk when I join for the first night, she's undoubtedly going to explain from the first day she left, she talks a lot just like you. lol. Thanks so much, my Love. The word Jesus is the most powerful word, and I know as God's children, we will have trials, but He's going to be with us. Thanks for the reminder. I have heard of Billy Graham, and I didn't know he has passed!

You make me smile whenever you talk about a warm massage. I so need it right now with the cold weather here, with those hands of yours, a Marine massage too. Sure it would put me in an instant sleep, and you know what a lady likes, honey.

You make me laugh so much, and my riding tornado is so funny. I can't stop laughing. I guess those divorce papers brought back old memories, I can imagine, and it has been a long since you are alone; it's not easy, but such is life, and I'm glad God has chosen me for you for this life journey. You are so right; when God is preparing His elect, it takes many years; sometimes, when people heard of 40 years or 100 years in bible stories, it's like it was just a story, but these years are actual, and it only takes a person with faith to endure. I have never felt this Love before, the one we share is indeed a God sent, and it's only our two hearts that genuinely understands.

I so appreciate all the sweet compliments. You make me feel like a lady each time you say all these nice things to me. How will I ever be able to think about another man? My heart is falling for you day by day, month by month, and I am sure years from now, it will be years after years and eternal because it will continue even when we leave this world. How did it go with Brian last night? Did he come back with the car? I hope he was a good guy.

I do agree with you about marriage. Many people expect a marriage to be like a planned miracle that they will not make happen. People are hoping that things will get in place after marriage, not knowing nothing changes.

It's the same old Thomas and me in the marriage, and without our collective work, the marriage can't work as we want, it's like our own lives, God gives us life, if we can't *make sound decisions, our lives cannot go the way we want it. When I talk about these things to my age mates, they think a young girl isn't supposed to be feeling so critical like I do, but then we are not staying young forever here. It's not a promise. You and I agree so much on many things, and I realize that our being together isn't just by accident; I'm not sure I can understand any other man as I do with you. We are so connected.*

Thanks so much for giving me updates on all that is going on there. I am honored that you think about all the future dreams for you and me and our kids, and I appreciate all your messages and know that there's nothing that can separate us ever. I'm such an exhauster now and will try to get things in order and go to the store and rest later.

All my heart and prayers to you.

Warm hugs and kisses to my handsome man.

2 January 2019

DiAnnie wrote;

Good morning my Love,

I hope you're having a great time, mine is going great. No work today; I'm just tired after yesterday. Guess you're as well. Normally after New Year's day, people get so tired. Anyway sorry that I didn't write back like I promised yesterday, good I'm doing that now.

Ah, my knees? They hurt when I don't expect that's why I said they act funny.. lol thanks for all the compliments concerning me loving God. I know where He took me from to be the good girl I am today, the reason I put Him first in my life. When looking physically around me as a young girl, there's seem to be many challenges, too many temptations, but there seems to be hope with Him. Sure not many young girls want to follow God, and I know you're right, I think one of the reasons seems to be that they still feel young and there's still time to give their lives to God, but the truth is the time is now! Yes, we have many similarities between us, our dads, birthdays, wanting a Godly relationship, the both of us is simple, and many more that I feel we did not accidentally meet.

Do you like to tickle? It would be nice in bed or whenever we both are alone. You're right. God does not call us home according to our wish but his, and no one knows, very sad, but then He loves us and knows best for us. I am excited as well, and things seem to be wrapping up fast for my trip. I'm preparing and will update you on how it's all goes. I am anxious and can't wait to see other places; I will have you with me in my heart where I go and be with you a few times. Who knows, we may travel in the future together.

Do you think I'm funny? You do more than me.. lol see you raise the amount to test my patience. What in the world would I want to do with $143 million! The $20 million was a big issue already.. lol so imagine more; I'm like you. I don't think I need that much money in my life, and I would change to be a silly girl who knows. Lol. Sure, with that huge money that you get like that from a lottery ticket, if not careful or mindful may change a person for the worse, so yes, I agree with you that you may be that minister that mistreats others. Hope not in our lives to mistreat each other.

You're good at changing subjects, and you still haven't forgotten about having those 12 kids too. Lol, I wouldn't mind having those many kids if I give birth without pain. It's the most challenging experience for women. So if you were a lady, I guess 12 children would be like killing me, hahaha. Sure, children are the biggest blessing in this life, and I really would be happy having just 3 or 4 with you, let's say 4, 2 girls, and two boys. They would give us enough grandkids, agree? Oh yes, bringing the children up in a decent manner is another challenging part, and I thank God for my mother. She did well for me. I see, so I believe we must've met in February or January. What is essential is the fact that we are still in touch and still loving each other. God is working everything out for the best.

Aww! thanks very much. I think my intelligence and intuition are not my being smart. Still, God's way of making my life the way He wants, you recognizing this means a lot to me, tells me you are a person who also follows God's directions and sees the good of others. I have always prayed in my life to be a help to others who are in need both physically and spiritually.

You'll like when I tie you up for several hours? I would tie you up and tease you because I will tie you up and get nude, and you will beg to have a hold of me. When you realize that I'm all nude or in my lovey clothes, just my bra and pant would have you all anxious to say, hey babe, sorry untie me, and it would only be because you see that I am lovey. I know that's just what you will do. Haha, your testicles are getting back to normal? From the operation of the vasectomy the other time? That's cool because when I get there, I would like you to perform well in bed, I'll be all yours, and I want you to enjoy me. You're not disrespectful at all, you're my husband to be, and you got all the

5

right to be naughty sometimes. I dream about us too, and it will surely be interesting when I am there sleeping naked in the same bed. I may do the same at some point, but not now. We will see. You are right; God does not hate it when a male and female wish to come together and be one, He created that, and sure it's the moral part He wants. You are also a romantic person, and when I think about you, a lot of love desire also comes to me, so we two are so in each other's thoughts.

I have asked myself this from time to time about gay men and women. What do they feel? Naturally, there's no feeling that exists when two women are even naked or lying in bed. I guess it's the same as men. Nothing is natural about such love lives for the same Love. Why the two didn't love for the other to give birth to that little girl, but they adopted? The laws are sick because they are man-made. Some of those judges, lawyers, presidents are in these acts, so they accept it. I have heard from many people that Arizona has those types of people very much. Only a male and female can have love intercourse and have children. God made it that way, from humans to animals.

Well, yes, thanks to my mother and God for making me the girl I am. If not, I don't think you would have loved me or me. You ask many questions, not bad at all. Yes, I'm doing okay right now, yesterday I attended a party for a girl from work, and it was a grand one, it was her birthday, so imagine birthday mixed with New Year and it was just a lot of partying. I'm very tired, and I know after this message I will get enough sleep for the day.. lol. My favorite color is purple, I got a few colors, but purple is. My favorite flower is Carnation. My preferable candy is Big Turk. My most precious stone is a diamond. hehe, my favorite food is Poutine.

I understand your heart very much for me, and I know you truly love me, and I do the same as well. Do you think you're a dumb Marine? Hahaha, not really. You're just the silly type of guy I love very much. Sure it's only God we should fear because He's the only one that knows our beginning and end, I appreciate your Love, and it would be great to protect my Mom and me. We are ladies, and most of the time, we ladies are vulnerable, and men take advantage when you least expect. You're genuinely a God-fearing man, and I appreciate you being a part of our lives. Honey, you don't have to explain how much you love me. I understand that and appreciate that true Love is always beyond human understanding, and that's what we share.

Thanks very much for the lengthy message. It always pleases my heart to hear from you. Enjoy your day and Happy New year once again. I included a pic during the party yesterday.

Warm hugs and kisses from the girl that loves you with all her heart!

3 January 2019

DiAnnie wrote;

Good morning my love,

I'm smiling right now as I read your message, lol you must have good eyes to see the quality of my dress. I appreciate your compliment very much. Well, diamonds are precious stones, I think the most valuable stone so far in the world, I have always dreamed of having one, but that doesn't mean I can't live without it. No worries about sending a package of all these candies and foodstuff for now, soon I'll be traveling, and I think it wouldn't be necessary for now. When I come to Arizona, I will have all these,

Yes, we will have one child at a time. Getting pregnant isn't a month, remember, it's a nine months process, so having one child at a time would be cool, you arouse because of what I said about what I will do to you? Sure, that's what I will do.. lol. Thanks for reminding me about being beautiful. I don't think I am sometimes; I am only trying as hard as I can to take good care of myself. I think you are a good singer, and yes, do the copyright after. I did enjoy your songs the other time you sang for me when you left the voice message. I said to myself that you sounded like Kenny Rogers.. lol.

Sure it was a great time on New Year's day compare to Christmas because I had to be with the girl from church who was ill. Another busy time is about to start, but at least I was able to rest yesterday. That was good for my health too. I know many girls my age does not think like me, and I am indeed far ahead of them, and I don't think it's because of me but the fact that God is in my life. Yes, no humans can be similar 100%. There will always be a little different, so that's not bad. Your favorite flower is a rose? What kind or color of rose? Let me know, okay. I know our fathers are with us, and they always want the best for us, and yes, there are some great similarities between us, and it's only coming from God's plan for our lives.

I wish I were there because I would give myself to you and have me all to yourself, and then you would be alright. I know soon you'll have all the sweet time with me and me with you. I look up to that too. I know there are temptations all around us, but being faithful to each other will make it impossible to fall into that. I am glad what you tell ladies about us. I also do the same. I do not even think of meeting guys because all they want is to enter your pants, and that's all. I need someone for a long-term relationship, not a one-night lady for any silly guy, so I don't even invite any of them near me. I want to see the end of what you and I have started. Please continue to be a one-man's lady and never change for any reason. I am doing the same, not going to change as well. I appreciate all your prayers for my mother and me each time and know that not a day that you're not in ours.

You make me smile how you keep talking about my knees of what I said, sometimes I don't know how to place my English, so I end up not making much sense, but I know you got the idea of what I meant about those knees acting funny on me.. lol right? I know you are not negatively laughing at me. If you did believe, I would tie you up, very tight too.

You're silly, Thomas.. hahaha you wanted to do what on the floor when you were huge? Blast your room? hahahaha this man makes me laugh so hard. I know you want my happiness, and I do want yours too, the reason I will keep loving you till the end. I'm planning to leave here by the 10th and spend my birthday with my Mom. I am only planning and unsure yet, Sure I will tell you my location wherever I travel—no worries about that.

I hope too that you will have your car today to go for your doctor's appointment. All my love and prayers as you go through your day.

Hugs and kisses from me, my love.

4 January 2019

DiAnnie wrote;

Good morning honey,

I Thought I write you a message before lunchtime, and I can check back to see if I got a letter back like I said last night that I was going to reply to your message. I'm just doing that now since I was so tired last night. How's your day going so far? Guess it's still early there.

Sure, you're right. Our love is something only those who have God in their hearts can understand. It's like Jesus loving everyone, be it good or bad. He died for everyone without having to die for specific people and leave certain people out; He only ask anyone to believe that He did for them, that's all. Sounds silly from a human viewpoint, right? But it is what will save the rest of the world, as stupid as that is.

Oh, I like your sense of humor. You drive me crazy laughing people here are asking what funny movie I'm watching on the computer. I wish they know I got a very fun guy in my life. I tell them yes, it's a funny movie before they stick their noses in my personal life. So I am just having fun by myself reading and writing you better that way. It would be my pleasure having good laughters with you all the time and not fighting necessarily. I want a happy life without fights, I understand no one wants a fight, but it is expected in a relationship. We won't pray for that, though. I love you with all my heart because you tell me that you will do all to keep me happy and even die for me. Not many men would want to say these words. It is how I know that you are so different. You're truly a Zoro, a hero too..lol.

Honey, please know that I do not think you're a liar. I felt so before when I didn't know you better, I know you are only full of tough jokes, and as soon as I know you better, I do not feel hurt anymore. I trust you very much because I know you love me and always want the best for me. So never think that I don't believe you, okay? I do, and you're the best man I have ever known in my life. I don't think any other can understand me as you do and me the same. As long you can be honest and tell me what you needed to do, it is okay.

Well, it's not like I don't know I'm beautiful. I know I do, but I do not want that to make me feel special over others because God made everything beautiful, so I try to remind each time not to be overconfident or feel any better than anyone. I hope you understand why God does not like those that blow their trumpets. He lets others appreciate you. Yes, I am beautiful, and you're also handsome, not flattering you because you truly are. Anyway, I will get busy now and will check back later. Enjoy your day, my love—much love from your girl.

5 January 2019

Thomas wrote;

You are a sweetheart, never have known this kind of love before and I thank God for that and you as well, I tend to disagree with you, a smile you may think that we are going to fight or argue when we get married. I disagree, just because others do and it is expected in a marriage, for most people that do not know God or who have never looked to be equally out spiritually, our making love with one another and our love life together is the cherry on the cake, neither of us is looking for that in our relationship or marriage together, that is not our priority I would say when you?

It is going to be a God-given gift and unique that neither of us has ever experienced before in our lives. And I am happy that I make you happy and make you laugh. This is what two people do that care about one another. We will have fun together and enjoy each other's love and companionship through the grace of God.

I realize I am a good-looking gentleman, and you are a very beautiful lady. When I was younger, and in my prime and physically in excellent condition, I still work out two hours a day because that's what Marines stay in shape. And I'm still good-looking, let me know if you had this similarity in your life when I was younger. Even today, when ladies look or talk to me, I can tell what they are looking for is a good-looking guy with intelligence and security, and I have a hard time looking ladies directly in the eye for this reason.

I have never looked at ladies directly into their eyes because I knew spiritually it was for all the wrong reasons. And when I got married, I was on drugs and alcohol, and it was for all the wrong reasons, and those last two ladies just about raped me to get me to marry them, and that was not morally right. And I'm sure you have the same problem with men when they look at you because all they want to do is get into your pants. Please let me know if I am right and that we are similar in this unforgiving world of immorality. Between two people?

And I want you to keep my beautiful sweet Guardian Angel that there is a 95 perchance that we can have children together, then there is always that 5% that we cannot. And I feel we have mentioned this to each other or talked about this before that you are comfortable with adopting children, just if you cannot have children or I cannot give you children.

Another thing my doctor mentioned to me, and I never thought of it, to get a venereal disease test, and I said I have not had love in about 17 years or made love to a lady, and I thought about it, and I agreed with her that I would do it. I know in my heart and my body that I am clean. It is free and a blood test, so I might as well. I'm not even concerned about that, although it would make me feel more completely sure.

You are a funny little girl, You are my girl, and I had waited years for you. God knew that before we did, unless, of course, you feel the need to get here in a hurry, big smile with a bigger grin, you would most certainly be satisfied as well as myself. I'm just curious to know how long we could stay in bed together making love? You might be bowlegged and a little bitter, triple smile people might ask you where you're walking the way you are? Triple smiles with a bigger grin.

I'm having way too much fun. How is your mother doing? And please make sure and let her know that my prayers are with her and yourself because God and I care, and I pray for the Love God has given us through Jesus Christ our Lord's name. I love you hugs and kisses I will write you another email before I lose these words smile.

5 January 2019

DiAnnie wrote;

Good morning my love. I hope you had a good night's sleep. Mine was nice dreaming about us, cuddling in bed together. When the place got real cold, I had this dream, I think about you much, and I guess too much of thinking about you comes in my dreams.

Awwe..lol, you got me laughing so hard this morning! I look forward to the good times we will have. I know there wouldn't be a day that we will not appreciate because of our love. You're so romantic, and I like you so much, honey.

Good, you're thinking the same thing as me, if a person who has not had love in 17 years sure if there were any disease would have shown, if it is necessary like I said you could. Let's keep praying about the vasectomy result. Nothing is impossible with God. If His will to adopt we can, two kids will be from one month old to love us like their own. Just in case, and I do not wish for that remember. Thanks for promising that we are never going to fight in our relationship, I hold you by this, and I, too, do not wish for that either.

Yes, I remember the lady you told me about that lives closer to you. I feel so sorry for her mother. Sometimes sickness drives people so bad that they lost control of their lives. Alzheimer's is one disease that is so bad with people unfortunate how many people have suffered so much from it. You're right. Her girl must do all possible to protect. It was your house next time would be at another place. You are a good man, and thanks for keeping her in prayer and not rebuking her.

I do agree with you, a house is not a home when there is no love one, meaning when a lady lives alone in her house is never home and same with a man, so it is when a man and his wife live in a house and their kids then the home is complete. You're so intelligent. I look to us having a happy home full of joy each time.

My Mom would be happy being with us sometimes, and having Brian as a kicking material would break my heart. Still, I guess he enjoys that as a simple-minded individual, there are people like that, and they're very interesting to be around, and having another fun guy like you it would be a home full of comedy..lol.

I appreciate the fact that we love each other and are never going to let this relationship down. I know you have had a bad past with women. I had mine with a guy, and thinking about our history would only bring hurts and pains, so for me, we move on our new path, leaving the past behind. If we think about the past, there would be hate in our hearts. We shouldn't look back, you have my back, and I got yours.

You're a lovely man, and I know years from now we will sit and look back where we came from, appreciating God for His wonders in our lives, being a testimony to people, and helping them depend on God's direction. With you, I'm never going to worry anymore because you're just the person for me, we go along so well, and I give God thanks for that.

So not sure how I'm going to stop talking about it because I'm still talking about it..lol. Guess this is not going to stop right now...lol.

Anyway, my love, I must get this place clean up and go to do some errands later. It's excellent hearing from you, and I wish I didn't sleep early last night to send this message off to you. Not bad since I can now. Gros bisous mon Zorro!

5 January 2019

Thomas wrote;

To my beautiful Guardian Angel, whom I care about immensely, How are you feeling today, sweetheart? I pray to God you are getting some rest? I wish I were there to give you a nice massage to make you relax and feel energized, satisfied, and secure with the compassion and Love of God between the two of us. Because you are my girl, and I am your Zoro, we are coming to open one year together, and I spiritually feel we have learned and grown and known a lot about one another. How are you feeling about our relationship so far? And our love for one another? Do you think it is getting stronger?

And are you not becoming stagnant? Or are you getting tired of this old Marine? Smile smile smile questions only my honey can answer. You have not even had the opportunity to tie me up yet. Triple smile or romantically love dancing in front of me in your underwear and bra. Smile with compassion and a sincere spiritual that came from God and heaven above through our Lord Jesus Christ.

Brother Brian thinks that we are never going to meet. He said I would enjoy meeting her when and if she gets here. And with my unshakable faith, for the simple reason he has to sneak up on a glass of water to catch it, he is so ugly—quadruple smile with a big grin.

I love reading the Bible, listening to documentaries, and studying prophecy, but what most consumes my mind is you, my beautiful angel, a guardian of my soul. Who has made me a better man, and I can only think God that you have come into my life at this point.

God has a chosen time for everything and everyone under the sun, and it is our time together, and we only come this way once, sweetheart. I pray that I can change this world by saving souls together with you and helping many, many others get to heaven. Peace and grace of the Lord be with you and your mother, through Jesus Christ our Lord's name, and how is your mother doing, by the way? Have you heard from her lately? And where is she at right now? Is she still with your uncle Samuel? Just curious and interested in the care of prayer to the Holy Spirit.

How the world is changing, how frightfully fast it is changing is not an accident that we met. It is no accident that we were born to live in this time. God chose us to live in this time to be ministers and preachers to others, no matter where we are or what we are doing in this world together, we can witness and set an example for others if for no other reason than just being together and showing God we care for his love in our journey together.

We've got what it takes to be here unafraid of absolutely nothing. We can be victorious in changing other people's lives; the world needs Christ and requires a witness of so many biblical scriptures so many do not know.

God loves us without reservation. We are so precious in his eyes; there are so many people not going to church and thinking they have time before Christ our Lord comes, they think, well, I can sin for a couple of years and then get right with God. How misunderstood they are, so many people are lovers of self, lovers of money, lovers of what others think about them, Lovers of conceit, lovers of themselves, Ungrateful and blasphemers of the Holy Spirit, how shallow is that life to live? Lovers of sensual pleasures, the world is in a mess in a very difficult time.

Everyone is a preacher or a minister no matter where we are or what we are doing, and then some people think that spending more money and wishing for a financial miracle in their lives from God is the answer.

With God and the Holy Spirit's help, we must walk in the spirit and act accordingly in the spirit. Setting an example for so many thousands of others and millions of others lost in such a rewarding time, and they cannot even see the light.

Many billions of people are gambling in the spirit, not knowing God or Jesus Christ or eternal destiny. We are the lucky ones, we have been saved through the blood of Jesus Christ, and there is no turning back for us. We have been blessed abundantly in the spirit of which so many are un- despicable and looking for answers in all the wrong directions. And it will be the few of us that have been saved through the blood of Jesus Christ who can save thousands of others through just witnessing our actions and our words and what we do and what we failed to do.

As Christians, we have work to do for God; God wants us to be conformed to his image to all that witness to Christians' actions that are moral and have a love of God within them. I will send this off to you now because I do not want to lose these words. You are such a precious beautiful soul in the eyes of God and consume my every thought of one day being together with you and me.

I Love that only God could have given any two people on this earth.

This is why we look up and pray and pray and pray, and I thank God through his grace that we have met at this time in our lives. Keep in mind we have a book to finish, I am. Working on it, I realize that you want me to wait and I pray you to understand that through the letters we write back and forth to each other. I can add to our book with the Holy Spirit's grace. I love you.

6 January 2019

DiAnnie wrote;

Good morning my Zorro,

I hope you had a good night's sleep and that your day is going to be full of joy. As you know, I'm here thinking about you. Did the snowmelt now? Guess it was a big surprise for you there since it is an unusual occurrence there. We have it so hard here and are so fed up with it, too..lol. I hope your time at the hospital yesterday was fine.

You make me smile so much when you called me all these names: Beautiful precious tasty little morsel guardian angel from The north country, my girl..lol oh wow, too much, and I just like you so much! Thanks for always asking me how I am doing and Mom too. I'm doing very great, healthy, which I'm glad about. Mom is also doing great and is supposed to be going to Malta soon. Well, I know you and know what makes you happy, been almost a year, and you don't think I will know my man? Sure I know you and care all about you very much. God brought us together to love and make each other appreciate Him and life in general reason I hate it when we fight. Life's too short to be hurting.

Not easy to make a move sometimes, but the experience is better than no experience. I know the next big travel is getting to Arizona and meeting you at the airport with my Mom. I can't wait to experience it. Sure I have no stress because it is with stress that people mess things up, so I am not stressed. Billy Graham was right. All those stress or negative feeling are Satan's way of driving us out from the presence of the Lord. I agree 100% with this. Believe the US isn't different Christianity or religion is fading away in many societies today. Still, I'm not surprised because the Bible says all this will come to the past to pave the way to the tribulation and coming of the Lord. We, as Christian, should stay firm.

Sure, I understand. The ones that are gone to rest are always watching over their loved ones, the human soul or spirit is very peaceful compare to our mortal bodies, so I agree our fathers are indeed watching over us. They were the reason we are together. God and them are making us appreciate each other. I like your observation so much. We think the same way very much.

It seems like you have so much fun when you go to the Veterans Administration hospital, you got good friends there, and that's cool. They love your sense of humor. Everyone is crazy in love with you for that. I'm your number one fan believe me..lol

Wow, you are so sweet honey, I kept looking at all these beautiful rings, and I have not chosen which one yet. I will examine some more and will let you know which one is suitable for me. You have good eyes sight, believe me, I'm so much in love with you! Will I let you know the best one, okay?

Sure, I know our income is limited. Still, we should be thankful that God makes us be among those who do not go to bed on an empty stomach. I have watched many documentaries and have seen so much sorrow around the world. If you look at some of these things, you thank God for what we have. Once a person knows this, they are always in a position to appreciate God. God is with us. Let's just keep thanking Him and working toward achieving much in life. You have worked and done your part; I'm still a young girl, and it will be vital to work hard for us and our kids and grandkids. Good, you have a young and hard-working wife, so no worries.

We pray for you all the time. My Love and God knows we love each other, I know, and my mother knows you genuinely love me. We keep praying for the best for us all. You are so interesting, and I'm glad you are making our home a little heaven just because of us. You such an amazing guy, my Zorro! I think you are making all the necessary things possible already, purchasing things we need, so I don't think there's any I would need. Maybe when I get there and see for myself, we will add some more things. But for now, all is fine with me.

You and Brian make me laugh so much. You get along well and have your silly fights. Brian is already an old guy, so don't expect him to change overnight. He has lived this way all his life. Let's love him for who he is. Like I said before, when I come, I'll do most of the cleaning. I'm a hard-working girl.

Anyway, my sweet man, I'll start my day now and keep checking my email if you have written back.

Love you so much, my handsome man.

All my heart, body, and soul for you and God. Warm kisses from your northern angel. You are my Southern Angel Zorro!!!...lol.

6 January 2019

Thomas wrote;

First of all, let me start by saying that when I went to the doctor the other day, she had mentioned that I gained 10 pounds from my last visit. Now, where was I? Before I so rudely interrupted myself? Double LOL,

My beautiful guardian angel from The north country with whom I am madly in love, you are who I pray to. You're my Jesus Christ, my Lord, and Savior. I find that my writing to the one I love the most is like writing to our Lord and Savior.

You are my foundation through the Holy Spirit that works through me and the spiritual gift we all have in our family. We build our relationship by spreading the word to others about Jesus Christ, our Lord. He came into this world with nothing and collected absolutely nothing throughout his life, only performing miracles and casting out evil spirits.

We all have to go through the storm, which makes us stronger, I have been through many storms in my life, and I'm sure you have as well, my beautiful honey. And I think about a goal one day of us being together, that others looking upon us will know that there is most certainly a God in heaven above. I would like you to visualize us being together. We will always have a handyman or caretaker or helper that God has sent to us, such as Brian.

Providing him with a place to live, and he will provide us with the service that God has sent him to us for. Now imagine beautiful, I work out every day for about one hour and 1/2, and I fast, and my prayers are mostly thinking about the two of us in the writing that I write to you.

You are my guardian angel, and whether you realize it or not have changed my life forever for the better, and for that, I cannot thank God enough for bringing you into my life and bringing us together. If we are of this world, we are of Satan. Everything outside of this materialistic world is of God, such as helping others, for the simple reason we have to give it away to keep it. I do not pray for money, and it seems I always have a place to give it away to someone who can use it. Money does not mean anything to me. God has always taken care of my needs one moment at a time. However, I realize that a ladies' needs for the materialistic world to make a warm home for the family require love.

And as I have stated before, the Holy Spirit is working through me, letting me know that when we finally get together, God will provide for us with an overabundance of blessings as long as we have the same goal in mind reaching out to help others through the Holy Spirit keeping Jesus Christ the Lord in mind. Another thing I am in a wheelchair most of the time, and I am slowly getting out of that, and I'm sorry that they provide wheelchairs for people such as myself, for the reason that a person gets dependent on a wheelchair and only makes them worse as far as moving forward physically.

I know this, and I am walking more and more every day, just letting you know that you may have to push me in a wheelchair and to see a beautiful young lady such as yourself pushing a good-looking Marine around in a wheelchair could only come through the grace of God that many others will be witness to. I am always smiling and joking. Sometimes I wonder what people think,?

Here's a man in a wheelchair with one arm and is laughing uncontrollably and very kind and pleasant to others, most certainly has to make them feel good about themselves. Although this Marine can love his girl from The north country as she has never been loved before because we have never known I love spiritual and coming from God above.

I'm looking forward to the experience, and I am most certainly not aboard Christian. I always have new ideas, and innovation in my imagination is fire 24 seven. There is no one I have found that I could not make laugh and take their minds off the trials and tribulations.

We will have storms together that will only make us stronger, like the apostle Paul, from prison he wrote 13 books in. the New Testament, and between shipwrecks such as one in Malta, and being stoned out of towns and whipped. The Holy Spirit working through him has carried the message for thousands of years for billions of Christians. And there are so many others in this world who are not even aware of the spiritual world drifting away before their very eyes.

Let me explain a minor miracle that instantly came to my attention but not brother Brian's. Remember I was telling you about that lady that had dementia and came into my home a couple of times the other day? Well, let me explain to you how she got into my house. She always stands by the giant garbage bin on wheels and stands there with a blank look on her face most of the day like a statue. Anyway, Brian went to empty the garbage, and he saw that she had his telephone charger around her neck that he dropped. He said to her that it might telephone charger and she gave it back to him. A minor miracle but a miracle, and then she followed Brian into my home, and that's how she got here.

Just letting you know, sweetheart, you are my guardian angel, and the reason I write so much once again is that I am praying to God through the Holy Spirit that works through a soul if we are in acknowledgment and recognition of our spiritual gift and spreading the word trying to get others to heaven. I'm in love with you, how are you doing? How are you feeling? And if it's any of my business, what have you been doing? If it does not forget I ask you, smile peace and grace of the Lord be with you and your mother through Jesus Christ our Lord's name amen I love you hugs and kisses.

7 January 2019

DiAnnie wrote;

Good morning to the most handsome man in my world!

Sorry I was unable to message you yesterday. I went to church and got back very late after visiting people from church. So here I am writing you now. How was your night? I hope that you slept well and had a good night's sleep. Mine was also great as I slept enough to have the strength for today. My day just started, and I'm fine, just looking to the rest of the day. It would be so lovely having you giving me a nice massage. I have missed that so much. Sure it is approaching a year since we met. The start was tough, but I can see how much we see the results of the hard work we started months ago. So far, I think God is directing us on the right path in our relationship, and I praise Him for that.

I like this old Marine day by day, and that is God's will. We are more robust more than before. I don't think I have forgotten about tying you and dancing and teasing you with my body..lol you will see if I did. What would you do to me? Well, Brian is a nice guy, I know, but he's thinking like everyone who does not know what we share inside. He has his right to think that we will never meet. Still, I know in my heart and with God, in the process, we will. I am not on Mars, and you are not on another planet, so I'm not going to overthink what anyone would think. Hahaha, I guess Brian felt like, hey Thomas, what do you think me for? Why can't I be able to have that girl, sure? He does not deserve me because he is not a responsible man at his age and is not taking good care of himself, so no, no, he can't have this girl..he would be a cool family figure, and I'll like him. Sure we have other exciting, but you also consume my mind most of the time; I can say everything.

I do agree with you, honey, sure; it's our time like I said before, I have had a sad past and never thought that any man would retake my heart, but you did, so it must surely be our time because God has allowed it to happen, we have no choice but to accept what God wants. Yes, my Mom is doing great, and she's in Belgium with a long-time friend of my late aunt from Dad's side of the family. Uncle Samuel is in Malta with his family. But before my travel, she will be back in Malta by then. You know she hasn't seen many people over the years, so it's the time, I think.

You're so right when we look around the world, and even in our various countries, many people have disconnected themselves from God. As God's people, we have a huge task to help those who are lost. There are many ways we can help them. All we need is God's guidance. Nothing is too hard for God when looking at things from the spiritual point of view. As long something is accepted in the spirit, it will happen in the physical world. Like Jesus, He was promised in the spiritual world and came physically. Only those who believe in God were accepted in the spiritual world before those who didn't think they saw Him physically. Our understanding is so different from those who are not yet saved, and you can't convince them so easily about the things of the spirit.

I know you are not able to get your mouth off me, and I don't think anyone can silent you from talking much, not even Satan..lol it's a gift for you to talk to people and bring joy to them, so not sure how God is going to allow the devil to cut off your tongue..lol. Those at the Veterans Administration hospital just like you and wish you were going there all the time. Many people are so sad with different trials these days, so bringing smiles to their faces is very good. That's a Godly life. Haha, Your dragon said sorrow... lol Zorro is what you are!

If you called me a nasty girl in a positive way, it is well accepted unless you meant to be negative. I know you are a fun-loving person, and I never think I will get angry unnecessarily with you, okay? You're the love of my life, and I like tough jokes because I do as well. I appreciate all those biblical passages that you send me. They do renew my heart and mean a lot to me. Thanks so much, my love.

To answer your question about what you learn from Anthropology concerning when a lady hears a baby cry that she can lactate from her breast, I have heard of it before but have never experienced that. So maybe true.

Well, about women being the number one child offenders are valid in many ways. The first person to make a child cry is the mother when the child cries for feeding. Maybe you're asleep, mothers are also the first to give their children training, and it involves some tough training for the child's good. It may not be very kind but always for the good of the child. There are many ways, and what you explain would be one as well. The story of Solomon and the two ladies with the child explains the heart of a true mother, or for any human being for that matter, it is you that feel much for what honestly belongs to you. The wisdom of Solomon spreads beyond our daily lives.

Well, to admit, when we first met, and the way and things you were saying at first really made me think you were just any other men, you felt the same with me, I didn't like such person and as time went on your tune started to change romantically and decently. Then my heart began to change for the good because I was just about planning to send my usual message telling men not to contact me again if they kept being disrespectful to me. I saw that you were testing to see what kind of a girl I was, I prayed, and a thought came to me to write and see. It was starting to get in place for us, so I think it was all God because if I was to send that message, I was blocking you forever, just as I did all the guys from that before deleting my profile.

I hope you understand, my love. Have a good day, and I look to hearing from you.

Kisses and hugs from your girl in the north.

8 January 2019

Thomas wrote;

I am doing fine to my guardian angel with whom I have fallen in love; thank you for asking, sweetheart. My day is going well. I'm on the third day of my fast and prayer and working out. That is the most beautiful letter, or should I say, email that I have put my eyes on. For God, I thank you for that, and your emails always make me a happy man; you are so precious, and a guide sent for sure sometimes; I still have to pinch myself and wake up because I think it is all a dream that will never come true. And that is my stinking thinking smile let it be God's will and God's time for us, and with our unshakable faith, miracles do happen.

Brother Brian is cleaning out the refrigerator and all the kitchen drawers, and a few weeks back, I had him clean out the steam shower in the Jacuzzi bathtub in our bedroom. I pray to God I had this home spick-and- span and immaculate for an angel. If I cut this email short, it is because Brian is coming back into the. House to do some more work in the kitchen. My home is always clean, and; I want it to be unique when you decide to come *to our family, a warm place that God has provided for us. You will never have to wheel me in a wheelchair. I should not say never, and we will always have a caretaker like Brian to help us with everything that we need to have done around the home or travel together.*

You are my girl, and you are my sweetheart; you are my precious God- given gift and a guardian angel, a miracle I prayed for as well as your mother and yourself, either consciously or unconsciously, we pray for one another. God knew the answers before our prayers before we even asked. Together with your mother, our small family will save many, and we will touch thousands of lives and save their souls and get them to heaven through the Holy Spirit and Jesus Christ our Lord. We are not going to do anything without the Holy Spirit working through our Lord and us. I love it when I used to talk about God in the Lord and strengthens my love for you; even more, keep in mind we are just building the cake, and the cherry on the top will be our sensual desire for one another. I have a spiritual feeling that it will be beyond our comprehension.

I will write you back again later. Peace and grace of the Lord be with you and your mother through Jesus Christ our Lord sent a man I love you.

9 January 2019

Thomas wrote;

My beautiful Guardian Angel, you make me laugh, and that is all good because the way you talk to me about our love with one another is so precious; it also makes me cry with compassion that neither of us knows what God has for us in that area I feel it will be miraculous and for more than we can comprehend in a spiritual sense. And I will not call you that word that I mentioned to you before. In my spirit, it is disrespectful to say to the one you love, especially a lady such as yourself. Now have to say to me, self? What would you say to your guardian angel that God has sent you? As a. husband to a wife, I feel it is not appropriate, although when a wave says it to the husband, I think it to be appropriate. Does that make sense? A smile I may have to cut this short again until Brian gets finished cleaning the kitchen. He just took a break for lunch, and you are right. He does not think that we are getting together, Maphibisheph, who is Jonathan's son, a good friend of King David that got killed with his father King Saul in a battle Gilda Moore; King Saul tried to kill David for 30 years chasing him around like a wounded rabbit, although Jonathan and David became good friends during the chase, anyway when a king got killed back in those days we are talking about 1400 BC it was customary for the new King to kill every family member of the previous King, so Jonathan's son who was a small child and the nurse grabbed him from his crib and as she was running after she heard the news of King Saul being killed in that battle, drop the baby and broke both of his legs, so for 30 years he lived in a cave until King David remembered his good friend Jonathan, and said is there anyone from the house of Jonathan that I may show my kindness for?

And I shuffle bureaucrat named Azeba, said that he was living in lodabar, which means parent pastures, it was the ghetto he was living in a cave when two white stallions pulled up and took him back to the castle where King David was waiting, and he prostrated himself on the ground in front of King David and said here is your servant. King David then gave him back all his father's property Jonathan and his grandfather's property King Saul, and he ate at the King's table for the rest of his life. Just a story of God's unforgiving grace.

There are many exciting stories in the Bible that most people do not even know about, and I am still learning about them. That's what I do every day while I'm not thinking about you. And you consume my every thought of being with you one day, and this is what I pray to God for. You and I are God's elect, and being God's elect, we will be taken care of with the blessings and grace of God through Jesus Christ our Lord's name. And for myself, I do understand why I am broke right now, and I'm poor then a church mouse, smile LOL that's why the church mouse has to go to work LOL smile double backflip. meeting at the Catholic.

God knows that I know you, and God knows that we have met and that our meeting was divine and inspired by the Holy Spirit. Hugs and kisses I love you

Thomas wrote;

The only reason you are going to be, my sweet little beautiful Guardian Angel, is because you are the one who is going to inspire our love. I would never say that that is just between you and me. I would never talk about our love life to anyone, and when they see the two of us together, they will know that there is a love, a miraculous love that God has granted to precious souls.

Although when I wake up in the morning and think about the two of us together, and it's your fault; LOL smile. I love it is your fault; it makes me happy and proud to have a lady such as yourself that God has so deservedly given us a love we have not yet known or experienced. And I cannot say that honestly because we do have this God-given love, and you and I both know that it came from God. I cannot keep my mouth off of you. It is one of those days, so expect a few more emails, sweetheart, smile with compassion thinking of you, I will get this email off to you because Brian should be back from lunch. It is time to kick the furniture kicked the old furniture, double smile with the big LOL; he does enjoy being around me because of my knowledge and wisdom and is always anxious to learn, and for that, I do appreciate him in my life right now.

You will like him; honestly, you will. He makes me laugh, that's the only reason I keep him around when I was going to leave him at the Veterans Administration Hospital standing there, and I took off in the vehicle. I looked at his face, and I cannot even explain the look, but it made me laugh and stop the car, and that was the day he lost my drivers license and credit card, so I should've gone with my intuition and left him standing at the Veterans Administration Hospital. Like I mentioned before, the look on his face I cannot even explain, bewilderment? I cannot even find a word for it, a little child lost? It had to be something like that to make me stop for somebody that I am about to leave for a perfect reason. I am happy to hear that your mother is doing fine and you two are getting ready to locate one another in Malta; that makes me happy, and I will pray for your safety as well as your mother's, keep in mind if evil should approach you to say "Jesus help me" as loud as you can, with God's love for the two of us I'm not concerned or worried or stressed or any negativity you know me better than that I pray to God that you have a good time and that you are happy through your journey and get to experience a lot of things you have never seen or experienced before.

Because I care and your experiences throughout your life will play a part in our book together. Especially our love over the last year, have you ever heard of anyone communicating one year without seeing one another? Just curious, and this is just a thought I had that I read about women can take a hormone that will start their breast lactating and that an adopted child can feed on the mother's breast milk. It will be God's will whatever happens, not ours, and if we think it's about us, we are in trouble. It's about helping others, and we do not have to go to church. Anybody and everybody who sees this will know that we are living testimony, and we will be out and about mingling among the thousands preaching the word in our way. That God has in mind for us through the Holy Spirit.

I'm happy you got to go to church yesterday and visit with some friends. My homeless apology for not writing to you sooner. I just wanted to hear from you and make sure you read the bombardment of emails that I have sent you; big smile well, sweetheart. I will more than likely write to you more. I have to get back to Billy Graham, a documentary, and I saw him, at a huge auditorium filled. A great evangelist for the Lord Jesus Christ. I'm not exactly sure how many millions of people walked to see him in China, and I forget exactly how many miles they walked, but it was a distance, and it was in the millions.

He just passed away at the age of 99 years old, and I have a feeling spiritually that when we have children together that I am not going anywhere until our children can protect you and provide for you. I want to see our grandchildren together. And I have a lot of work to do for God I am still behind the eight ball with him; believe me when I tell you this. I have scared so many people in my life and so many things I have done to others that I am immense. Make to God because of His grace and love. He knows this. And God would not have put us together to see us apart from one another. This I know because my unshakable faith tells me so. I love you, sweetheart. You're my girl xoxoxo.

Thomas wrote;

Beautiful, I have not heard from you, and I'm sure you are either tired or busy this I know, I wish I could be there with you when you get off work so I can give you a nice massage and have you go to sleep and wake up feeling rested. But I am here, and you were there; I have had tornado parked in the garage or should I say stall for quite a few years; I'm not sure if bowlegged would be the appropriate word, smile not sure if you can handle tornado?

Big smile with compassion, seems to be restless and hard more often than not, I woke up this morning dreaming about the two of us together, and I had a dream, double smile with the triple backflip, do you know what a wet a plan and wakes up. Smile with triple compassion big smile waiting patiently for my girl from The north country, my treasure

I woke up to powder my nose when I sent. You the last email, and after rereading it, I wanted it to be a surprise for your birthday, a story that I read in the Bible that is very appropriate to our lives as well as your father's and my father's and Brian, believe it or not, I will still write the storie for your birthday, it is a miraculous story and a cool one that I was reading last night, and I'm not sending it to you until your birthday. If you do not feel comfortable with giving me your father's name, I can understand; way back in the emails somewhere, as I recall, you did let me know your middle name. I feel a little embarrassed that I do not know it because praying your full expression through the Holy Spirit prayer seems to get answered. This is my fourth complete day of fasting, and if all you are drinking is water and some coffee, I now have the Clearwater squirts, smile, and I can call that nasty, although the odor is fairly fresh as compared to usual, something every human being has in common, so I do not mean to write you this way, just letting you know,

Peace and grace of the Lord be with you and your mother to Jesus Christ the Lord's name amen. just to let you know that I'm not fibbing to you, this is for real sweetheart, I love you I will wait to hear from you.

10 January 2019

DiAnnie wrote;

Good evening my love,

It was a long day and great to be back home. I realized you had messaged this morning and not too long as well, I was on my way and didn't check my mail at work today, so it's nice I can now. I have missed you since last night..lol been like a year for me! I think I'm getting attacked by you day by day, and it's a good sign that our relationship is going in the right direction. I think that is what people ask for from God, to have someone you can cry and laugh together with, and God made it possible, so all the praises to Him. I'm feeling alright, my love; thanks for always asking about that, and I hope you're as well, you're always on my mind, and not a day that passes by that you're not present in my heart.

Wow, you're such a nice and lovely romantic person. Only a caring man such as yourself would give his lady a nice massage after a long day at work like the one I had today. Sure, distance hurts most of the time, but I know the time is near and not so long to have all this God-giving cares you have in store for me. Haha, a parked Tornado would be dangerous because it wouldn't have any mercy as it is so eager to function since it has been parked a long time..lol.I would handle a tornado if only I am not going to have a bowlegged..lol Oh, poor boy! That's so sad that you did; I am all yours and here, and you are there having a dream while my body is here fresh and waiting..lol No worries because I am keeping myself and I will feel like a virgin when we meet because it has been long since I haven't had a touch of a guy.

Okay, honey, I will be interested in the story you want to write for my birthday, it would be nice to read it from you. Too many surprises, lol. Sure, I know the bible stories are very appropriate to our daily lives. They help us to reconnect with God each time. I'm glad you went through your fast successfully, May God is praised; I'm planning on doing some fast before my trip. I'll let you know. A whole day without food wouldn't be bad for the sake of prayers and fast.

Well. Yes, I heard from Mom, and she's still in Brussels with my aunt. I had good day honey, what about you? Oh sure, I do miss talking on the phone, but good we can still communicate. I wish I had enough for a phone but no worries, let's settle the important things. I hope to call you soon. I missed that too, and I admire your understanding so much. Not many guys match you, my love.

I really wanted to be there before, but you can go ahead, it's for our good, and I wouldn't stop that; I will look to getting what you're going to write and when I get a less busy time I can read it.

Anyway, my love, I will look forward to hearing from you. I give you a gross bisous, means in English, I give you a big kiss!

Love you very much, my handsome man.

Thomas wrote;

Genesis 24—Abraham and Isaac

Abraham was now ancient, and the LORD had blessed him in every way. He said to the senior servant in his household. The one in charge of all that he had, "promise me, I want you to swear by the LORD, the God of heaven and the God of the earth. that you will NOT get a wife for my son from the daughters of the atheist, among whom I am living, but, go to my country and my relatives and get a wife for my son Isaac."

Brian asked him, "What if the woman is unwilling to come back with me to this land? Shall I then take your son Isaac back to the country you came from?" "Make sure that you do NOT take my son back there,"

Abraham said. "The LORD, the God of heaven, who brought me out of my father's household and my native land and who spoke to me and promised me on oath, saying,

'To your offspring, I will give this land'—he will send his angel before you so that you can get a wife for my son from there.

If the woman is unwilling to come back with you, then you will be released from this oath of mine. Only do not take my son back there." So promised his master and swore an oath to him concerning this matter.

Then the servant left, taking ten of his master's camels loaded with all kinds of good things from his master. He set out for and made his way to the evening when the women went out to draw water.

Then prayed, "LORD, God of my master Abraham, make me successful today, and show kindness to my master Abraham. See, I am standing beside this spring, and the daughters of the townspeople are coming out to draw water. That when I say to a young woman, 'Please let down your jar that I may have a drink,' and she says, 'Drink, and I'll water your camels too'—let her be the one you have chosen for your servant. By this, I will know that you have shown kindness to my master."

Before had finished praying, came out with her jar on her shoulder. She was daughter, who was the wife of Abraham's brother.

The woman was gorgeous, a virgin; no man had ever slept with her. She went down to the spring, filled her jar, and came up again. The servant hurried to meet her and said, "Please give me a little water from your jar." "Drink, my lord," she said and quickly lowered the jar to her hands and gave him a drink. After she had given him a drink, she said, "I'll draw water for your camels too until they have had enough to drink."

So she quickly emptied her jar into the trough, ran back to the well to draw more water, and drew enough for all his camels. Brian watched her closely to learn whether or not the LORD had made his journey successful without saying a word.

Took out a gold nose ring when the camels had finished drinking, weighing half an ounce and two gold bracelets weighing 1 ounce. Then he asked, "Whose daughter are you? Please tell me, is there room in your father's house for us to spend the night?"

She answered him, "I am the daughter of" And she added, "We have plenty of straw and grain, as well as room for you to spend the night."

Then bowed down and worshiped the LORD, saying, "Praise be to the LORD, the God of my master Abraham, who has not abandoned his kindness and faithfulness to my master. As for me, the LORD has led me on the journey to the house of my master's relatives."

The young woman ran and told her mother's household about these things. Now had a cousin named Jonathan, and he hurried out to the man at the spring. As soon as he had seen the nose ring and the bracelets on his cousin arms and had heard DiAnnie tell what the man said to her, he went out to the man and found him standing by the camels near the spring.

"Come, you who the LORD blesses," he said. "Why are you standing out here? I have prepared the house and a place for the camels." So the man went to the house, and the camels unloaded. Straw and grain were brought for the camels and water for him and his men to wash their feet.

Then food was set before him, but he said, "I will not eat until I have told you what I have to say." "Then tell us," Jonathan said. So he said, "I am Abraham's servant. The LORD has blessed my master abundantly and has become wealthy. He has given him sheep and cattle, silver and gold, male and female servants, camels, and donkeys.

My master's wife Ruth has borne him a son in her old age, and he has given him everything he owns. And my master made me swear an oath and said, 'You must not get a wife for my son from the daughters of the atheist. In whose land I live, but go to my father's family and my clan, and get a wife for my son.'

"Then I asked my master, 'What if the woman will not come back with me?' "He replied, 'The LORD, before whom I have walked faithfully, will send his angel with you and make your journey a success so that you can get a wife for my son from my clan and my father's family.

You will be released from my oath if, when you go to my clan, they refuse to give her to you—then you will be released from my promise.' "When I came to the spring today, I said, 'LORD, God of my master Abraham, if you will, please grant success to the journey on which I have come.

See, I am standing beside this spring. If a young woman comes out to draw water, and I say to her, "Please let me drink a little water from your jar," and if she says to me,

"Drink, and I'll draw water for your camels too," let her be the one the LORD has chosen for my master's son.'

"Before I finished praying in my heart, DiAnnie came out, with her jar on her shoulder. She went down to the spring and drew water, and I said to her,

'Please give me a drink.' "She quickly lowered her jar from her shoulder and said, 'Drink, and I'll water your camels too.'

So I drank, and she watered the camels also. "I asked her, 'Whose daughter are you?' "She said, 'The daughter of, my mother, bore to him.' "Then I put the ring in her nose and the bracelets on her arms, and I bowed down and worshiped the LORD. I praised the LORD, the God of my master Abraham, who had led me on the right road to get the granddaughter of my master's brother for his son.

Now, if you will show kindness and faithfulness to my master, tell me; and if not, tell me, so I may know which way to turn." Jonathan answered, "This is from the LORD; we can say nothing to you one way or the other. Here is DiAnnie; take her and go, and let her become the wife of your master's son Isaac, as the LORD has directed."

When Abraham's servant heard what they said, he bowed down to the ground before the LORD. Then the servant brought out gold and silver jewelry and clothing articles and gave them to DiAnnie; he also gave costly gifts to her mother Anna and her cousin Jonathan.

Then he and the men who were with him ate and drank and spent the night there. When they got up the following day, he said, "Send me on my way to my master." But her mother and her cousin Jonathan replied, "Let the young woman remain with us ten days or so; then you may go."

But he said to them, "Do not detain me, now that the LORD has granted success to my journey. Send me on my way so I may go to my master." Then they said, "Let's call the young woman and ask her about it." So they called DiAnnie and asked her, "Will you go with this man?" "I will go," she said. So they sent their sister DiAnnie on her way, along with her nurse and Eugene's servant Brian and his men. And they blessed DiAnnie and said to her, "Our sister, may you increase to thousands upon thousands; may your offspring possess the cities of their enemies."

Then DiAnnie and her attendants got ready and mounted the camels and went back with the man. So the servant Brian took DiAnnie and left with their caravan.

Now Thomas was traveling. He went out to the field one evening to meditate, and as he looked up, he saw camels approaching.

DiAnnie also looked up and saw Thomas. She got down from her camel and asked the servant, "Who is that man in the field coming to meet us?" "He is my master," the servant answered. So she took her veil and covered herself.

Then the servant told Thomas all he had done. Thomas brought her into the tent of his mother Ruth, and he married DiAnnie. So she became his wife, and he LOVED her, and Thomas was comforted after his mother's death.

11 January 2019

DiAnnie wrote;

Hey Babe,

Here thinking about you constantly, and whenever I see a message from you, it gives me joy that I have heard from a special someone in my life. I hope you had a great day, did you? Mine was busy, but it wasn't bad, always fun at work and it's also great being back and relaxing as I write to you, you I guess you know that feeling of working the whole day and being home free to relax? That's what I'm doing now, especially on the weekend too..lol.

Does your heart sing when I send you a long message? When I do, what runs in your mind that makes you sad? Sure I notice there was silence from you, and I wondered what happened until I got a message that you're devoting some time to writing our book. I, too, didn't get your first message sooner. I see that I have a like four from you, so I don't think you kept your mouth off me..lol. Yes, I'm so eager and counting the days left for my birthday. You writing about that makes me happy. I know it is sad that our Dads are no more, but not a day that they are not present with us from the spiritual side of life. They are our angels protecting us.

I will try to open the attachment later and see what I will do, and I just wanted to get my message off to you, so you will know I got all your messages. I will be able to comment in my following message. I wear between sizes 4 and 5 in rings; depending on if I try to lose weight or put the weight, I'm slim because I control my diet most of the time. I'm glad you are putting more effort into the book and meeting the producer in Hollywood. I'm praying that everything goes well and it's not going to be like the same as those book promoters that never helped you.

God, I'm so silly! You remember when you came from the hospital after your vasectomy, and you had those swollen testicles? The sense of having me around is perfect because I do just that here and you giving me a nice massage and caress makes me blush. I can't wait to have those kisses and fall asleep sound in your arms.

Well, spending time with a love maniac like you wouldn't be wrong, respecting me and loving me, and the rest will be yours. I am yours, and it includes all my body..lol which part of my body do you like? You are so romantic, though. You are a very rough and tough guy, but it's fine having such because such guys are protective. You make me feel horny reading your sweet words, and you know how to steal my heart and mind just for you!

Haha, sure, it's my fault that you get so hard and you do the same to me because all your romantic and sensual words got me drawn to you, so I can't resist too. Sure God loves us because we love each other so dearly. God is not against love; He only wants our decency. He is not abusing what He created precious.

I know our meeting was never by accident, there's a saying that says: God programmed everything and whatever we see in our present life is just a fulfillment of what has been worked on ever since by God, like you're watching a football match and there's a replay, that's how it is with God and us, He play and after we see the replay, His past is our present.

Sure, I think there are a strong connection and great similarities between you and me and our both families. I didn't know the birthday of your dad, and I still wonder what a coincidence! How come it got in line so well that Thomas, Dad, and I have the same birthday? God has many ways of reviling Himself to us; our family, especially those who have gone to rest, are also watching and protecting us. When I come there I will prepare Poutine for you, it is a popular dish here, you will like it, and good I know your favorite color now.

Ah, you're so funny, Thomas, you called me a little girl? I'm a big girl. I know you are an old Zoro which I agree, but I'm a big girl as well..lol People say I have a little girl's voice. Still, I don't believe that because my voice changes sometimes depending on the situation. I may have a huge voice if I'm angry. My voice is different when I wake up from bed or happy, so you never know..lol. Yes, I have gone through some tough times with my Mom. You know, growing up with a single mother isn't so easy, but we do our best to be happy. Thanks so much. Each time you pray for you and my mother, that's very nice of this great man I love so much with all my heart.

What an exciting story of that couple you read about online. God works in many ways more than what we see from a human point of view and understanding.

Oh yes, I speak French most of the time, and it makes me happy when I have to write all these long emails in English makes me better each time. That's a good thought. When I come to Arizona, it's not to say I have said bye-bye forever to The north country, so I'm glad that you will allow me to visit sometimes. I love you so much.

I promise that we will always work together as a team and will continue to pray and have God guide us. There are no worries, I have gotten used to you, and I think we are moving in a way that I will not have to worry about, the start is always difficult, and we have passed that stage. Sure, I do trust this old Marine Zoro and love him too.. lol. I know, and I always pray for our financial stability. God is with us, and I know.

You guys are really on a cleaning mission.

That's so cool to have a decent home. Good Brian can flow with you and understands that you are not the wrong person to him. You only want neatness for our home and him. I do admire that so much. I look to us three cleanings and making fun someday. Yes, better to get rid of stuff that is no more useful. I do that here as well, mostly on Saturdays. I wanted to ask you, how are those stuffs you put on Craig's list?

My attraction to you is that you are a God-fearing person, a fun person, and someone willing to change to a better person. You have changed so much reason I am drawn to you.

You are so silly, but I like all that and love you so much... .enjoy your night, my love. I will get some sleep now. It took me almost an hour writing, so I will go in the shower and get some sleep. I look to hearing from you tomorrow.

Un gros bisous pour toi mon amour! Kisses.

Thomas wrote;

Beautiful, thank you so very much for the long email. You are most certainly a God-given gift that has come into my life and may be in for a better man, this I know. And for that, I am so proud of you, and you are a great young lady and so knowledgeable with wisdom, far beyond your years. You are what they call an old soul.

When you open that attachment and read it, I think it will bring tears to your eyes. It's about Abraham sending out his servant to find a virgin wife from his family a distance away. And Isaac stays home with his Father while the servant goes to the family clan and finds the virgin daughter Rebecca. The servant takes her from Abraham's brother, is the complete story that I could not believe when I heard it on the TV program called shepherds Chapel. Genesis chapter 24 – are brothers in the story. That would make Isaac and Rebekah first cousins.

A couple of thousand years ago, this was legal as it is not today. Also, I made up a cousin that you had in the story "Jonathan," not a lot of reading but a decisive meeting of the love you and I have between us. And after you read the story, please let me know how you feel about what was written,? I kept it as factual as possible. I change the names and places.

You had a long day, sweetheart. Indeed when you leave to come to Arizona, you will understand and see that I will treat you like a queen with respect and honor you with kindness because you are my girl, my precious treasure from The north country.

You are right. I am working on that book, doing a lot of research right now, a lot of reading, and a lot of information I'm getting from online, and it takes a lot of time, so please do not ever think that I am avoiding you I would never do that. Just send me a note, and that will say everything is okay, and I would try to keep my big mouth off you. Well, I do not have a big mouth, a talkative mouth, sweet soft lips tenderly kissing you.

And when you get here, God willing, I know you will realize that a bachelor has been living here for a long time and that it needs a young lady's touch. And another thing I would never be rough with you, I would be kind, polite, and respect you for who you are because I know you are a guardian angel sent from God and I'm not peace and grace of the Lord be with you and your mother through Jesus Christ our Lord's name amen hugs and kisses.

Thomas wrote;

Beautiful, I'm taking a break, and I miss you so much I thought I would write you an email, I could give you a nice massage after work and caress you and hold you and kiss you softly, let you go to sleep, and feel completely rested when you awake.

One day we pray this will happen. How have you been, and how is your mother doing?

So I reordered the trinkets that you may or may not like. If you do not want them, you can always give them to someone you do not like, a triple smile with the double backflip or your mother made like them. . If you noticed I had kept my mouth off of you for a while and I miss my mouth not being on you. Smile

Have you ever thought of just spending quality time with this love maniac? A double smile I miss you because you are my girl from The north country, my sweet precious treasure, my tasty little morsel. I am going you and taste of sweet will give you a nice body massage.

I cannot help myself, honey, see what you do to me it's all your fault.

Double smile and God will condone whatever we do because God loves us, and if God did not love, not one of his creations would be here right now, it has to be moral, and I do believe that we are to Christians that love God through Jesus Christ the Lord's name.

There is no way you're going to get me to think that God did not bring us together and since we have not met in person as of yet, although we have been together for one year online. And it's going to be your birthday in a couple of days as well as my father's. Who I feel spiritually has condoned our relationship together. There are so many coincidences that did not happen perchance. I know our spiritual gift is helping others, letting the Holy Spirit work through us, and I will love you as you have never been loved before, and you will love the way I treat you.

And you know, or should I say realize that I do like a dark lavender that is almost purple, my favorite color. And I would love to try to indulge in some of that food that is your favorite. Let me think Poutine and the candy bar or the candy, big Turk? It sounds like something I throw over my shoulders, gets me off balance, and keeps me running backward. LOL, triple smile with the double backflip in my dreams.

With respect, honor care, consideration, communication, conversation, and just listening to you. I would love to hear your voice. I could do that for hours. You have such a sweet, lovely, sensual little girl voice, although I know you are not a little girl. You have had to go through some rough times this I can feel spiritually. This is why my prayers are with you and your mother that I may bring a little stability into your lives.

I just read about a couple online that there was a 40 year age difference, he was 40 years older than she was, and they love one another, and they always have, and both agreed and said that they have never had love experiences in their lives as they have had. With one another, anyway beautiful, I'm looking forward to one of these days when God willing brings us together.

And I realize you have a life you have lived in Calgary and Montréal and more than likely around friends that speak French. I would never refrain you from going to The north country whenever you wanted to be with your friends. I'm sure you have materialistic items there that are your treasures in the life you have grown up with that will be very difficult for you to leave permanently this I do understand.

We will work through it together, and God will be with us this I know this is what I feel the Holy Spirit spiritually working through me, and our unshakable faith will all be okay. No worries, no stress, because that is a moment of happiness that will never get back, you are my girl, and I will treat you like a queen. And there will never be a Negative word between us, and you can trust this old Marine and know that he will be there for you when you need him and your mother to protect you both. The first thing I'm working hard on is placing a little stability in our lives through the blessings of God our father.

And that he has brought us together not to have us live a life of survival. This I strongly feel that we are going to be okay. We each have our spiritual gifts, and we will work together to help others. With the Holy Spirit working through each of us, there is a plan for us we do. not know about yet far beyond our comprehension or imagination, I pray to God that I have the abundance of blessings when God willing, you decide to come to Arizona for a visit. Or however long you would like to stay with us in your home. Keep in mind that it is your home. You will always have your home in Arizona,

Brian took down all the curtains in the house yesterday, and we wash them, and we are taking stuff off the walls emptying drawers, getting rid of stuff. Things I will never use, I am not one to hoard or hang onto things because we came into this world with nothing and we are leaving the same way, And this is what I pray for stability that I can bring into your life and make you a very happy, beautiful young lady, God willing provide you with anything and everything you need for a home to make it a home. And with our faith, mine is unshakable we will have an overabundance of blessings from God to help others in their spiritual journey as we trenched through the happy road of destiny. Cheerful young beautiful lady.

I still have to ask the question once in a while and do not take it the wrong way, please. "What is it that attracts you to me"?

I feel you would just like to tie me up and dance around in your skimpy undies. LOL, smile with compassion. Well, honey, I'm going to lay down for a little while they get back up and work. I cannot keep my eyes off your picture, and I especially like the picture of you with your mother; that is a very gracious and loving picture. I love you. Hugs and kisses. You need a nice massage, don't you? You like that, don't you? You love the way I am going to make love to you and will take care of you.

12 January 2019

Thomas wrote;

This is a God-given love between you and me. And as of yet, we have not even experience that love. That will continue to grow in a Christian spiritual way that we cannot even imagine or comprehend as of yet. I am only speculating, and I should not have read that article. All I want for you and your mother is your happiness and health. To be happy, joyous, and free. And our trials and tribulations with God and the Holy Spirit through Jesus Christ our Lord on our side, God can do for us what we cannot do for ourselves.

Keep in mind no worry, no stress; one moment of negativity is a moment of happiness we will never get back, okay sweetheart? I love you so much I cannot keep my mind off of you or my mouth. I am a very sensual loving man to this love I have never experienced. I will treat you very gently, and everything will be slow and soft and very, very romantic between the two of us. Give you a nice full body massage, and very slowly and gently massage your scalp. Softly and gently and romantically, this is how I will treat you, and I cannot feel any other way to treat a guardian angel than in a precious holy gentle soft, slow caressing you the way your spirit would love to be loved. Because I care, and God loves us both as well as your mother. I love you, honey.

Letting each of our Holy Spirit's connect, a God-given gift of grace that we have never experienced before. I will never experience this feeling I have for you ever again, you may have the opportunity at some point in your life, and you will know what to expect from a man. God will come like a thief in the night; we know not when.

So if God chooses to call me home before you. I want you to find that man who will treat you like I will treat you in the way I talk to you. You have to promise me this, okay? This is what I would want for you. And this is what God would like for you to make you happy. I have no intentions of going anywhere anytime soon. This is why I am good-looking and young looking for my age. As God has prepared our holy relationship together. I love you, beautiful, have a good evening. I pray you are doing well and feeling okay? Have a good day, and God bless you. I love you. Hugs and kisses

13 January 2019

Thomas wrote;

Beautiful, you are my girl, my treasure from The north country, my guardian angel that God has put into my life. Without you, I would not be going to heaven. You have Come into my life through the Holy Spirit. It most certainly inspires me to be a true child of God. and carry the message to many others. As Christians, we will save a lot of souls.

When I was reading about that lady 40 years younger than her husband, I felt sorry for them because they were being treated by outsiders and family members as well. And they love each other so much. So we may have an uphill battle together at times. This is one reason that I suggest that we take one thing at a time and meeting face to face spirit to spirit we will know a lot more about one another.

Although I feel we know each other well through the last year of communicating together and talking on the phone. This is one reason when we come together or decide to go to Arizona, God willing. Now, this is only an idea of mine, and you let me know what you think. I am not saying this to hurt your feelings or make you sad, okay? You know how much we love each other.

And possibly one we can count on as being a good friend. Now think about this, that I do have a spare bedroom and spare bathroom. And it is your home.

This is between you and me. We may have to live a life of anonymity for a while. And live a Christian life. Marriage or engagement? Let people know that I met you possibly in an Alcoholics Anonymous meeting, and we became friends. And you are from The north country. And you are just staying here in Arizona and our home for a while. I do not want anybody to make you feel that were hurt your feelings. That would upset me and make create a lot of chaos and turmoil. So you can go back-and-forth from The north country to our home in Arizona, and nobody will know the difference. They will think that we are friends.

And God willing when and if you happen to come up pregnant with our child. The kitty cat will be out of the bag then. We will take it one moment at a time, and everything is okay. Okay? Let me know what you think, sweetheart, and I have never experienced the love I have for you. And it is a Christian love that you and I both know that God put us together. I'm open to any suggestions you may have.

This is Christian love, and I feel God will take care of it appropriately. Anyway, it was interesting reading about this couple. The lady was 40 years younger than the man. And they were going to have a baby together. That was her big quest in life. And you could feel the love they had for each other from reading this article that I had read. The article got over 40,000 hits. And a lot of feedback from various people that read the article. I would say 95% of them agreed with their marriage. And said to everyone else, family, and friends to mind their own business.

I just feel that the only trials and tribulations that we will have to go through together. Sad but true, it is from family and friends. Those are jealous and think it will not work between us. And more than likely, I will get most of the negative feedback because it is usually an older man that always wants the younger lady.

Thank God I was a Sgt. in the United States Marine Corps. And God will give us only what we can handle. And when the going gets tough, the tough get going. I'm ready to protect you from anyone or anybody, As well as your mother. I do not care what others think about me because God did not go on vacation and leave them in charge. Thank God.

And please keep in mind this is your home. And I realize you and your mother without a father in your life and a husband. There were some very difficult times for you and your mother, I'm sure. No one to fight or die for you and your mother. It must have been very difficult. And I'm writing our book. Feeling I can only go so far with it. And

I will go as far as I can. Spiritually I am going to need you to help me with that book of ours. Peace and grace of the Lord be with you and your mother through Jesus Christ our Lord's name amen.

Honey, you know I love you, don't you, and I'm not saying these things to hurt you, just something you may think about, and let me know your feelings because you are a very intelligent, beautiful young lady. And I rely on your intuition and feelings, and emotions to make certain decisions. That's why we are a team, just you and I against the world. And we do not want to leave God out of the equation. After all, God has set us together to help many other souls. That is beyond our comprehension. Nothing happens perchance, and we have come together like putting a hand in a glove. We could not have brought us together without God. I love you, my precious Guardian Angel. Hugs and kisses.

DiAnnie wrote;

Hey Babe,

Here thinking about you constantly, and whenever I see a message from you, it gives me joy that I have heard from a special someone in my life. I hope you had a great day, did you? Mine was busy, but it wasn't bad, always fun at work and it's also great being back and relaxing as I write to you, you I guess you know that feeling of working the whole day and being home free to relax? That's what I'm doing now, especially on the weekend too..lol

Your heart sings when I send you a long message? When I do, what runs in your mind that makes you sad? Sure I notice there was silence from you, and I wondered what happened until I got a message that you're devoting some time to writing our book. I, too, didn't get your first message sooner, and I see that I have a like four from you, so I don't think you kept your mouth off me..lol

Yes, I'm so eager, and counting the days left for my birthday and you writing about that makes me happy; I know it is sad that our Dads are no more but not a day that they are not present with us from the spiritual side of life, they are our angels protecting us.

Sure I know on birthdays so many people would like to give surprise visits, so I know I will be busy but not for you. I will try to open the attachment later and see what I will do, and I just wanted to get my message off to you, so you will know I got all your messages. I will be able to comment in my following message.

I wear between sizes 4 and 5 in rings. Depending on if I try to lose weight or put the weight, I'm slim because I control my diet most of the time. I'm glad you are putting more effort into the book and meeting the producer in Hollywood. I'm praying that everything goes well and it's not going to be like the same as those book promoters that never helped you.

But you were a good boy, and I'm not prepared to have you go now because I need to experience all the promising future with you. The sense of having me around is perfect because I do just that here and you giving me a nice massage and caress makes me blush. I can't wait to have those kisses and fall asleep sound in your arms.

Well, spending time with a love maniac like you wouldn't be bad. Just respect me and love me, and the rest will be yours. I am yours, and it includes all my body..lol which part of my body do you like? You are so romantic, though. You are a very rough and tough guy, but it's fine having such because such guys are protective. You make me feel horny reading your sweet words, and you know how to steal my heart and mind just for you!

Haha, sure, it's my fault that you get so hard, and you do the same to me because all your romantic and sensual words got me drawn to you, so I can't resist too. Sure God loves us because we love each other so dearly.

God is not against love; He only wants our decency. We are not abusing what He created precious.

I know our meeting was never by accident, there's a saying that says: God programmed everything and whatever we see in our present life is just a fulfillment of what has been worked on ever since by God, like you're watching a football match and there's a replay, that's how it is with God and us, He play and after we see the replay, His past is our present. Sure, I think there are a strong connection and great similarities between you and me and our both families.

I didn't know the birthday of your dad, and I still wonder what a coincidence! How come it got in line so well that Thomas, Dad, and I have the same birthday? God has many ways of reviling Himself to us. Our family, especially those who have gone to *rest, are also watching and protecting us. When I come there I will prepare Poutine for you, it is a popular dish here, you will like it, and good I know your favorite color now.*

Ah, you're so funny, Thomas, you called me a little girl? I'm a big girl. I know you are an old Zoro which I agree, but I'm a big girl as well..lol People say I have a little girl's voice. Still, I don't believe that because my voice changes sometimes depending on the situation. I may have a huge voice if I'm angry. My voice is different when I wake up from bed or happy, so you never know..lol. Yes, I have gone through some tough times with my Mom. You know, growing up with a single mother isn't so easy, but we do our best to be happy. Thanks so much; each time you pray for you and my mother, that's very nice of this great man I love so much with all my heart.

What an exciting story of that couple you read about online. God works in many ways more than what we see from a human point of view and understanding.

Oh yes, I speak French most of the time, and it makes me happy when I have to write all these long emails in English makes me better each time. That's a good thought. When I come to Arizona, it's not to say I have said bye-bye forever to The north country, so I'm glad that you will allow me to visit sometimes. I love you so much.

I promise that we will always work together as a team and will continue to pray and have God guide us. There are no worries, I have gotten used to you, and I think we are moving in a way that I will not have to worry about, the start is always difficult, and we have passed that stage. Sure, I do trust this old Marine Zorro and love him too..lol. I know, and I always pray for our financial stability.

God is with us, and I know.

You guys are really on a cleaning mission. That's so cool to have a decent home. Good Brian can flow with you and understands that you are not a bad person to him. You only want neatness for our home, and for him, I do admire that so much. I look to us three cleanings and making fun someday. Yes, better to get rid of stuff that is no more useful. I do that here as well, mostly on Saturdays. I wanted to ask you, how are those pieces of property you put on Craig's list?

My attraction to you is that you are a God-fearing person, a fun person, and someone willing to change to a better person. You have changed so much reason I am drawn to you.

You are so silly, but I like all that and love you so much....enjoy your night, my love. I will get some sleep now. It took me almost an hour writing, so I will go in the shower and get some sleep. I look to hearing from you tomorrow.

Un gros bisous pour toi mon amour! Kisses.

DiAnnie wrote;

Hi Thomas,

I'm sorry you did lose your precious message you wanted to send, it's not still bad, and I'm the one to apologize for my delay. Things have been a little busy for me but thank God I'm able to message you now. How's it going with you? I hope you have been doing great, always thinking about you and missed you greatly, and it feels so good to hear from you each time. With the help of God, I'm fine and not much to complain about.

Reading your message, I see many funerals, but as you say, not to feel sorry, yes, I agree no matter who we have lost in this world, we will surely be together soon in eternity. It's sure a celebration of life after death. Well, you and I are thinking the same way, we are not going to die now, there's still a great future ahead for you and me, and I look forward to being your wife and spending our lives together with our kids, you would be the very first man to have a child or children with me. I think I have heard about Neil Young, the musician from Pasadena. You must've enjoyed life being close to people who had great concerts!

Well, I'm not nervous or will ever be. I know you're a great person and what I understand about you each day tells me you're a very caring and romantic person, and I would never be nervous, let's be patient about the hospital, hoping they tell you positive news. Have you heard any news from them yet?

Oh, the airfare must be so cheap. I'll find out about it as well. I just finalized a few things as well about applying for a passport and other documentation. Prices change daily, so I hope when the time is right, we will be lucky.

Do you love my middle name? Thanks for liking it. But I haven't picked it for a long time, but I appreciate it since you do now. Yes, I too can not wait to be in your arms, I can feel the strong desire you have for me from afar, and I pray that all we have asked for will come to pass.

Thanks so much for all the nice words. My love and you have a great day. I wrote you on yahoo messenger as well and hoped we could also catch each other on there. Hearing from one another from both ways makes me happy. Love you so much—hugs and kisses from me. Have a great time till I hear from you.

Yours DiAnnie.

14 January 2019

DiAnnie wrote;

Good morning my Arizona Zorro,

Sorry I was so tired last night, and good that I can message you this morning before going to work. How do you feel? I hope you had a great night. Mine was excellent, and thank God for strength for the day.

Thanks for asking, my love, I'm feeling great so far as I woke up not too long, so I'll be looking out for the rest of the day. Well, I thought I was going to get some rest, but a sister from church drove by and picked me up, so I did go anyway. I guess what we plan, sometimes God decides on another thing. I was like Jonah in the Bible yesterday.. lol. That was a charming question from Jesus to the Pharisees, though we are supposed to rest on the Sabbath day, but if it was to save a life? The intelligence of Jesus always shows man's hypocrisy and makes the wisdom of man useless before the eyes of God. Oh yes, we believing in the same God makes us flow along without difficulties, and I thank God for that. Imagine if one of us was an atheist? So I know God brought us together for the simple reason He wants us to work for Him.

You're right, and we do write long emails to each other. It is challenging to have you write all those excellent and sweet messages and ignore them, which makes me answer every bit you write. It is important also that I tell you all that is going on in my heart. And it's through writing that we can express ourselves more. Well, I haven't been baptized in the water yet, but I am looking forward to doing that soon. To me, this baptism was the tradition of the people of Israel.

However, it is important but hearing the gospel of salvation and being saved and realizing that you have eternal security and cannot be revoked is sufficient to me than being put in the water. Yes, I know what the Catholics do by baptizing children. I think in a way it's not appropriate, and a child knows nothing, so the best way is to grow and come to the realization that Christ died for you once and for all and left with you to accept and be baptized to fulfill the Jewish tradition.

Sure we wait patiently, and you are the only man in this world that truly understands me. I am proud to be a part of you, and I know it's all God's love and directions. You will be a French man in no time as long I am with you because I am patient when it comes to teaching. I'll surely laugh at times when you make a mistake and maybe knock you down for wasting my time? lol

Good Marines are neat people, so it would be cool to have a clean bedroom and bathroom in our home. Wow, that looks like our rooms and home will be a small Paradise in Arizona! I can't wait to see everything there.

You said to peel my eyes, so that's what I'm going to do, so if you write me and I can't reply, know that my eyes are having a problem from what you told me to do. Lol, I guess you thought you were silly, right? You got a very silly girl. Lol. Sure I do tell my mother every time about you, if you will be a good student in French accept the bad words as well, because after the good ones I will give you the bad ones..lol don't use them on me because you would feel the ropes coming to tie you up..lol

Yes I remember you told me before about county being the richest. I wonder how a poor guy like you can live there? I know you were blessed for your family to have a home there, so I guess it's easy living there for someone living on a low budget. God is good that at least you live day by day. I love country life, but the city is my favorite because you learn new things each time and see many things and many people. Small towns are full of little gossips, and you will hear them..lol not like big cities. I don't have a driver's license, and I attempted driving before when I was young, and it's where I got a shock and had knee pain, not sure I told you a part of this back, but I would be glad to drive a car and having an international driving license. We will see.

Oh, sure, I am an outgoing person, but believe me, I will slow down when my belly starts to show. No one is going to advise me. I will do that with no fight. It would be so cool having people like me; I'm a people person, so I believe people will be attached to me faster.

I know you are just as anxious as I am, and we need to be patient. I'm excited but waiting till everything unfolds. Haha, you and Brian do have good fun there. Please let it be that way. Whenever I'm watching American football, my favorite team is the Steelers, and I think they are in Texas.

No worries about the bedroom, I know as long there's no lady there yet, it wouldn't be arranged like if a lady is there. It happens with us women too when living alone. I know you're a neat gentleman, and when I come over, all will get in place to their right positions.

Anyway, I must get ready now to go. It was so great hearing from you once again.

Enjoy your day till I hear from you. All my heart and love to you. Your sunshine.

Thomas wrote;

It is beautiful, for the intelligent wisdom and knowledge and a great guardian angel who has taught me the narrow road to heaven. I'm not sure if I got an email from you today. I was not expecting when I am busy writing. And you know me? Mr. motormouth smile with a triple smile. I read some more in the Bible on the book of Genesis, and remember Isaac married that beautiful virgin, Rebecca?

Anyway, along their travels, it was customary for the king of whatever land or country were traveling in to have the most beautiful women either married in his harem or concubines. Anyway, Esau told someone that Rebecca was his sister instead of his wife. And the king came to Isaac and said, why did you say that to me. And Isaac told the king why then Isaac prayed to God because God had promised that many nations would be born of the numbers of the skies through his seed line through his Father Abraham.

And Rebecca is part of that seedling where Jesus Christ came from, and when Isaac prayed to God, an angel of the Lord appeared to the king and reprimanded him severely. So they bowed down before Isaac and let them go their way. This is why I start up my emails with beautiful. So do not ever think that you are not. I feel very fortunate to have met you and communicate with you over the past year. For making me a better man and traveling that narrow road that will eventually lead to heaven. Many will not make it.

Matthew chapter 7 verse 13 — enter through the narrow gate. For wide is the gate, and broad is the road that leads to destruction. And many enter through it.

Luke 13; 23 – 25, someone asked him, "Lord are only a few people going to be saved?" He said to them. Strive to enter through the narrow door. For many, I tell you will seek to enter and will not find. When once the Master of the house has risen and shut the door. And you begin to stand outside and to knock at the door, saying, "Lord, open to us, "then he will answer you. "I do not know where you come from."

Isaiah 35; 8 – and a highway will be there, and it will be called the highway of holiness; it will be for those who walk on that way. The unclean will not journey on it; we could. I Will not go about it.

Matthew 7; 21 – 23 – not everyone who says to me. "Lord, Lord," will enter the kingdom of heaven, but the one who does the will of my Father who is in heaven. On that day, many will say to me, Lord, Lord, did we not prophesy in your name and cast out demons in your name. And do many mighty works in your name? And then will I declare to them, "I never knew you, depart from me, you wonders of lawlessness.

Luke 13; 26 – 28 – then you will begin to say, "We ate and drank in your presence, and you taught in our streets." But he will say, "I tell you, I do not know where you come from. Depart from me, all you workers of the evil" in that place, there will be weeping and gnashing of teeth, when you see Abraham and Isaac and Jacob and all the prophets in the kingdom of God but you cast out. If you say you love Christ and your rebellious towards his word, you are lying.

Luke 6; 43 – "why do you call me, "Lord, Lord," and do not do what I say?

John 14; 23 – 24 – Jesus answered him, "if anyone loves me, he will keep my word, and my Father will love him, and we will come to him and make our home with him. Whoever does not love me does not keep my words. And the word that you hear is not mine but the fathers who sent me.

Mark 4; 15 – 17 – some people are like seed among the path, where the word is sown. As soon as they hear it, Satan comes and takes away the word that was sown in them. Others, like seed sown on rocky places, hear the word and at once receive it with joy. But since they have no root, they last only a short time. When trouble or persecution comes because of the word, they quickly fall away.

Matthew 23; 28 – in the same way, on the outside, you appeared to people as righteous, but you are full of hypocrisy and wickedness on the inside.

James 4; 4 – you adulterous people, don't you know that friendship with the world means enmity against God? Therefore, anyone who chooses to be a friend of the world becomes an enemy to God.

John 3; 8 – 10 – the person who lives a sinful life belongs to the devil because the devil has been sinning since the beginning. The reason that the son of God appeared was to destroy with the devil does. Those who have been born from God don't live simple lives. What God has said lives in them, and they can't live sinful lives. They have been born from God. This is the way God's children are distinguished from the devil's children. Everyone who doesn't do what is right or loves other believers isn't God's child.

Sweetheart, this is what you have taught me, the above verses. How can I not love you for who you are? Wherever are you? Who are you with? You save my soul. Will you realize it or not? You are one of God's children and a guardian angel I needed desperately. Peace and grace of the Lord be with you and your mother to Jesus Christ our Lord's name amen. With soft massaging hugs and sensual wet kisses, I love you

Thomas wrote;

Beautiful, I'm so proud of you for the man's simple reason that you have made me in a direction we are going for eternity. And I can't wait until you start teaching me how to speak French. Seriously I'm looking forward to that. The only language I have learned from my workers and in school grammar school was that we had to take a Spanish class.

I feel French is a more sophisticated and more sought-after language than professionalism, and I think it is a spiritually beautiful language. One time and I have to smile when I say this and almost laughed, you may not think it's funny, but you get upset with me, and before you hung up the telephone on me, you set a whole bunch of language that I did not understand, and I thank God I did not, LOL smile.

Anyway, sweetheart, I love listening to you, you are so precious, and the way you speak English gets attention in a very positive way. This is why I would love to learn French and to listen to you talk in English; it would be like Christmas morning for me and the spiritual gift given from God that I would certainly appreciate. Because my wife is so intelligent with knowledge and wisdom and teaches her husband in a profound intuitive way that touches my spirit and I thank God for that. How are you feeling today, sweetheart? And how is your mother doing? And thank you so very much for the long email that you sent me. Are you keeping your eyes peeled? LOL for? I say extra prayers for that anyway because you are my girl, and you're worth it. You are more than worth it.

I wish I could send you more in one day. I will. God, I pray to Jesus Christ the Lord's name that my sweet, beautiful DiAnnie and myself will be blessed abundantly through Jesus Christ the Lord's name. This is what my wife and I pray foramen.

As well as DiAnnie's mother, we pray for her safety and accept her prayers graciously and humbly through the grace of God. And God, we cannot thank you enough for the opportunity you have given to us through your grace and the Holy Spirit. We pray to help others spiritually also eternally that they get to heaven of the souls we touch. And we thank you, Father, for giving us the opportunity to live where we live and the bounty we eat and the love that has so graciously been granted to us, in a way that was beyond our comprehension or imagination. We bow our knees with humbleness and appreciation. Amen

You know, equally yoked spiritually, we will be a testimony to so many others, and so much more will be revealed to each of us together. That we will have to praise God continuously and look at each other in amazement, knowing exactly why things happen and that nothing happens perchance everything will be a miracle revealed to us in our lives together.

So if a light shows up as it usually always does, I pretty got also that it will be consistent in a spiritual way. Because of the love we have for one another that was gracefully granted to God our Father, that if we should happen to get separated somewhere along the way, that we will remain strong spiritually with each other.

And I understand that, because I cannot imagine a beautiful young lady at yourself, that has roots in Montréal and Calgary speaks French and has friends and materialistic accumulations, that will be very difficult to part your life for this man. I cannot even imagine, although I have really considered moving to Montréal to live with you or Calgary, and that may very well happen one day, only God knows. I just want you to feel free, sweetheart, and I just felt God willing that when you come to visit in Arizona with your mother, I am not holding expectations for you staying other than for that visit?

That would be entirely up to you; I just have a feeling that you will be going back and forth, and we will have to be blessed by God with abundance.

Is tomorrow your birthday? Are you excited? I am smiling that your name was written in the book of life then. Peace and grace of the Lord be with you and your mother through Jesus Christ the Lord's name amen. I love you so much, warm, gentle hugs with soft sweet kisses

Thomas wrote;

Beautiful, you are the funniest little kid I know, smile darn foreigners double smile, the Steelers are from Pittsburgh Pennsylvania, not Texas, a smile there are two football teams in Texas, the Dallas Cowboys the Texans. I love you so much. You make me smile. And I have researched baptism. Baptism cannot save us, and only Jesus can. Although baptism is the faith with works making one feel cleansed through the Holy Spirit and makes one feel closer to Jesus Christ our Lord. So from what I understand, it is a personal preference. It is how we feel spiritually about baptism. I am in no hurry myself. I know for a fact I am saved through Jesus Christ our Lord and the Holy Spirit condoned by God our Father.

About the items I had for sale, I did not get one bite. It sounds like I am going fishing, smile LOL, and love me, don't you? You are such an intelligent, beautiful young lady and so precious in the eyes of God and myself. For one reason, I am so happy and relieved that you mentioned to this bachelor not to do any rearranging in our bedroom until you get here. That was a pleasant surprise and relief, a smile I was going to do a whole bunch of work moving things around, so things are spotlessly clean for when you get here, and you can point your cute little finger and let Brian our servant know where you would like things to be.

And I am excited about your trip, for the simple reason you will appreciate the freedom we have here in North America as opposed to other countries. You are my girl. Think about the similarities once again. There are more that will be revealed between the two of us, our ancestry are both from the continent of Europe, and we now live in the North American continent.

As far as her nationality goes, we do not know who was in the woodpile throughout the thousands of years, so I look at myself as a child of Christ not being prejudiced, we are Christians, and that is the strongest equally yoked holy union that God has brought us together for. And to be joined with someone that is not a Christian will never work. It never has and never will, I have done a lot of research about couples where one has been a Christian, and the other has not, and 100% of the divorced or separated.

How are you doing today, beautiful? And believe it or not, I am interested in what you do every day. When you let me know what you are doing or have been doing or how hard you have been working, or where you are going, it just gets me closer to you in a way that I'm sure you can understand? Any child of God who speaks two languages, such as yourself, is far more intelligent than I am in some knowledge and wisdom regions.

Although there are 186 languages throughout the earth, no one knows every language there is except God. This is why some people are gifted in speaking in tongues because that is the language that can be understood universally. That's not my spiritual gift, and I accept that. One of the spiritual gifts that I'm excited about is the Holy Spirit answering our prayers and bringing us together. And the full potential of our spiritual gift together has not yet been revealed. I have lived in big cities before, and I'm anxious to live with you in a big city. I understand what you mean about small towns.

However, it would be an excellent place for you to rest and have our child. Then after that, we are gone, unless you would care to leave sooner? Whatever God has in mind for both of us, it will be powerful in saving other souls. I could have mentioned before, and I feel you agree with me that because of your outgoing personality and energetic, vivacious figure, men are more drawn to you than women.

Because being a single woman, you are a threat to other ladies that are in a relationship. And there's nothing you have in common with those ladies. This has been my observation with the ladies I have known in the program of Alcoholics Anonymous that I attend from time to time. It's a way to get to know people and carry the message of Jesus Christ, and that's the main reason I go. From the year 1935 – 1939 – all alcoholics had was the Bible.

And they love the book of James so much they were going to call it the James club. The program consists of Jesus sermon on the Mount, Matthew chapters five chapters 6. chapter 7. Psalms 23, Psalms 91, first Corinthians 13, nowadays because of the end times, where so many people are secular humanist, atheist or anti-Semitic, they believe that they are their gods is okay to do, mainly love immorality and homosexuality, etc., etc. I also realize that because of my outgoing personality and sense of humor and knowledge and wisdom of Christianity through spiritual discernment, there are quite a few ladies attracted to that. So I feel when we are together and married, God willing, that the two of us together will be a spiritual gift of our love to God, and God's love for us will be boundless and endless and blessings. Peace and grace of the Lord be with you and your mother through Jesus Christ our Lord's name amen, I love you beautiful you are my girl from The north country you are my treasure you are my sweetheart you are my honey you are so precious. And do you realize I have been waiting 17 years for you? Smile with complete compassion and thanking God. Soft, gentle hugs and sweet soft, tender wet kisses

15 January 2019

Thomas wrote;

Beautiful, I'm not sure if I mentioned to you before that for a short time in the military, I was a pilot, and I had a platoon of Marines with me, 34 men plus my crew chief and one gunner, anyway as I was flying along the countryside headed for a target, three of the four engines went out and filled at the same time, the plane was falling apart, everybody on board was scared to death, I immediately stepped for my cabin with my parachute on, and told all the Marines do not worry, I am going for help, LOL LOL only kidding, I made you laugh. However, it would not be funny if you're one of the passengers. Smile

We are very fortunate to be Christians and to be living with the faith and happiness that we have and the joy for life. Some so many people want what we have and are willing to go to any lengths to get it just to be around souls such as ourselves, and know that we store our riches in heaven and that one day we will be multibillionaires with Jesus Christ and God our Father through the Holy Spirit in heaven.

I pray that you have a great birthday, I wish I were there celebrating with you, and at this very moment, I will never have this opportunity again to write these words to you. And for the joy and the change you have brought into my life, keep in mind you are an extraordinary birthday girl. That only through the grace of God you have been brought into the soul of Marines life. And I thank God every day for you and your mother that has come into my life and made a difference. And you knew it before I did. I still have a hard time, even with my unshakable faith to realize how much love I have for you, and I know I will never have this kind of love again ever.

It's a Christian love I have always wanted and dreamed about, and you do not realize how miraculous that first email you sent me was to me. I keep praying to God that I can live up to your expectations. And bring love into your life and the way that God would want me to. Not only for our sakes with your mother's as well and our children. The love I have for you and the love that you have for your mother and myself bring us together in a holy way and so graceful in the eyes of God.

Sweetheart, I want you to have the best birthday ever, and keep in mind you are so precious to me, and I love you so much. For every birthday that you have had, I will give you one kiss for every year of every birthday you have had. My mind is smoking, I could figure that out it may take a while, LOL smile with compassion now that would be a lot of kisses I think, and I would not give them to you all at once, I would give them to you when its time and I would pray that you make sure I do.

Because you are my miraculous girl from The north country, my precious treasure is a brilliant, knowledgeable young lady with the graceful beauty that I'm growing more assertive in love with day by day. You have a great birthday, sweetheart, and know that I will be there with you, and I realize you will not have time to write tomorrow, because possibly there will be friends that will want to celebrate your birthday with you, so keep in mind I am there in spirit with you.

Do not worry about writing tomorrow. I will send you a short email, and now I might be lying there; LOL smile, praying for God's forgiveness. Peace and joy of the grace of Lord be with you and your mother through Jesus Christ our Lord's name amen. I love you a very soft, caressing, gentle hug and a slow, softly sweet, loving kiss from my heart.

DiAnnie wrote;

Good evening my sweet man,

Thanks for all the lovely messages and early birthday messages. It makes my heart happy, and I know I have two special people in my life that are not so far away, no matter the distance. You and my Mom are the people I'm talking about because you are my actual family. Mom sent an early message today, and you did the same, and those flowers make me so happy from looking at them in this email. I did lookout for the package today, but it hasn't arrived.

I overheard someone telling me today that the post-The north country is on strike, so I don't know how long is their strike. I guess it will depend on their delivery to the emails that arrive. So I'll keep you updated on that. I will reply more to your sweet messages, but I thought to get back to you so you know I'm here thinking about you as well. Enjoy your evening, sweetheart and thanks so much for all the nice words and early birthday greetings. They mean a lot to me. Hugs and kisses from your girl. Hugs and kisses from me.

Thomas 'n DiAnnie

17 January 2019

DiAnnie wrote;

Hi, my love,

I am so grateful to God for having you and my Mom in my life; you are the cutest people I have ever seen. I know years from now, we will be thanking God for our meeting. God is so good. I am going to start praying for your telephone interview. When I get home, I will have a special prayer for you again, and I will send a short message to my mother about this. I think the prayers of the two of us are sufficient to be answered. Just believe that it has been answered, and it will come to the past.

God knows our hearts even before we were born because He knows the past, the future, and the present. He saw our hearts hoping for happiness, and when we least expected it's when He brought us across one another. I know your mission in writing books isn't about profit-making, but interesting people go and buy it when a good book is written.

Although you didn't think about that, God makes such things possible so that you can be a help to less fortunate people. It is truly a lady's security lies in materials, but also a good woman thinks mainly about the future, life with her and her husband and kids, and living according to the wishes of God, so I mostly look more broadly not just of what I need right now, you being a good and a decent man, you see and understands what your lady needs and you are trying as hard as you can to make her happy, that's what I value the fact that you love me truly. There are always challenges to start a good thing, and we have had our share in the past. I can see how smooth we are going, my Mom does realize how much we are happy, and she asks me about other things pertaining to our relationship, and I tell her all is on course, so we need prayer and ask God to continue what He started.

Thanks for asking, my love. My day is going well. I got a little break, so I thought to use the time to write you back to let you know I got your message. Oh yes, in the past, with too much work, I felt really like a slave.

I had too much work and the two days of rest were a great relief, and I wish it was two years without work and spending all this time with you..lol.

I look forward to having things settle for my travel this way it would be another good time, and when I come to Arizona, and the day I'll tell my manager that I want to resign, it will be emotional, but there would be no choice but to be with my man. We have a lot to share and ahead.

Thanks so much for the messages. I did read the one you wrote to Mark Johnson, and it was a nice piece there. You're such a great writer, and I admire you so much.

Anyway, babe, back to work now.

Love you millions and sweet kisses till I hear from you again. Your wife to be.

18 January 2019

DiAnnie wrote;

Good morning to the sweetest man in my world!

It was a long and joyous day yesterday, with too many calls and friends asking me to come over, so it made me so tired, and I'm glad the long-awaited birthday has finally passed. Lol, I got the two packages, and I wouldn't believe the timing was so much in line with my birthday! The chocolate and the rest were the most exciting gifts, you are so lovely, my love, and I like to thank God first and you for being so sweet! You're truly the man of my life.

I took almost 30 minutes plus reading all your lovely messages, and here I am, all smiling, you and Mom are my biggest fans, and I am yours as well. Ah, I didn't. Steelers was a Pennsylvanian team. Thanks for educating me. People learn in many ways. Your response on baptism is so right, and we do think the same. I believe the best thing we can do is serve our God. That's the most important thing and bring more souls to His kingdom.

Ah, the sale didn't even get a bit. Sounds funny but sad that people do not wish to buy anymore. I think things are getting difficult these days. Sure a bit sounds like you went fishing, and nothing saw your bait, lol. You know I love no other man, but you and I cannot even think of anyone, better to continue what we started and be happy. Oh, you'll realize when I come over I'll arrange the room. I have some ideas about interior decoration, so I will apply my skill set to our room romantically that we will feel as if we are in a bit of heaven whenever we are in there. You don't need to give yourself much work. When I come, Brother Brian and I will do it all, we will need to purchase a few items for the room, but we will see.

Yes, experiencing how life is in other places and here in our part of the world is something interesting, the freedom isn't the same and stamina are also different, so I look to seeing all that. We have a lot of similarities, and I realize that our lives are also going in the same direction, so much to be thankful for, and years from now, our testimony will be what many will see to appreciate God and life and not feel all is lost, there's still a lot of good times when we think it is over. I agree with what you said is about understanding, especially when it comes to religion. In this world, a relationship is mostly not possible when two people belong to different faiths. It is as sensitive as racism. Only God-fearing people can endure such.

Well, thanks for asking about how I am. With all the ups and downs yesterday, it is expected that I will feel tired, so I am exhausted and did ask for two days off work yesterday and today so I will get enough rest today. I realize that yesterday was also a great day in your life, the birthday of your father. I take this time to pay my respect to him and wish him a happy birthday as well, and I know he's resting at the right-hand side of the Lord along with his friend and brother Philippe, my Dad, and also your mother. They are our angels watching over us.

Once again, thanks so much for the birthday wishes, they mean a lot to me for a special someone such as you to take all your time to write all these lovely and lengthy messages to me, and all those surprises in the packages are well appreciated. I wish I would write and write, but I'm falling asleep as I write..silly me, but it's okay.

Love you so much, my handsome and my Arizonan Zoro. You the center of my heartbeat right now. All my love. Hugs and kisses from your girl.

19 January 2019

DiAnnie wrote;

Good morning my love,

It is always great to hear from you. It is a relief that all is going great. How is the weather over there now? No worries that you did not get back to me sooner. I know *you always. I was just worried since you told me that you had a big storm there. I know you're busy recently with the books and the interview you're supposed to have, so I truly understand. Are you a lucky person in playing the lottery? I have never won a lottery before or know anyone who has won, so it would be great if you did ever win a lottery because people would want to know you everywhere. Having me by you would mean we both are going to be known everywhere..lol.*

I can imagine. I was wondering about that as well. I am praying that day by day, and with faith, I know that everything will come in place. Just keep putting in an effort. All will materialize. With God, all the dreams we have will surely come to pass. we would use most of the funds to help less privileged people worldwide.

Thanks for asking how I'm doing, I'm doing great, just that things are busy recently, and also my trip is on my mind daily, and waiting patiently for things to pick up. Right now, I'm trying to gather as many items and stuff to sell and have enough to be able to travel, not sure if you remember that my Mom and I did put kinds of things in a container to ship and have items sell while we are away, so I am doing too many things at once, not easy but I know all will be arranged. I am thinking about still going to Calgary to get those items in my shop to be put in the container, so I may go there for two days and get back here on time.

You're the nicest man I have ever seen in my life, and you make me happy especially asking about my Mom each time. This tells me you care for my mother and me and very lovely friends. Mom is still in Belgium. She will travel to Malta as soon I am ready to travel because she will meet me at the airport. I will extend your greetings to her.

Good to know that you are fasting and prayer and working out; please don't overdo anything. This does make things go wrong most of the time. You're so right; loving God was why each of us was called to Him, so I admire you for always being in the Lord. That's our real hope. You're so sweet, my love! I missed massages and really can't wait to have a nice one with your romantic hands and to feel so good for the simple reason of being with you. I think about you each time, and I pray and look forward to the day we will finally be together.

I will get some things done shortly and look forward to hearing from you. Love you so much, Thomas. You are my Zoro! Hugs and kisses from your girl that loves you truly.

22 January 2019

Thomas wrote:

Beautiful Guardian Angel, my precious girl from The north country, the treasurer of my life, if God is before you, who can be against you? I know there is always a love that is with you in my heart, and it comes from God our Father through Jesus Christ our Lord. Even with my unshakable faith, there are times I question in my mind as to why such a beautiful young lady would want to be with an elderly good looking gentleman? And I'm sure in your mother's mind she may question the same doubt as to why? Although I do not know your mother as you do, I know mothers want the best for their children. And I'm not sure why I doubt God's love for the two of us.

There are so many similarities and so many things in our lives that are not coincidental and could only come from the Holy Spirit through God and Jesus Christ the Lord. And I do not worry or stress about our love for one another; I do care about where you are at and what you are doing, and how you're feeling, especially your happiness is the key to my serenity. It's your happiness in life, and I can only pray to God that through his blessings, I will be able to provide for you in a way that will make you happy.

That's the furthest thing from my mind. I only want the best for you, so as I have mentioned before, if lightning strikes, and perchance God willing you happen to run across that man, I will most certainly understand. You will always have a love in my heart that I have never experienced or could have ever comprehended, and for that, I thank God. I just felt the need to say these things to you and not make you sad or hurt your feelings. I tell them with compassion for your happiness and your financial stability in life that there are men like me out there that are younger and could make you feel more secure than I can at this time.

Please keep that in mind, and if that should happen at some point in time, I will certainly understand. Okay?

I would never want to own you or control you only want you to feel happy and free and not feel obligated to our relationship until we meet. And even then, you may not be satisfied for one reason or many reasons, and I would not want to hold you back from the love that God willing you deserve. I pray to God you understand what I am saying or what I am trying to say. You will always be my girl, no matter who you are with, whether be another man that can make you happy, could you be happy in the present situation and face it for life? Life could show up, and we do not know when or where.

We have communicated and gotten to know one another quite well over the last year together. And I have experienced the love that I have never known, and just to have had that feeling that could only come from God. I think Jesus Christ for this opportunity to have loved this woman who I have never met. Think of yourself, sweetheart, and please think of your happiness,

And if you were with another man, my feelings for you will never change. You most certainly will not be forgotten even if you are with another man. I will only make your life more gracious and make you feel more secure and happy.

And I have mentioned to you this before, this may seem like a sad letter to you, but I do not feel about setting you up for disappointment. That would break your heart and your mother's heart as well. That this is a man I spiritually care for, but I am not happy with, for he cannot provide for me and make me feel secure in life.

I pray to God that you understand what I am saying. Breaking my heart by being with another man would not be as bad as breaking your heart for me, not making you happy or provide for you or your security. That is the bottom line and what I am trying to say.

And before you respond to this email, I want you to think about this, logically with the wisdom and knowledge that I know you have as an intelligent young lady of beauty and charm that only God knows your heart. You will always be my beautiful girl. You will always be my guardian angel, my precious treasure from The north country, and the Guardian Angel that God has sent into my life to have maybe the man I am today to get to heaven,

And that feeling I have not had since I have been 22 years old, and I have it all to think to you for. And if that is the only reason you came into my life, you have made me a very happy man for those reasons alone. There will never be another lady in my life; there will never be another love like the love we have had together. You are the reason I am going to heaven. You are the guardian angel that God has sent to me.

And I will always be in love with just you. And if you should happen to find another man and it does not work out for one reason or another. However, you have never been married, and so I know you are more intelligent than to marry anybody for any reason other than equally yoked spiritually. Patiently I have been waiting for 20 years, and patiently I will be waiting for another 20 years because I'm in. love with you, and that will never change. In my care for your mother remains the same, peace and grace of the Lord be with you and your mother through Jesus Christ her Lord's name amen. God bless with love and prayers, your Zoro.

Please do not feel by me writing this to you. I do not care for you or love you with all of my heart and would love nothing better than to make a life with you. And then some are not going to agree with our age difference. And be very jealous and have everything negative to make us feel bad about each other. That is Satan's work, and those are Satan's people in the world. They are full of those people. Keep in mind also that I am the United States Marine Corps Sgt., one tough man. And for that reason alone, I feel we will not be as bad as you might think I am making it out to be.

I would die for you, and I would protect you and love you and do everything in my power, God willing to keep the devil away from us. The devil knows me. He knows what I am capable of doing, and therefore he does not come around me because I have danced with him for too many years. In other words, I always wear the United States Marine Corps black leather vest, and I have the United States Marine Corps tattoo on my forearm. And that tells everybody to be kind and nice. Or die, smile. God will only give us what we can handle. I consider my guardian angel, who I know is as tough as I. am when the tough gets going. We are a parent to reckon with, and God is on our side, but the devil will try not too hard, you know, is better.

24 January 2019

DiAnnie wrote;

Good morning my love,

It was so lovely hearing from you once again. I hope you had a good night's sleep and that you are thinking about me as I do here. I woke up not too long and thought to send this message off to you to let you know that I got all your messages. I will be going to Calgary tomorrow morning and will be back hopefully Monday night, so prayers, please.

When I say I'm your wife to be it is not just for fun, but it comes from deep within my heart. I know God has a purpose and a future ahead for us, and I do not doubt all that *you are the man for me. I don't know about you, I have no idea you share the same thoughts with me, but I see the love for one another is genuine and not the regular love people say they share that comes only from their lips. Ours is heaven-sent, and people with canal mind can not comprehend our love because one must first have the sense of God to understand the things of God.*

I do agree with you in some part of of your messages about people giving us hell because of our age difference, and, normally, a natural human being will do such because one not having Christ honestly in his or her heart will never read between the lines but to judge as it is human nature, only people that have Christ and think deeply do not think the way everyone is thinking. So I know people will find it difficult to understand what exists between us.

I know there are people here and there that are already against us, for example, friends that I know that I do not speak to anymore because of being against you just because they think I should be messing around with guys that they go around. You have people there who have never met me but are already against me for the reason that why will a young girl such as I can fall in love with an older man, so you see if we both put our minds on what people are thinking and not us then, believe me, we will never have the future we plan together because people are good at destroying than helping build.

Do you ask if all you said will make me sad? In a way they do, no right-minded person will hear such things from the person they love so much and feel happy, even though I understand you are not saying all this to push me away, I know there a lot we share, and similarities and I too do not believe anything we have in common is coincidental, nothing in life is perchance. When we believe God, we see clearly that everything or anything that happens to our lives results from what He has planned. We only see it coming to the past. I was a young girl have had an early pain in my love life, and you have had your share.

You have been alone twenty-some more years, and then there were things you were struggling with, such as being addicted to porn, not knowing your status till you did the vasectomy, so if it wasn't God, I don't think all these were able to come along like that. Know that I truly understand that you can not provide for me the way you want. Still, then I'm not complaining, I know you can't walk on the sea or part it, and we all fall short sometimes in life. Whatever you do for me, I do appreciate it. Honestly, you think I can jump into a guy just like that because he has money?

I look first for the chemistry that exists and the love he will have for me and respect and the same way round, other girls do not think about all this. They want a good life and not the character of the person they are going around. Most girls fall in love with killers, and before they realize it, it is too late. I take time to fall in love and look at many things, so I don't think I can see any guy and love them like that. Loving you wasn't a day, if you remember. Our love took some time and still building, so what makes you think someone can have me so easily like that? Don't get me wrong, honey, you are Thomas, who is full of love, and that is what matters to me.

I pray that we both are healthy and the best things come our way. Those stories you talked about were very touching, and it makes me feel that miracles do exist. We only have to believe.

Take good care of yourself, my love and prayers always for you. My Mom extends her regards to you and appreciates your concerns each time for her. I look forward to hearing from you.

Much love from your Zorrrowess..lol Kisses and hugs from me, my Zorro.

27 January 2019

DiAnnie wrote;

Good evening My love,

Sorry that I was not able to answer all your messages. It wasn't intentional at all, and I am currently in Calgary the moment gathering my stuff and will be going back to Montreal on Monday evening. I left yesterday morning in a hurry, not being able to do anything. Good that I can get to a library to write you, it was a hectic day packing things but not bad since it is for a good purpose.

I hope you are doing great there and everything is okay with you as well. Like I always tell you, I do forgive you any day because I love you; I know sometimes you doubt my love for you, it is normal as it is human nature, I only get hurt because I wonder why you do that? Do you think that I am too better or too good for you? I do not see myself as someone being young or beautiful over others, I follow my heart, and I think it's the wrong I have done in this relationship.

You sound like everyone sometimes, but I don't think I can change that. I'll let you change your perception about me by yourself, not me. I have done my part, and I believe you need not repeat this, doubts are for unbelievers, not for people like us. From the onset, I told you that I do not fall in love with anyone like that. When I say I love someone, it is from my heart, and believe me, I do not love you for anything. I do not also look at how you are, and I look from within a person. The heart of a person is worth more than their outward appearance.

Many things have changed since you met me. You were never the nice person you are today. You didn't know how to address a lady adequately, but all is changing, and I am thankful that you are a new person because of me. God is happy when because of His love, one of His children can be a good impact on another, so I never have any regrets about ever meeting you and having you in my life. They say we disagree to agree, which matters, and with this, we will continue to move forward.

Hahaha, I was about to be scare that you said the girl you saw in the Department of Motor Vehicles looks like me. You thought it was me, sounds like my ghost was there and I'm here alive! lol, believe me, when I will meet you for the very first time seeing you in your Marine vest, I'll indeed say the same thing, I will say thanks to sir for serving your country! this honor is the most significant honor you would give to a living legend who gave his sacrifice to his country.

Good, the girl you saw and I share similar caring souls. That's what a human being is supposed to be like, to care for one another. It was interesting to hear what discussion you had with the Canadian girl Simone. That was so nice. Our stories are similar. The difference you are not in another country fighting war. We both love each other just as she and her boyfriend love each other. Sure we will have our kids, and I realize that people quickly like you, and they get into conversation with you so quickly.

It's a lovely gift, and not everyone can do that. You are such a friendly person.

Thanks for your good wishes concerning my trip, it was a hurry, and you realize I have not even written you before leaving, good I have the opportunity to get here to write to you. Calgary looks so strange after being away for a while, and I guess that's what happens when you stay in another city or place for some time. Well, honey, as I said, you are always forgiven. All I look forward to is meeting you and making the best out of what life has to offer.

Life is so short to fight. All my thoughts right now are for us to be happy. Fun is the medicine for a stressful life. So let's focus on the positive side of life and stop the negativities. If we both agree that our meeting is never perchance but that of God, then no need to have Satan enter into our lives and make unnecessary fights. I know you are a decent and lovely person, and I know some of these doubts are not intentional. At times you say things are not learning, which I understand, and if you realize, I do not fight anymore when you do because I am getting to know you better and understand you. This way we become better people. When two people in a relationship can understand one another better, there's nothing to separate them in times of any problematic situation.

You are so right about the verse of the bible you heard from your ministry program; there are people in the bible God-blessed, and they didn't put to use that blessing, like good kings and bad kings in the old testament, we have the will power to please or not please God, which one you follow depends on our relationships with God. I'm glad that after you go astray, you can realize through the word of God, a real man admits his fault, and women love such men because our hearts are that of little kids when you can understand a little child. You will have no issues with a lady. That's the biggest secret of women, so please don't use this to hurt me, okay?...lol I'm only telling you the truth of how to treat a lady and not hurting her feelings.

My love, one thing I always tell you is never to put your situation over your faith. We are not the only ones facing financial difficulties. It is everywhere, but when we depend on God, He opens doors to bless us. I know you are someone that stands difficult times. Still, then you also complain, I do too not trying to be the holy one here, God saw we both are stressing for financial stability and has reconfirmed the monies you were once denied, so this must tell you that nothing remains the same, God hears us when we call Him honestly.

I am doing all I can as well to have things get better that when we meet you are not going to be the only one providing for our needs, we both have to do that, I am an independent person and does not believe in just sitting and the man doing all the difficult part. Let's keep praying things will get better no matter what, and life will be fine. We have God. That is what matters. I know life for a Christian is like a hill and valley, but He blesses us abundantly within this. You are so right. We have two choices to make either take the way of God or the way of Satan. After the earthly life, our next life is in eternity, so I know it is where our hearts are. Thanks for the supporting scriptures. I do appreciate them as they renew my faith each time.

Oh, I'm not going to feel like a stranger with you, we have known each other for a while and are so used to one another, I don't think I will even be shy when I come there, you feel when you let me tie you with the ropes, you will supply I will hang you? Don't be scare, are you? I'm not going to hang you, and not every time I'm going to tie you up. It is when you do wrong things like those sad messages you wrote the other day. When I'm there, I know it's not going to email, but you will want to say silly things. It's when I'm going to tie you up, never to repeat them. Or I may hang you just for a few minutes to realize that life is better than death and having this cute girl loving you and not making her feel bad...lol, you just as silly as I am and believe people will be fed up with us. We are not going to also listen to them. We live our lives and do things that please us. Having Brian making us laugh is better..lol.

Sure the girl was right. People think whenever they heard people talk about free medicine in The north country. They feel it is a paradise. Still, in reality, other things make The north country a difficult place sometimes. I think I told you some of these things, but maybe by then, you didn't know I was telling you the truth. She knows about life in The north country. You were a baby when you were here? It is not compared to the reality of people that know themselves living here..lol, You were just a baby Zorro when you were here...lol, not the old, old Zorro you are now..lol.

Well, I'm also excited about my trip to Europe and other countries, I'm anxious, but things do not happen overnight. It's one at a time, so I look to getting back to Montreal and getting ready for the long-awaited trip. Mom is missing me so much, and I too. Anyway, I will get back home and have things ready. I must put everything in place so there wouldn't be any delay in getting back to Montreal. Have a nice day, my love.

CHAPTER 2

Romantic Memoirs From Heaven, February 2019

1 February 2019

DiAnnie wrote;

Good morning my love,

It was a busy day yesterday, but rest assured that I am never busy for you even if I take a day to write you back. You occupy my mind 24/7, and there's no way to resist it because the love for each other is natural. How is my handsome man doing this morning? I hope that you had a good night's sleep, mine was great and here I am thinking about you as I write you before leaving.

Well, I know boredom is for people that keep burning issues in their hearts, not you and me, because we always speak out whatever that bothers us, so there wouldn't be any room for that. One reason I am grateful for having such a man like you. I know Satan is very creative in having people worry, but with God's word built in me and you, we will always stand up more substantial. You're so right, my love, the word of God, is undoubtedly our foundation, and with this, all is sure.

Hahaha, this man is going to kill me with his sense of humor! Lol, you think you're a bit virgin because you have not had a lady for the past years? Well, you're a virgin in a way, but then, believe me, let me make myself available in your bed right now, nude too, you're going to shock the hell out of me! Lol, I would be surprised how this little virgin Thomas is so huge and knows so much about lovemaking..lol, you're that old Zorro who has been with ladies, so don't pretend to feel like a virgin. You know a lot.

I know it's not easy going whole 20 years without a touch of a lady, same things happen to ladies as well, you missed having the touch of someone, God didn't make a mistake He made us natural with huge desires too, so I know where you're coming from and what you mean, this is on a serious note because I was kidding at first. God has a purpose of bringing us together, and here we are going deeper and deeper in love with each other. I have experienced love before, but I have never experienced this kind before with the love that exists between us. I always tell myself that it is a God- given love that only those with the hearts of God can understand. My heart is so deep into you that I do not think I have anyone so close to my life than you and Mom.

People wonder these days what is going on in my life that I always smile on my face. In my heart, I tell them Thomas is responsible for my joy and God above all. I am enjoying your book very much as I read it when I get home.

You are such a great writer! How is the cleaning going in the house? Hey, no laziness because when I come, and things are not arranged, I'll arrange them, but then you and Brian will have a grade of F for the poor performance..lol. Sure my Mom would say in French: Oh mon Dieu ces Deux Hommes!..lol means Oh my God, these two guys! She would be surprised just like me, but no worries, I'm only kidding. I'll see if anything of the stuff there doesn't need would interest me. No need to change your bed, leave everything important thing in the house, and I'll let you know what we don't need. I love neatness, and you are a neat person, so not much to worry about, I think. see, I'm becoming just like you..lol

Well, I know I'm not in a hurry. I'm not going to travel forever. We have our future, and getting together is what matters after all my travels. Arizona is my last stop in our home. I am patient, but you also understand me, okay? It's like you're a mind reader, and you know my Mother so much without even meeting her yet! Lol, she likes you very much and wouldn't mind so much about the home. I told her, you are a very neat person, so we have no worries at all. 61 isn't a little age, so I see why Brian doesn't work much. Lol Does Brian cooks very well? Anyway, when I'm there, I will do all the cooking. I want you to eat healthy dishes, both American, Canadian, and Italian, and I have some ideas for Maltese dishes. You will see, I am a good cook. I work in a restaurant for nothing! Lol.

So lovely hearing from you, my love. You have all my heart, and looking forward to hearing from you. I must get ready now and will check my email later this evening. Enjoy the rest of your day. Hugs and kisses from your true love.

3 February 2019

DiAnnie wrote;

Good morning Sweetheart,

I was already in bed last night when you messaged, so sorry I didn't get back to you sooner. How was your night? I hope you had a good sleep and your day is going to be a fruitful one. Mine is going great so far, and I had a good night's sleep as well.

I'm looking forward to the rest of the day. Not going to church today, so I'm just here relaxing, watching Netflix.

Hmm, I wish I did read your sweet message last night before going to bed. At least I would have dreamed about the massage you wanted to give me. It would be so lovely experiencing your huge and soft hands massaging my back. Lol, I know you will not just want to massage because going all the way to my lower back and going close to my buttocks would lead you to something else. I know my Zorro!..lol I'm right?

I think of you all the time as well, and it is not easy thinking without thinking about such a sweet man in my life. You're present in my heart and my mind each time. The love we have for each other is beyond human comprehension, and not many people understand what goes on in our hearts. Let's not try to understand how people feel but how we think and God. I love this man so much! Let's continue to love each other and praying to God for His protection for us all the time. I'm also glad that I'm in your life. I love the way you appreciate me. I do the same as well.

Sure, It would be so much fun and relief having you holding me on a freezing night, and believe me, you're so right. I would never miss the cold weather, and I would appreciate the climate of Arizona any day! Lol.

Thanks so much for the sweet message. Enjoy the rest of your day, my Zoro! Looking forward to hearing from you. All my love for you Alone on Earth, and God has the rest for both of us.

Hugs and kisses from me.

4 February 2019

DiAnnie wrote;

Good morning my love,

There are no worries for not getting back to me sooner; I know it was never intentional; there are other things to do at times. I do also get busy, and I do not write on time sometimes, so I understand.

I hope you had a lovely Sunday yesterday and that you slept well. My day was great yesterday didn't do much and did relax well for work today, and I had a good night's sleep as well and all healthy. Thanks for your prayers each time for me. Mine are always going to be with you.

Nice that you will be a good boy when you're massaging me. It makes me smile seeing how lovely and innocent you seem, accurate when someone is suffering from a headache. They need some comfort in their mind and feel some quietness and go to a sound sleep. So having you near me and massaging me as I feel so good going to a sound sleep would mean the world to me! This would be more than taking medication that will give natural healing. I feel much better now, though, so I guess just reading all the sweet messages gives me some relief..lol.

I'm in love with you very much as well, and I agree with you. We do have many years left to enjoy life together. I look beyond the 35 years you think about, having the world's oldest man wouldn't be a bad idea..lol, I wish we would live forever!

I look forward to us raising our kids together and possibly our grandkids; I have my Mother shower them with love and feel a sense of grand Mother and us great parents after our kids give us their kids. Sure, you don't seem to be getting older. When you tell someone your age, they won't believe it, seeing how younger you look, I know I'm not going to get older soon as well with my skinny body..lol. I didn't know the pic you were going to send me in the shower, and I guess you forgot.

You guys must be doing a lot of cleaning because it is going to days. You are still cleaning. It seems like you are making our home a little paradise before I arrive. My Mother would be happy to see all the things you mentioned that you would put in her room as she visits us. She's a simple- minded person and appreciates even when things don't seem to be at their best. She thinks making another person feel comfortable is better than discouraging them.

Mind you, she does speak out when something bothers her, so expect this..lol. I think it's like you read my mind, purple would be fine for curtains, white isn't bad, but a color that would be hard to get dirty is better than white. So the dark purple would be cool, sure I'm going to have a little heaven in our home, you didn't talk about your room, and I hope it will be friendly as well because I will always be there even though I have mine..lol. My Mom's favorite color is red and white, but she would like whatever is neat, so no worries. What color are you going to give the doors that are not yet painted? Brown should be cool. Just my opinion, okay.

Honey, I have always hated the snow since my childhood. With my knees pains, I hate it even more, so I'm never going to miss the snow no matter what. The only thing I believe I will miss is The north country because it is where I am born and raise and knows it's not a bad place after all apart from the snow..lol I guess they say" No place like home" so, with that, I will still miss Calgary and Montreal no matter what, I'll get used to Arizona and the U.S. and in term develops the liking and in time appreciate life there, I think it is normal to feel this way as a person.

Even you would think the same. Sure you're right, living in countries where snow is huge is very expensive living, good you had your own experience of living in the snow. We will tour your county and see places, you're right, small-town people got their problems as they are not used to see new people, so their minds are limited to their environment. You're my only best male friend right now, and my Mom, my best female friend, and I don't regret anything because those that bring you joy are your true friends, not those that make you sad.

True, the secret to a long-life marriage forgives each other continuously. Do you realize why I always forgive you when you say bad things to me? When I tell you it is over, I remember Christ forgives reason the whole world is supposed to save, so why not forgive someone that I love and loves me. Billy Graham was a motivational preacher and speaker of the word, I read about him, and you talked about him. I have watched some of his preachings on YouTube.

No worries about you having some evil thinking of what you said about my Mother. I will not tell her anything; I know you're a silly man..lol and you didn't say those things negatively. I know you were kidding. From the description of how you wish to design the room, my Mom will stay in sounds so cool but a bit terrifying with the pictures of all those vast Animals..lol. Mind you. She will appreciate it, as I said earlier.

You are so interesting, and I love all those wicked senses of humor. You are just the right man for me. I like how you keep me laughing when reading your messages, and I remember it was the same when we used to talk on the phone as well, although we fought at times, but I really missed the time and hoping soon I can have those phones and take one of those good phones to stay in touch with you like before. Anyway, babe, I will get ready to leave now. Enjoy the rest of the day.

All my heart and soul for you.

A big hug and kiss from the girl that loves you so much.

5 February 2019

DiAnnie wrote;

Good morning my love,

I always have a smile on my face whenever I hear from you. Sorry for the delay, but you know that during weekdays, things get such a busy reason I'm writing at this time. I hope you had a good night. Mine was great, and here looking forward to another day. I'm thinking about you as I write to you.

Thanks for asking. I'm doing well and did have a nice busy day yesterday as usual, but you always occupy the rest of my thoughts, and glad to write back. The question of how to get to Egyptian heaven sounds funny. I never knew Egypt has its heaven..lol.

Good to know that your town is a cool place. I wouldn't be happy seeing people sticking their noses in other peoples business, I believe in life everyone supposes to be concern about his or herself and be friendly, so I'm glad people there are not what I thought, thanks for letting me know so that when I come there, I wouldn't be mean to the people. I know being homesick isn't going to be forever, my love, like I said, it is normal that when you move to a new place to miss where you came from till you get settled and start to like it, so I know when I come, I'll get used to living there in no time especially having such a lively guy like you around. I know we have our own lives, and things will be busy for us too. Please know that I'm not worried about moving over to you. I like to experience new things. I know with my Mother and I with kids and you and brother Brian we will be a big happy family.

No worries, Zorro, I know you were kidding. I do not tell my Mom everything. Even if I did, she would just be laughing, saying, wow, this man must be so fun-loving! she likes fun as well, nothing too serious, trust me, same with me as well.

Wow, the curtain looks so beautiful. I like them, and the color is so beautiful! You got good eyes in choosing things, well my love our program never change, like we have always talked about, Mom and I will come and meet you, I will stay some times and then I will go here and move back to Arizona, we can't live apart we must live together to have our lives move forward, having kids and a home and looking to the future can not happen when we live apart, I have no problem at all coming there I'm more than happy making my decision, I don't know about you, what do you think? I like you to take this being homesick matter from your head. It's no issue at all to me. I like your picture very much too. You are a handsome man!. How was the meeting you went to? I hope it went great there. All my heart for you, and enjoy the rest of your day.

Hugs and kisses from me.

7 February 2019

DiAnnie wrote;

Good morning honey,

It's always excellent hearing from you, and I enjoy reading all your messages. How are you keeping this morning? I hope you had a nice sleep and that everything will be fine as you go through your day. Mine started not so long, and I am also looking forward to having a great day.

We both are God-giving gifts to each other because there's a lot we share in common, and we do get along so well, which I appreciate so much, and I know you do as well. Like I always say, it would be so difficult not forgiving someone I love very much. We had our fights in the past because by then we didn't know about one another, which was normal for a new relationship but trust me, I'll always have a forgiven heart for you no matter what, I must respect you for who you are but mind you, never take advantage of my forgiven heart to hurt me intentionally because you will not be happy if I took my decision to pull you back. Lol, I know you wouldn't do that, so rest assure that we are going great. I wouldn't want to hurt my Zorro, whom I have learned to love with all my heart.

I know the feeling of having your partner closer. I do think about it too, but we must be patient till I get to you, and we will have all the time for each other. Though I enjoy your sense of romance, it makes me horny too, but I must control my feeling till I meet my man, Thomas. Sure, I am looking forward to going on my trip, and it makes me anxious, but that's normal.

Are you fighting once again with your relatives for you the park? You sound like there's something not going right there, my love. Please tell me what's going on. The devil is busy in many ways, but we can overcome Him with wisdom as children of God. God gives us the power to use knowledge to defeat the devil, so always remember that.

I like communicating with you as well, my love. The more I stay in touch with you, the more I feel closer to you. So whenever there's a delay, know that it is never intentionally oaky?

People sometimes forget so good to remind them. We all do once in a while..lol, and you have so much on your mind so that I can imagine as well. I do relay your regards and prayers each time to my Mom, and she so appreciates you and say to take care of you and prays for you all the time. She says you are a very good man, and the devil hates the good-hearted because they love God. Our parents are our true guardian angels watching over us. We all are family in Christ. God put us together to love each other till the end. Anyway, my love here thinking about you as I make my way out. Have a good day till I hear from you.

I love you so much. I can't wait to be

8 February 2019

DiAnnie wrote;

Good morning my love,

Sorry for my delay. It wasn't intentional; I have just been busy trying to message you back as quickly as possible before leaving for work. I hope you had a good night, mine was stressful, but I'm getting fine. I don't feel by not getting back to you sooner means that I'm mad at you, not really, the only thing is working overtime, but I got no choice. I must hurry up now. Have a good day, my Zorro.

9 February 2019

DiAnnie wrote;

Hello Honey,

Good, I could get some quality rest last night, and I slept enough this morning, so I am relieved..lol. How are you doing on this day? I hope you had some rest because I realize that I don't think you slept much with all the messages.

You bring so many smiles to me with all these names just for my one..lol you know how to play with words to make a lady so happy. Are you serious that you want to become a Canadian citizen? If yes, why? I would become a United States citizen once I start to become a resident of the U.S., and I guess it's the same that applies to someone from the U.S. that wants to be a Canadian citizen as well. Once married, it's not so hard to do. What is important right now is for us to meet after my trip, so no need to stress for now, okay? You got my message yesterday, I was not so sure you did because I was in a hurry, but you didn't say anything about all I talked about yesterday in my message.

Are you kidding me? You guys are still cleaning the house? It must be more than cleaning the Solomon temple in Israel..lol don't tell me it's going to take you a month cleaning.... lol not you but Brian, for sure if you were in good shape, I know you would have finished because I know just from your look you are not a lazy guy at all Brian does. I so appreciate all the time you guys are taking making the house the best for our arrival.

I know what to expect from a bachelor's place, so don't think I will get mad when things don't seem to arrange I'll arrange things as a lady. Men are not so good at arranging things as a lady would, so stop worrying so much about how my Mom and I will feel about you, I believe you guys think you are cleaning in the best way you can, but when I start to rearrange things and begin to put things in their right places you would realize a lady's way of doing things is so different! You guys are only doing the general cleaning. helping me, so I know you will be right there scratching your head of how much you guys didn't arrange..lol hey, no shame, all I need from you that day is thanks for the hard work babe..lol We will not throw all the stuff away I will see which ones are useful to avoid losses. Brian wants to finish his work faster that's why he brought the idea of just putting everything in the closet! Brian a smart lazy guy, hahaha.!

Well, from the first day we met, I knew we were met to be. I was not sure when you started those silly nutty messages until I realized you were not that way and Mom told me to be respectful to you when I told her about you. It was all God's plan because I am very quick to let things go, but God was in it, and I couldn't let this sweet mango even though he didn't present himself as a sweet man..lol. So although we were born on different dates and years, God's plan was now. That is the other between God's calculation to that of a man. That is why God said His thoughts are not His thoughts, neither His ways are our ways.

I saw the list of the things you want to purchase, and I think you don't have to purchase many things because we may not need them all, so when I come, we can start purchasing the most important ones. I know you are a neat person and a man that knows quality things but doesn't buy so much yet. I think Brian thinks like a normal unbeliever. I can blame him for that because it is natural because when he accepts God's thoughts, he can reason like you and me. He should count himself lucky for knowing a Godly man like you.

Because of me, you're making heaven, and because of you that Brian will make heaven, so he should count himself blessed. I know he will understand when I come over. I will make him my best friend. Lol, Brian only gave his compliments to my Mother because my Mother is very choosy in picking what type of guy to fall in love with, and since my Dad passed, she has only picked one guy, but he was a big jerk, so we let him go. So if a miracle happens and Mother ever is blind enough to fall for brother Brian, French and providing for her would be a big wall of Mexico between my Mom and him..lol. If yes, I'll be patient.

Sure, I would be glad to help you and even do the driving around to get the things we need. Just be patient, and as soon as I arrive with my Mom and we start living together, we will do most of the things for you. I know it is hectic for a man alone doing all, especially what a lady is supposed to be doing in the home. You are so right. Wherever my Dad is, he is more than pleased to have someone watch over his daughter, and having the Sgt. in the Marine Corps doing that is a relief, even over my Mother as well.

I look to the day that we are looking in each other eyes with passion and thanking God for the opportunity given to show each other love. Years from now, we will look back and see where we came from and become a testimony to many people.

Thanks so much for all these sweet messages. Waking up and seeing messages from you do bring so many smiles to me. You are my true love, my hero, and of course, my Zorro!

I will try to get a few things done and will be looking forward to hearing from you. All my love to you.

Hugs and kiss from you best friend and wife for life.

Can a Canadian Legally Marry an American Citizen in America? Federal immigration and visa law cover marriages to foreign nationals within the United States. As citizens of a foreign country, Canadians must follow these rules or risk denial of their visas and deportation from the government. If you are a U.S. citizen and considering marriage to a Canadian, familiarize yourself with the basics of immigration law. Considerations

Foreign citizens may come to the United States after obtaining a visa. There are different visa classifications for tourists, guest workers, diplomats, refugees, family members, and fiancées. A Canadian wishing to marry a U.S. citizen inside the United States and then take up permanent residence in the United States must first file a visa application in The north country. Suppose the couple does not intend to stay in the United States. In that case, the Canadian may arrive on any legal visa, participate in the wedding ceremony, and then leave before the visa expiration date. The U.S. citizen must follow the rules and procedure for immigration as a Canadian's spouse to The north country.

K-1 Visas

The Department of Homeland Security and the United States Citizenship and Immigration Services process visa applications. To marry a foreigner in the United States, the U.S. citizen must first file Form I-129F with the USCIS. After this application is approved, the Canadian must file a K-1 visa application at the nearest U.S. consulate within four months. If successful, this will result in the issuance of a K-1 visa at the consulate. Immigration law bars foreigners from arriving in the U.S. on a non- immigrant visa, then applying for permanent resident status. Therefore, the Canadian fiancée must wait until the K-1 visa is approved and issued, then come to the United States.

Marriage Deadline

Once the Canadian fiancée arrives in the United States, the couple has 90 days to marry. The couple must obtain a certified copy of the marriage certificate to adjust the status for the Canadian. The USCIS will not extend the 90-day deadline; if the time expires and no marriage occurs, then the Canadian will be "out of status" -- without a valid visa -- and must leave the States before the wedding takes place. Permanent Resident Status

After the marriage, the Canadian must apply for permanent resident status. As the spouse of a U.S. citizen, a foreign national has the right to live and work permanently in the United States. To achieve this, you must file an I-130 application for permanent resident status, which will result in the issuance of a green card and Form I-485, an application to adjust position. While waiting for the issuance of a green card, an applicant may not leave the United States except under particular circumstances. Anyone holding a green card may go and return to the United States freely.

10 February 2019

DiAnnie wrote;

Hello, my love,

I hope you are having a good Sunday, I just got back from church, and nice I can reply to all your sweet messages. How are you doing? I hope everything is going great, not much going on here as all my heart is on my upcoming trip and getting things done before leaving.

You make me smile every time I see a message from you with all these exciting words. This tells me a lot about your character that you're truly a loving man who God has sent to me to show me the love I have never known as well, we were in the same boat, and God saw how much we were weary of all we have endured in this life and decided to bring us together so I most of the time thank Him for our lives. You are as important to me as I am to you, and we love each other very much, which fulfills the Love of God for us. You are a great man to admit.

My love, let us be positive and not even think that anything would ever get in our way, we are going to enjoy this earthly life together and heavenly life as well because we have been faithful to God and truly knows what we wish and will surely give us our hearts desires because we always seek Him. I know you appreciate me very much in your life, I am honored to be the person you appreciate, and I know I do the same.

I know, right..lol you can arrange the things you can. When I come and see that all is not to my expectation, I'll be laughing at you so hard, and Mom will also laugh, so do your best to shame us so we wouldn't laugh okay, I know not much I'm going to expect from the cleaning of a bachelor, but hey sometimes people can prove themselves so go, babe! Having a good laugh wouldn't be so bad, if you the right thing or not even so impressive I'll motivate you that's our nature our family. I know you have been a hard-working man before your present conditions, so I know you're not the kind of person who likes sitting around doing nothing. I see all those books you have written, and I can how much work you put into them.

So you're serious about being a Canadian citizen? Come on, my love; you're kidding me, right? Lol, anyway, when you visit The north country with me someday, I'll help you obtain your citizenship here. My Mom and I will help you, but you must be a resident for a few years, so would you wish to do that? Sure, I know the program Brian is talking not sure it's the exact one, but you see, when the diplomats go to an international meeting or conference, there's an earphone each person put on for translation purposes. So when you are speaking English I can get what you're saying in French it is very relaxed but must be expensive, you can't use that all the time, there are simple errors so you must be patient and learn French from us..lol.

Hahaha, silly man!! Do You think we can rob a bank the 4 of us? if I ever tell my Mom, she will be like quoi? (what?) lol, We won't succeed because having two ladies who love God so much and a man who loves God would never wish to do such. Maybe brother Brian would go alone, but then when he should think about all the nice things you have taught him, he will say, hey Thomas, you must be going nuts rob a bank? So we will be left with zero people to go.

You got me laughing so hard reading about this. I love your sense of humor so much, and all you want us to do is to please your girl? Well, she does not need all those terrible things to be happy. She loves you without so much. So get those evil thoughts out of your head Zoro..lol I'm glad Brian is getting closer to the Lord. That's what really important for him right now, and our real hope is to have God in our lives. Tell him our real hope is life after death. Being with God in paradise and living forever and one thing brother Brian must think about having a lady somewhere because Anna is very picky..lol.

I so enjoyed all your messages, honey, and the word of God, how you explain things in a very simple way.

Well, Valentine is in most places, and we have the same here for lovers, but loving someone every day is more day thinking or loving them on a special day. Love should be all the time like we do, not just on Valentine's day. I like how we are never bored with each other and our love growing so much each day. It's like we just met because we are new to one another always. Let's keep growing and looking forward to the future. Love you so much, honey.

I will try to take a nap now and will check my email later.

You are so sweet, and I love you so much. Hugs and kisses from me.

12 February 2019

DiAnnie wrote;

Hello My Love,

It is always a pleasure hearing from you and knowing how you feel and what is going on at your end. I'm doing alright just been busy and glad I can send a couple of messages to you now.

How is the cleaning of the house still going? Don't tell me you are rebuilding the house from scratch and telling me you are just cleaning..lol hope not. Sure my Mom and I will laugh, but we will appreciate your effort in working so hard. We know men are cleaning and ladies cleaning isn't the same so that we wouldn't laugh too hard. Well, I was not paying too much attention to all the years you have been a bachelor and can imagine it been long and believe I will understand if things are not in place the way I wish.

The idea of being bank robbers no matter how much you teach me, I don't think I'll be so clever to know and would just put you in trouble because our first mission would indeed fail..lol If the thought of me made you got such a bad idea then please don't think about me too hard okay?

Lol, hahaha, a machine gun school for my Mom. Are you kidding me? And us selling brother Brian would mean the trouble will surely hunt us because he will surely be caught from the way I see him..lol. This plan would never work because all the parties involved will not comply for a straightforward reason. After all, we better spread the word of God than this lousy ideal. You make me laugh so hard, honey. I'm glad that brother Brian is understanding how God works, not believing in his thoughts.

Thanks so much for your prayers for us every time, and know that not a second and minute that you are not on my mind and prayers, I think about you all the time, if there are delays in writing some times understand it's because I get real busy most of the time. Oh yes, my love, I can't wait until the day I'll be called Mrs, a woman is born to take the last name of her husband, which is the biggest fulfillment of a lady, so I pray all the time. I'm smiling right now just reading this sweet message.

You have me laughing so hard as I read about your dream. And you know what? What surprises me more is you dreaming and falling from your bed, hitting the floor, going back to bed with the hurt, and still dreaming about the same thing. It makes me laugh how this Zoro is interesting! Lol. The dream was very interesting, though..lol.

Seem like this house will be a brand new one altogether with some much done already and having your nephew coming from Alaska to help you. Many people love you, and I think the secret is that you got a great sense of humor and good at heart. I'm glad God brought us to each other's lives. I love you so much, my love.

I extended your regards to my Mom, and she prays for us all the time. Thanks as well for your and I wish you a good day till I hear from you. I must get busy now, okay. Much love from me.

Hugs and kisses.

Thomas wrote;

Sweetheart, I love you to pieces. I love my wife,

I find it interesting that meeting ladies in Alcoholics Anonymous and even some promoters to call me on the telephone. I always ask them if they are married with children for some reason I'm always interested to know that they have children and how fortunate they are, the reason being is I would like to mention Jesus Christ in their life, And the main. The reason is most ladies are living with a man, and they are not married to him. And that's when I say, "you do realize that you are living in fornication and adultery"?

And what amazes me is these ladies I do not talk to that many, like at the dentist office or the doctors, etc., etc., they are not married for the simple reason they have never been asked to be married, or they cannot find a good man.

I find that interesting, and it is hard to believe with all those stupid men out there wanting to get into lady's pants for that reason only. And this is why I feel ladies are far more intelligent than men because these ladies are not just going to hop into bed with any man or marry him.

I'm not sure I don't live their lives, and I do not know them that well or at all, and then I think of my beautiful girl from The north country who has never been married as well, similar to one of these ladies. You ladies are very intelligent. I thought it would be easy for a lady to get married, I guess it would be easy for all the wrong reasons, and many ladies do get married for that reason, I think.

You are so precious, and I love you so much. I appreciate you for who you are, an intelligent lady in my life with knowledge and wisdom from Jesus Christ, our Lord and Holy Spirit working for both of us. More and more, I prayed to God about how fortunate we are to have found each other. And I think God with Love and I cannot thank you enough because her love keeps getting stronger.

Peace and grace of the Lord be with you and your mother through Jesus Christ our Lord's name, and please let your mother know that my prayers are for her happiness and health as well as yourself. How are you doing, beautiful? How are you feeling? I know better than to ask you if you are busy, you are my wife, smile.

Fortunately or unfortunately we are very busy people you and I are. I do keep dreaming about us together, and it is becoming stronger, and almost every time I dream, I dream of you. You're my girl from The north country, my precious tasty little morsel that is so pleasing to my palate I can taste sweet juices that I will tenderly place upon your neck and love the smell and the taste you are, my precious angel.

You're the only Christian lady I will ever love with Christian Love you, and I have never known or will ever know or experience again. This is what I feel spiritual. And it's not so much about the love part of our love for one another, but it is what will be revealed to us in a miraculous way that will always be new.

And God is not going to let us be beggars. We have a mission to do together to help others spiritually and find Jesus Christ, and I feel it's going to be on a big scale, such as writing our books together or even bigger.

This is what shall be revealed spiritually, and we will be blessed abundantly, and our children will be very special to this world. And your mother such a gracious precious soul that God has put into our lives for a very loving, caring, kind reason.

13 February 2019

DiAnnie wrote,

Wow, I just read all the lovely and sweet messages, and I can't stop smiling, I'm not sure we met on Valentine's Day, but from the messages we shared then I can see clearly that our lives are not coincidental at all, it is all God's plan for us. I can see that God made this possible even before we met. Thanks so much for all the sweet Valentine's messages. The day hasn't been reached yet, but you made me happy already.

Thomas wrote:

You are my guardian angel, my Canadian girl of home I love, and you are so linkable, Sweetheart, a tasty little morsel, very pleasing to the pallet. I can taste such sweet juices right now. mmmmmmm

14 February 2019

DiAnnie wrote;

Hello, my love,

I'm here reading your messages and smiling at how much fun it is communicating with you. How is your day going so far? I hope that everything is going great. My day is going great, busy but I can't complain since I got some time to message you.

Sure, you look younger, and I thought it was only to me, but I can see that others can see how blessed you're with this young body of yours. I guess when people tell you, it sounds like they are flattering you, right? Not so you don't look so old as you think.

You're so funny, honey, and you want to know if someone is married when you talk to them? It is somehow embarrassing when you ask such questions to strangers, but then you are just that tough Marine who does not care ..lol I know you so much now. When people are not married, it seems they do not want to, especially women but believe me, and there are only a few guys such as you in this vast world that are different. Some men are also unfortunate not meeting the nicest ladies who are God-fearing.

I'm glad that our meeting has made you an all-new person, not going into porn anymore or dating sites, better we start what will continue till the end of times, you are not leaving anytime soon and me as well, as we continue to depend on God we will surely see good things happen to us, I'm speaking with faith. I have never pay any money on a site because I know love is natural and good. We didn't have to pay to love each other. Sure nothing is perchance, and all was the exact plan of God. Only those in Christ can relate, not those still in their thoughts.

Thanks always for acknowledging my intelligence. I appreciate that very much. When someone sees and tells you your qualities, it is better than you blowing your own trumpet; I always want people to see what I am not for them to be a force to appreciate me. I give God thanks each time for such a man like yourself as well.

I look forward to the day you and I will hold hands, kisses, and sleeping in the same bed. I know it's not so far away. I'm so anxious. I know it is normal because we will finally be laughing together, Mom watching, and Brian is smiling. We will be a beautiful family with so much love from God.

Anyway, my love, I will get back to work, and as we celebrate Valentine's Day from this very moment, I give you all my love and all my heart, and I like you to know that you are an essential part of my life. With regards..hugs, and kisses from me.

DiAnnie wrote;

Happy Valentine's day, mon amour! I shouldn't be working, but I have no choice as we have customers here today and asked to perform. I just asked for my coworker's phone to write you a quick message to wish you a happy Valentine's Day. I look to hearing from you soon. I'll check my email. If not, when I get home, I'll enjoy your day on this lovely day. Hugs and kisses.

16 February 2019

DiAnnie wrote;

Hey Sweetheart,

Glad I got some rest on a relaxing Saturday and can message back now. Nice to hear from you because I wondered what happened. I thought since you told me that your electricity was cut off it hasn't been restored. It's always a pleasure to hear from you and to know how you're doing as well. Any plans for today? I will try to get some more sleep after I'm done writing you, get something to eat, take my shower and get a nap.

Well, babe, I'll always want to hear of how you are doing no matter what because I care just how much you care for me. When I hear that all is going well, I am relief as well. Sure we genuinely love each other, and our love for one another never gets expire or old, it feels like we just met, and that's how I want it to be till the end. Thanks for always asking about how I'm doing. Your girl is doing great, and how is my man doing as well?

I couldn't stop laughing reading your dream you had, and It seems like you always dream, right? I don't dream often, and I wish I had this gift of you dreaming. I mostly think dreams are imagination to the highest degrees, but dreams are real, so I believe them in the spiritual realm.

It has been long since any of the guys I have befriended with or went out with ever bother to call me or seen each other. I don't even know the current events about friends or male friends because I am more focused on you, my Mom, my job, and the trip and how to meet you and start our lives together. So in that dream of the guy being jealous of me, I was only wasting his time because my love for this man called Thomas is so real, and I am not sure any guy can take me from him. If this must happen, it must be a power beyond my control..lol. Not wanting to go to the guy in the dream is so valid because I want to believe you dreamed in the first place..lol, the rest is something I don't even think about.

Anyway, my Zoro, I'll try to get a few things in place around here and get to take a nap after I am done later. Thanks for always keeping smiling. You're just what I need. I look forward to being happy with you all my life. Enjoy the rest of your day, sweet man.

Big hugs and kisses from your girl.

19 February 2019

Thomas wrote;

My beautiful Guardian Angel, the miracle in my life. I will never grow weary of being with you—my sweet precious heavenly angel. I will always love you. You took my breath away the first time I looked into your heart and realized that you are one beautiful lady sent from above as one unique spirit. There's nothing single about being together with you. With you, tomorrow is inevitable. Before I met you, my angel, my life was miserable, and now I have the God-given opportunity to make up for those lost years by spending and to cherish every moment with you. I love you so much. I found happiness, joy, peace, and contentment.

No matter how worrisome a day might be, it is a moment of pleasure we will never get back. The thought of you always makes my life worth it. I love you so much. When we get together, God willing, nothing else matters but you and me. I love you beyond the stars, into the light of eternal heaven. I wish I would have met you sooner so I could have loved you longer. Everyone longs to give themselves completely to someone. I have a deep soul relationship with another to be equally yoked spiritually.

But God to the Christian says, "No, not until you satisfied and fulfilled and content with living, loved by Me alone and giving yourself totally and unreservedly to Me, to have an intensely personal and unique relationship with Me alone. God said to me, I love you, my child until you discover that only in Me is there satisfaction to be found, you will not be capable of the perfect human relationship that I have planned for you.

You will never be united with another until you are matched with Me, exclusive of anyone or anything else, complete of any other desires or belongings. I want you to stop planning, stop wishing, and allow Me to bring it to you. You keep watching Me, expecting the most significant things. Keep learning and listening to the things I tell you. You must wait. Don't be anxious and don't worry. Don't look around at the things you think you want. Just keep looking off and away up to Me, or you'll miss what I have to show you. And then, when you're ready. I'll surprise you with love for more beautiful than any you would ever dream of.

You see, until you are ready and until the one I have for you is ready, I am working this minute to have both of you ready at the same time. And until you are both satisfied exclusively with Me and the life prepared for you, you won't be able to experience the love that exemplifies your relationship with Me, and this is perfect love. "And dear one, I want you to have this most wonderful love. I want you to see in the flesh a picture of your relationship with Me. And to enjoy materially and concretely the everlasting union of beauty and perfection and love that I offer you with Myself. Know that I love you. I am God Almighty. Believe and be satisfied."

How are you today, Sweetheart? How are you feeling? I have to reread God's message to me and us in the prayer I prayed before God came to my heart and brought you into my life. You are so precious, for that when I think of you and dream of you and have visions of us together living with one another. I have to look at you as you were God with that same kind of love, I have to love God, and then I can love you how I love God. And for this kind of love, who can say that it will not be perfect? What God has brought together that no man takes apart. When we were reunited together with the first email, you sent me. God knew right then that we were ready for each other. Although me being skeptical and of this world from time to time getting sidetracked.

That will never happen again, Sweetheart. I will never doubt your love for me. And I pray to God you know that I love you with all my heart and do not doubt my love for you. This is a spiritual gift from God, and only through his union and miracles our way to Butte with one another. I think about the miracle of our meeting and being together. And I have to thank God for you and your mother in my life and our fathers, who all had something to do with this, and it all had to do with love. That's nothing money can buy. There is no amount of money for all the money in this world or everything of this world. I would even consider trading for our love for one another. It is that powerful and that beautiful.

Do you have Valentine's Day in The north country? Just curious, in the United States, it is the 13th of this month, and that would be Wednesday, the day I get my Social Security check. Coincidental? I do not think so. You're my girl. You're my precious beautiful, scrumptious delicious, delectable, delightful tasty little morsel, young gorgeous lovely Sweetheart of a girl from The north country. There are so many indescribable words as far as our love goes, and we have a whole lifetime to find them together.

And I will find them all our lives will never be boring moment by moment day by day we have a lot of energy to live for one another and for our children your mother and others we are going to help spiritually with the Holy Spirit working through us this is what I pray for. I do not pray for materialistic items or blessings in abundance; I have the unshakable faith it just shows up when we needed It. So everything is okay right this very second, honey, my Sweetheart. I love you. Hugs and kisses

20 February 2019

DiAnnie wrote;

Good morning my love,

Thank God I can finally get back to you. It has been a hectic time for me, and I realize I haven't written you back for a few days. And here are all your sweet messages I'm about to respond to before leaving for work. It feels so much better reading all your lovely messages and getting back with you so that you know I'm still alive..lol, not going anywhere; God isn't ready to take any of us yet..lol my health is super, and here giving praises to God. So my not messaging you was intentional; I like you to understand that. You are such an understanding person, and it's a critical quality in you that it is not easily found in other guys. Don't change for any other reason because that would break my heart.

You are also a busy person in a way. The difference between you and I is you stay home to research, read, and instruct Brian. I have to wake up each morning for work five days a week, so we both are busy people. You would have been busier than me if you didn't have that accident, so God has His way of saying; hey boy, I will have you in a position to calm you down, and that is what He did. Will you be sad? No, praise God for who He is in any situation. God knew that He was sending a helper who will show you not just the care but love. I know you and Brian are trying as hard as possible to have the house in order, but men's work isn't like women's work, so do what you can.

When Mom and I come over, we will do our part. So home is not a home when the wife isn't there, so I know soon things will get in place, and that bachelor's pad will be no more..lol. Wow, you shoot a target on the door to play? Sure, that was not funny. A Marine is the only one that would do such play by shooting a target on their door. That is a tough boy's play..lol, when I'm around, no shooting on target on our home, okay? You are such a crazy man!..lol. We will laugh to death when we see those holes and how you cover them even though you didn't need to shoot at all..lol.

Well I understand, the wants or needs of a person are unlimited and believe me even if you had all the money in the world you would still want more done on the house so do the most important ones, I will understand no need to stress about making thing so hectic okay. I know God will bless us with abundance and try as hard as I can to put things in place before meeting you because life shouldn't be one-sided, I so let's just put our faith in God. All will be fine. I pray for those two books to succeed and what we are going to write as well. In the most difficult times that you know, if someone loves you, life isn't about the good times only, even in the worse times is when people appreciate each other. God has a great plan, and I think all we need is patience. We have a great future ahead with our children.

My love I like you to understand one thing, being a husband and a wife is not necessarily about putting a ring on the finger first before knowing that you are husband and wife, that's what many people think, it is true in a way, but when two hearts do not join in honesty that the two people in the relationship belong to each other.

Still, just the rings and documentation that you are a married couple is a waste of time. Hence, as we are not yet married, I know it would sound silly to others who do not believe what you and I believe in. I consider myself your wife, and I don't feel pressured at all about you calling me your wife, even if you called me your wife now. The ring is not yet there on the finger. We know that we will still get married no matter what, so I'm not bothered at all. You dream all the time, babe..lol. In your dream, those guys that were disrespectful to their elders are not from God. I know it wasn't associated with me because I would never be disrespectful to my elder because I got a good moral upbringing from my Godly mother and father, and I thank God for that.

I think I remember a little about that when you told me, hope he's a nice person to women and not someone that is not nice to women. The good part is that he's going to help you fix things on the house, which is fantastic. I pray for his safe arrival.

Well, honey, we all have our life qualities, and it is only God that gives these qualities reason that not everyone has them unless God is with you. I am a forgiving person because I was taught to forgive like a child of God. One good quality you have that I have already mentioned is patience, and it is only a faithful person who can have such, so that's the big difference between you and I and others. Whenever someone hears about us, they believe they would say negative things about me, or if I talk about you to someone, they say negative things right away because they do not share the same qualities. So I better not talk about us to anyone, and it feels better now.

Only those in Christ honestly will understand the love we share. Not the world, my passion, and I love you the way you are. You have changed a lot, and that makes me love you more. We share so many things in common to let us know our meeting was never perchance but something directed by God before we were even born. I am so surprised how you list all we share in common, birth dates, meeting, our parents, European ancestry. All these little things make me believe we are just the right person for each other. You are so crazy, babe. Do you think my Mom and I will kick you out from our home and kick you on the street? I will cry if the Devil fools me to do such ever. How would I ever want to hurt this old Zorro? Never because I love him with all his shortcomings, I better pray to God to change you than kick you on the streets.. lol I am already proud of you that you realized how much because of me that you have changed a lot.

I look forward to hearing from you, my love. I will get ready shortly to get out. Thanks so much for all the sweet messages. You are always on my mind and heart all the time and know my delays are never intentional. The work is so recent, and I get so tired when I get home, but it is okay to get in touch more again. Love you so much, Mon Zorro, and enjoy the rest of your day.

Warm hugs and kisses as I feel very cold right now..lol, Your girl.

Thomas wrote;

Beautiful, I always have dreams. I do not worry about you not writing to me because you're so busy working. And you're right. If I were physically capable, I would be working too. Just as hard as you are, it not harder. I always have been an honest hard worker, as I know you are as well. That's another thing we have in common.

And I thank God for your understanding that we are husband-and-wife without feeling pressured. You are with me and all my dreams, I had a dream about your father last night as I woke up this morning thinking about its purpose. There never seems to be a purpose with dreams all the time.

Your father was a renowned minister, and I remember you being in his ministry as his daughter and just as beautiful as you are now. And for some reason, we were both hungry and needed food. And dreams are never in a familiar location, we were down by the ocean somewhere, and I said to everyone in your family, help yourselves to any food that I have. How can you have food in the refrigerator in the ocean? I don't know. Smile

Anyway, you ask if I had anything to drink, and I said I believe there is some juice in the refrigerator. And you open the fridge in a remember you seeing some grape juice that you wanted to have and I said help yourself, and you were so happy, and we were so in love as usual in my dreams.

When I thought we were broke and had no money, your father being a renowned minister, put $25 into my hat as it was being passed around the church. We were outside somewhere by the beach. I remember your father was a very nice gentleman and everyone wanted to be around his ministry. And then I woke up, some dreams I do not mention to you because they are so crazy and I should mention them to you because they might have a meaning to you. Like I have said before, you are always with me in my dreams, like you are my conscience.

Anyway, Brian and I are working daily on this house.

Brian and I work on projects as I have mentioned before, and just when he thinks he is done. And you are undoubtedly correct. I would not shoot holes through my door, I should say to our bedroom door. When you are here, I would never even think of doing that. That's what makes me think how much of a bachelor I have been all these years living alone by myself and just having fun like boys do when they are alone without my beautiful lovely wife with me.

I would not even think of doing those things. I might mention them to you when we are together, smile LOL I might say, "DiAnnie would you care to shoot some holes through our bedroom door?" Smile LOL, we can at least laugh together, and we will always laugh together and have fun together. This I know for sure because God loves us both, and it is only God's love that has brought us together.

And what I find sad is that we cannot explain our Christian love for one another to other people. Because, as you had mentioned, they would not understand, and that is sad. The only one who knows about you and brother Brian. And I do not say a lot to him, other than I have told him that he will have to start speaking French, stop smoking cigarettes, and memorize the Bible and become a Christian and quit swearing if he is going to have any chance at all with my wife's mother, Anna. Smile LOL

Keep that between you and me, not your mother, because I use that to keep Brian busy. It's kind of a boy saying. And absolutely no disrespect to your mother at all. I pray to God you understand, smile with care and kindness. Thank you so much, sweetheart, for writing when you had the opportunity and have patience and only write when you feel like it. I will certainly understand.

The only thought that crosses my mind occasionally is that you might be in the hospital with pain in your knees. Sometimes I think that, and our faith in God is so strong that everything will be okay when we finally get together, have unshakable faith, sweetheart, as I know you do, your my Christian girl from The north country, my beautiful Christian girl of whom I love very much and care about with all my heart. Peace and grace of the Lord be with you and your mother through Jesus Christ our Lord's name amen, hugs, and kisses.

23 February 2019

DiAnnie wrote;

Hello to my handsome man and my best friend,

I guess you have looked on the way quite a while for my message, sorry promise was not fulfilled like I plan to keep in touch more, not my fault honey it's loads of work. Good, I can write you at the moment, it makes me happy when I can. How are you doing today? I hope that you have been keeping well since we last heard from each other. I am doing great as well health-wise and spiritually as well. Work has me the stress recently, but I guess I shouldn't complain as long I want to survive..lol.

I was reading about your dreams, and I said to myself, this man has a good head on his shoulder! Remember, every dream isn't just anyone who can do that. You may be an inventor some days as long you can write down dreams. Sad, I do not remember most of my dreams. Maybe I sleep too much when I get from work; if not, at least I should have a dream one or two, but I do anyway once in a while. Oh yes, we do have this workaholic spirit in the two of us that I will not deny..lol.

Sure your dream about my father makes me want to agree because he was also a man of God, and as a girl coming up, my Mom and I attended our gathering, so you must have a perfect head. What are we always doing around the ocean in most of your dream? Lol, sometimes we are in the mountains, to this must be Arizona? Ah, I guess we will spend most of our lives in Arizona..lol.

You two must be working so hard on the house as if you have never worked on it before. I guess there must be many things you didn't put in place till now. We will do our part of the work, but I guess I will be the interior decoration part. I can imagine boys working to have the home in place for us makes us feel special in a way. When I told my Mom, she said, hey, are you serious about this? Why do you have Thomas working so hard to say to him, it's okay, we will do the rest? Lol, I only said I'd, but we can't do the men's part of the work. Am I right? Lol.

Brian may be fed up sometimes working, I guess. You know when a lady person does a piece of work, and you come to tell them that you haven't done anything! It feels as if you will die unless that person has an honest spirit like you have made Brian become. Those boys saying makes me laugh so hard imagining the response of Brian when he's tired. Lol. Living or being a friend with a Marine must have its ups and downs, and I hope it's not going to be the same with me.

You know I wouldn't say I like pressure..lol. Sure I feel sad too that we can not express our joy to others. I think it's better to be happy as two- person than having a multitude happy. Those involved in the relationship are the sad ones because gossips are everywhere and people are so fast to stick their noses in other people's affairs, so if it takes us to be the only happy ones for what we share, better that way than to stress. Sure, I know Brian knowing you and I will be together and kidding with him that he may have Mom all to himself in his dreams would make him a better person keeping busy..lol you know how to have him happy in a fiction movie..lol, sad for him. If this will keep him busy, trust me, I will keep this between us, not everything I share with my Mom. I know you don't mean to be disrespectful. Thanks always for mentioning Mom and me in prayers each time, not a second that passes that you are not in mine and Mom as well.

One gift I do not have is interpreting dreams. If you noticed, whenever you dream, and you tell me, I find it difficult to tell you the meaning. Still, these dreams with us continually together are the sign that our meeting is sure, dreams with kids are good dreams because it's a sign that God is going to work a miracle that people would wonder how come you have given birth, once a person's dream is not mostly opposite than these are sure good dreams, not everyone that have the same dreams meaning, some people dreams come true and some in the opposite, so which one are you?

It seems like those curtain you bought are nice from your excellent explanation..lol sure we believe what we can afford, so no matter what you buy in our home, as long it is okay, I wouldn't mind complaining but if we both agree that this isn't the right one believe we will have to change it. Bit by bit you will be done with the designing of the house like I said don't work too hard because some things will be changed certain part of the house will have to look more feminine..lol.

I know living as a bachelor all these years you will not be 100% perfect, so I expect that not everything will be good in my eyes or Mom so there is where we will come in. So you got your license now? I love your sense of humor you had with the instructor. You beat their questions, some of these questions in the driving schools are sometimes out of place, but they are important too because you have people that go against them, and you ask how can this be!..lol So I'm glad you were able to make her laugh, I trust you in that one lol. Brian seems to know you very well, and I like that, how I understand you so perfectly.

You enjoy your day, my love, I will try to do some things around here and see if I can get out later or get some more rest. My day seems like night from being so exhausted..lol

I kiss you and give you a big hug! I love you so much. All my heart, honey.

24 February 2019

DiAnnie wrote;

Hello, my sweetheart,

It's such a joy when I get a message from you. I feel so much relieved when I know how my man is doing. Sure our chef is God, and I always enjoy all those lovely messages from you, especially with all those compliments. These make me feel special, and I know I have a loving man who appreciates everything about me. You are so different from millions of guys out there. Your character is so unique. I hope you are having a great Sunday, my love.

I think the thought that came to you of Mom, and I stay in the same room for a while isn't bad at all, though it's my home in the first few days when we arrive we two will be strangers in that home so to have Mom feel the relief I'll spend a few days sleeping with her. It seems like you think just like me, and you are sometimes far ahead of me—you such a good man, my love. Wow, 3000 ft is huge, and you have lived alone for quite a while. Have you always lived there alone or the others there have been with you for a long time?

Right I agree. Right now, it's a house till the heat of a lady is in there before becoming a home. We will see if anything needs changing. I know there will be something somehow to change. Learning a bachelor has lived there a long time. Men can be disorganized more, so I know what I'll expect..lol.

Are you serious? Hahaha, you talk in your sleep? I hope you'll not wake me most of the time because those who dream and talk in their sleep are annoying sometimes. Do you snore? I hope not. If you do these, know your mouth may be bandage with a piece of cloth when sleeping. I guess you start to get scared now, right? I'm just kidding. Everyone has their performances when sleeping. You may not know what you do unless someone tells you. Good, you have Brian and Christine tell you you talk. I'll help you when you start to do that. Also, I do snore sometimes, especially when I'm so tired. We will see when I am there. If Christine is a nice person, for sure, we will get along.

Wow, you are so sweet babe, you mean you have bought everything brand new for us for our rooms? God, such a clean and neat gentleman! Sure, I'll get enough rest today just wanted to reply to you, so you know someone here is thinking about you. You are always in my prayers and thoughts, and thanks for keeping Mom and me in prayers each time. Have a nice day, my Zorro.

26 February 2019

DiAnnie wrote;

Good morning my sweet man

I was caught up with loads of work yesterday, so I'm glad to message you right now before leaving for work. How was your night? I hope you had a great night full of sweet dreams about us. Mine was great, sleep much, and didn't dream. When a person is too tired, they do not have any time to dream..lol.

Good, you do not snore because if you did, you would get the shock of your life! Lol, if you snore, I would light a cigarette to your mouth, and you will smoke while snoring guess you would want to kick the hell out of me, right? Lol. I snore sometimes, so I believe I give you a secret that you would use on me..how silly I am! Please don't mind me, okay I was only kidding because I know you as silly as I am, and you would surely light a cigar and put it in my mouth while asleep. I know what this Marine is capable of doing..lol You are right; I realize when I sleep on my side, I do not snore, so I guess I'll start to sleep on my side, but when I come there, I will mostly lay my head on your chest and fall asleep.

Okay, that's a good idea to wait before purchasing those things for the room, maybe by then I'll do a research and see which would be more feminine for our rooms, Mom and

I. Sure I know, my love, you constantly come up with good ideas just as I sometimes do, I know you are a respectful person. I like how much you take things one reason I love you so much.

Well, the best thing for me is to spend a little time with Mom in her room before starting to come to our room.

I know Mom will tell me why I can't go to sleep with Thomas? This way, she is at ease. I hope you understand. I can't believe you guys are still cleaning lol it's like you have not clean since you build that house do you? Lol. It seems like life for a single man is more stressful than that of a lady to me. No worries, we will continuously do cleaning, and our home will be a little paradise on earth. That's so sad to hear that Christine is still committed to your family even though she lost her man. She must be a lady with a heart full of gold.

You make me laugh so hard reading about your past hard jokes with friends. When I look at your pictures, I can see a bad boy Thomas when you were younger. I am thinking now why in the hell I tell you I do snore! Hey, I was kidding. I do not snore, don't take me seriously! not sure you're going to believe me, right?

Honey, Here thinking about you as I get ready for work shortly. Have a nice day and think about me as well. A big hug and a kiss from your secret admirer.

CHAPTER 3

DiAnnie, shocks her fiancé, Unannounced.

On a warm spring day, Thomas sits comfortably at his computer writing an email to his soulmate and the love of his life, DiAnnie. When hearing the front door slide open, not thinking much of it, for this reason, Thomas never locks his doors, even when he leaves for a few hours. Those who know Thomas walk in all the time, which he is used to without looking to who it could be. He is mentally enthralled with this love for his soulmate/fiancé, not looking at whose walking down the hall towards him. He was sitting at the 26 1/2 inch desktop computer and the corridor that leads back to the master bedroom/office. Suddenly, hearing a female voice that has a slight accent is standing right next to Thomas. The curiosity of a female in Thomases home he glanced.

The female voice said, "do you know who I am"? Looking and not recognizing this beautiful young lady he had never seen before or met. The hall light was behind her, not portraying the features of her face clearly. In the theater of Thomas's mind, there is no way this could be DiAnnie. He had to look twice and still did not recognize this beautiful female smiling with the most beautiful smile, with tears streaming down her face.

Thomas knew immediately and miraculously who this was; Thomas immediately stood up and grabbed DiAnnie in shock and disbelief. Both of them, suddenly with tears, held onto each other like they were never going to let go of one another. Thomas says, "God are you kidding me," thank you, God, thank you, God. And they just held one another with tears of joy and spiritual love they have never known through the grace of God. A lifelong dream that has materialized and has not disappeared. Christmas morning with a gorgeous Guardian Angel treasure, most certainly from heaven.

Thomas and DiAnnie did not even want to know how she came about getting to their home from the North country to Arizona. After just holding each other for the longest time, not saying one word. Diane Annie mention that she promised her mother that she would call and let her know that she arrived safely and everything was okay. She said her mother was really excited for the both of us was praying for us and she could tell her mother's depression was not even noticeable her mother was extremely excited and happy for her.

And then Thomas asked, "sweetheart, how is your mother Anna keeping? And she is in a safe environment and a safe place and feeling well when you left? And Diane Annie mentioned that she would not have left if her mother was not safe with some friends she was staying with. And Thomas then asks, "you have not seen your mother in quite some time, and I know better than to ask a question if you miss her. Realizing, of course, DiAnnie will meet her mother in Malta, at her father's brother's home, where Anna was staying presently.

Thomas for the first time excuse himself while he went and drew the curtains and locked the front door. And then unplugged the phones so they would have absolute privacy for this gracious meeting.

Like the Holy Spirit was leading them and guiding them both, they walked over to the master bed, and both of them lay down next to each other and just held one another on the bed. There were still no words mentioned, and it was a miraculous spiritual gift supernaturally from God. They both just held one another for the longest time with tears of joy between the two of them.

DiAnnie was tired from her long journey, and Thomas was mentally drained in disbelief and shock. Still, no words were said for quite some time. This romantic romance of love they have never known, or even dreamed of, in their wildest imagination. Both of them later stated that it was like being in heaven on earth. As expressed in the Lord's prayer. "On earth, as it is in Heaven." DiAnnie was so relaxed and extremely tired and exhausted from her long journey she fell asleep in Thomas' arms. And Thomas just watched DiAnnie for the longest time. With no other thought than of finally coming together with love, they have never known—God's love. Thomas and DiAnnie have no desire of fornicating. Thomas knows it would disrespect his love for Diane and would be like slapping God in the face. Sex outside of marriage is a sin.

1 Corinthians 7: 2-4. *Nevertheless, to avoid fornication, let every man have his own wife, and that every woman have her own husband. [3] Let the husband render unto the wife two benevolence; likewise also the wife unto her husband. [4] The wife has not power over her own body, but the husband; and likewise also the husband has not power over his own body, but the wife.*

Communicating continuously daily for a year, Thomas is not as exhausted as his fiancée DiAnnie. Although Thomas came into DiAnnie's dream, she had awakened on her own, only to hold Thomas tighter. Thomas whispered softly into her ear after massaging her neck gently in the upper part of her back. Asking her if she would like to take a nice hot Jacuzzi? (a deep Jacuzzi with eight jets, never used after being remodeled) And she agreed, that sounds very relaxing.

Thomas just remodeled this comfortable three-bedroom, two-bath home for DiAnnie and her mother, Anna. Although there were unopened boxes of brand-new things stacked in the bedroom, that was remodeled for Anna. Thomas thought he would surprise DiAnnie, asking her if she would care to go into her mother's bedroom and open one of the boxes, where there were luxurious Teal Turkish Persian towels. And DiAnnie agreed with enthusiasm and seemed to have got a second wind. Thomas smiled and mentioned to DiAnnie, and you might want to save opening a few boxes for your mother when she arrives. They both smiled and laughed, and DiAnnie agreed.

And then Thomas mentioned, not able to see his fiancée for she was in her mother's room, Thomas asked, "you are opening all the boxes, aren't you? And you have already found the Persian Turkish towels. Thomas had a feeling he was talking to the wall or to himself. Smiling. And Thomas was laughing, and so is DiAnnie. And he said you might as well open them all, and do not forget the two dresser drawers that are packed with brand-new sheets, pillows, towels, and God only knows what else. And please do not forget to go into the walk-in closet where the other dresser drawer is and more boxes.

They were both laughing and having fun, and Thomas suggested opening all the boxes, and we can seal up the boxes again and make it look like they were not open of things you would not like to use. And they both agreed and smiled.

Then Thomas finally asks the question, how on God's green earth did you get here? And she explained that she made reservations about a week ago. All the time communicating back-and-forth, Thomas had no clue what his fiancée was up to. Nor did he even suspect she would have the courage to move forward with this kind of surprise, never meeting Thomas before.

And then she mentioned that we exchanged addresses a long time ago. So looking on MapQuest, she knew exactly where these comfortable homes were, and she had taken a taxi from the airport. And she had a trunk that had a handle on wheels setting on the front deck.

The restroom has a complete steam shower with a seat and a pulsating shower-head and a three-way full Hollywood mirror with lights overhead. In the meantime, while talking, Thomas was running the water in the Jacuzzi for his fiancée. And placing a natural fragrant lavender bubble bath into the Jacuzzi.

And Thomas was so excited and so happy and so satisfied just listening to his fiancée opening all the drawers, opening all the boxes, and looking throughout the home.

And straightening up a few things in the home that he would have liked to have done before his fiancée DiAnnie arrived. She surprises Thomas, the priority is not the house. DiAnnie felt right at home, and that was complete satisfaction for Thomas. And they both felt and knew that in their hearts, everything was okay and perfect. Thomas always tries to keep his home clean and takes a shower daily. And it just felt like this three-bedroom, two- bath home was made specifically for both of them, as well as Anna, DiAnnie's mother.

As Thomas ask do you have any baggage? And DiAnnie said yes, it's on the front porch, and Thomas immediately had his caretaker who lived about 150 feet, in a mobile home from their home. Dialed him up directly and ask him if he would not mind rolling the trunk into the master bedroom while DiAnnie was in the Jacuzzi.

While DiAnnie what is taking her steam shower and Jacuzzi, Thomas explained to his caretaker who had arrived and explicitly requested that they not be disturbed. Only unless the house is burning down, please do not sit and watch the house burned down while my fiancé and I are inside relaxing. Smile.

After destroying her mother's bedroom, opening boxes, and going through things destroying the home. Thomas was laughing; he could not stop laughing.

And went to the kitchen to cook a gourmet meal for his fiancée. Thomas just happened to have a thick T-bone steak that he had purchased the day before in the refrigerator. The T-bone steak on one side of the bone, shaped like a T, is cut of meat called "Filet Mignon." A flavor that is to die for. On the other side of the T-bone, a cut of beef is called a " New York Steak." Thomas thought they would share an equal portion of the two different stakes. The flavors are unbelievably entirely different. Yet gourmet.

Freshly cut artichokes, boiled in a pan of water until the leaves are tender, dipping each leaf in either mayonnaise or butter, scraping the tender leaves with your teeth. And baked potatoes either with sour cream or butter, with the side of asparagus. Thomas prepared a gourmet salad, cutting up the lettuce, tomatoes, black olives, some dill pickles, cucumbers, and keeping them all separate indifferent side dishes. It is always convenient for others to dish their salad the way they want to prepare it for themselves. Several salad dressings. And some warm dinner rolls.

They would have two types of ice cream for dessert: cherries Jubilee or sherbet. Thomas grated some almonds and place them in a small bowl, with a little warm chocolate or raspberry syrup, whipping cream with a cherry on top.

There was an assortment of drinks; Thomas does not drink alcohol, from the allergic reaction called alcoholism. Nineteen years clean and sober. However, Thomas does realize that some do not have an allergic reaction to alcoholism. Thomas always keeps a bottle of rare wine out of sight for the occasion. A bottle of red wine, California Merlot or Cabernet sauvignon-And a bottle of white wine, Chablis Premier Cru Montee de Tonnerre.

Also, beverages would include coffee, tea, milk, a variety, and a selection of soft drinks, including bottled water.

DiAnnie taking her Jacuzzi, Thomas took it upon himself to go outside and get a bouquet of freshly cut flowers. He was lighting a couple of candles on the dining room table and setting the atmosphere of romance that could only have been experienced by two of God's precious children.

After some time, DiAnnie went into the steam shower first and then into the Jacuzzi. Coming out of the restroom refreshed and relaxed, the timing was perfect. We were both a little hungry, and to her surprise, brunch was being served. She came out of the restroom in the most gorgeous flowered pink and white dress, looking like an angel, a precious treasure. What Thomas appreciates about ladies is the time they spend making themselves to look beautiful. Thomas appreciates ladies for that, and men should appreciate these ladies and let them know how proud they are of these gorgeous God-given gifts. That they would take so much time looking beautiful. Thomas is going to treat DiAnnie like a queen every day of her life.

Now it was Thomas's time to surprise with the brunch he had prepared for his fiancée.

Thomas recommended they say grace and thank God, instantly holding hands and bowing their heads graciously, not only for each other, bringing them together in the way that the Holy Spirit could only have happened through miracle. And Thomas continues to thank God not only for this beautiful precious Guardian Angel treasure from the North country, and all the friend's relatives and people that have asked us to pray for them and that need prayer, then for this meal that we are so graciously thankful for through Jesus Christ our Lord's name amen.

DiAnnie could not believe the meal Thomas prepared, and she was starving. And Thomas patiently waited for DiAnnie to take the first bite of food before he started eating. The conversation was electrifying, and Thomas just listened, and you can feel the magnetic spiritual connection of the love between Thomas and DiAnnie. And they both graciously ate until they were satisfied entirely with the dinner and the desert.

Thomas was reading a true story one time in the past. There was this family who was moving across three states about 400 miles. Because the husband had a new job and had a deadline, he had to meet that he could not be late for. So the husband, wife, their two children, and their two German Shepherd dogs started on their journey. Along the way, they stopped at a rest stop alongside a river. The male German Shepherd wandered off. And they looked and called for this dog. And because of the loud sound of the river, the male German Shepherd could not hear the family yelling for him, and they had to leave.

They made signs quickly, put them up all over the area, and asked everyone to please keep their eyes out for their dog named Eric. Heartbroken, they had to leave. They arrived at their destination, their new home.

About two days later, they heard a scratch at the front door. It was the male German Shepherd. His paws were bloodied; he was skinny and lost a lot of weight, although very happy to be with his family. And the family was so excited to see their male German Shepherd dog.

They slid out a bowl of food and some water for Eric. And it was the custom of this male German Shepherd not to eat until his female German Shepherd named Carla would eat first. So Eric sat patiently and waited for Carla to eat before he ate.

Spiritually what I learned from this story is. "When you go out to dinner with the man, and he eats first, he is very selfish; get rid of him immediately." No matter how long he has to wait for, that lady to take the first bite. That is an excellent character within this good man that shows respect and consideration. That could only come from a male German Shepherd dog named Eric.

Thomas then suggested that his fiancée call her mother, letting her know that everything was okay and perfect. Mothers worry about their only child, and her mother was even happier and excited after the second call. And both Thomas and DiAnnie agree to keep calling her mother.

They were both exhausted; they both decided to go to the master bedroom on the master bed, take a nap and get some sleep together. And they left the house destroyed with the kitchen chores in the open boxes, and it just felt like home.

Thomas and his fiancée lay down on the comfortable master bed, holding each other in talking cheek to cheek, as Thomas massage DiAnnie's neck very gently and her upper back, and it wasn't long before she was asleep. Thomas followed shortly after that in the dream they have prayed for their entire lives of this love.

Sleeping off and on, they each kept waking up, holding each other and continuously were in each other's dreams, and thanking God, knowing that this love was divine love, through God's grace for God's children. Both of them slept late into the next day, Thomas whispering softly into DiAnnie's ear, would you care to get dressed? We can take a ride in our automobile, and I can show you some magnificent sites. Thomas has always said that he lived with the Holy Spirit. DiAnnie finally understood what Thomas meant when he said that it becomes a part of your soul. And with unshakable faith, you know without a doubt that the Holy Spirit Jesus Christ our Lord left us with lives there.

Thomas can finally hold his fiancée DiAnnie high publicly praising his fiancée, and for the first time feel not alone, and be able to tell the world about this God-given gift and this love they have never known. The world will soon realize they have witnessed a miracle.

Both Thomas and DiAnnie decided they would not clean up anything because her time was short with Thomas. She had to leave in about four days to meet her mother in Malta. They had some legal matters concerning their father's estate that the lawyer had to take care of in Malta at a specific date.

DiAnnie suggested to Thomas that they spend a few days together and not go anywhere. A beautiful young lady's wisdom said I would be back and not gone forever, and we have a lifetime ahead of us. Let us spend this short time together with one another and not go anywhere or see anyone. Thomas could not have agreed more, and it is better to have just overwhelmed him with her suggestion.

She said on the way back to the airport, while you are driving me, you can show me a few of the sites and things we will do when we come back into each other's lives with my mother. DiAnnie also said with sincerity and tears running down her cheeks, and I do not want to leave. What could Thomas say? He felt the same way, although he knew that her mother was expecting her in Malta and that her mother missed her daughter just as much as I'm going to miss my fiancé.

Thomas said, "sweetheart, you have to continue with your schedule, and they both knew they had two separate, and they did not want to, especially the five days they have spent together went by so fast, they were both in a state of shock having to leave one another. It was like grieving the death of a loved one and going through the five stages. Denial, anger, bargaining, depression, and finally acceptance. They realize that the love that God them together for calling beyond their comprehension or imagination will be revealed to them slowly. Thomas and Diane Annie devote their lives to God and service spiritual discernment helping others, not-for-profit or prestige, proceeds donated. And if they both live by the Bible. BIBLE— basic instruction before leaving earth. There will never be a harsh word between them. Staying out of the world and into the word, their life will be "on earth as it is in heaven."

1 Peter 3; 7. *Likewise, you husbands, dwell with your wife according to knowledge, giving honor unto the wife, as unto the weaker vessel, and as being heirs together of the grace of life; that your prayers be not hindered.*

So you husbands listen, disrespecting your wife and trying to control her and co-hearse or manipulate your wife, your prayers will not be answered. Treat your wife with great respect and honor. She is an extraordinary creation of God and should be provided for, cared for, protected, loved, and prayed with.

1 Corinthians 7: 10-11. *And unto the married I command, yet not I, but the Lord, let the wife depart from her husband. [11] But if she leaves, let her remain unmarried, or be reconciled with her husband; and let not the husband put away his wife. And husbands, there are times your wife will have to depart from her husband, although if she leaves, she will not get remarried because she is honest and you can trust your wife. And a wife and husband praying together will stay together and will not be a house divided against itself.*

1 Corinthians 7: 27. *Art thou bound unto a wife? Seek not to be loosed. Art thou loosed from a wife? Seek not a wife.* Thomas is engaged to be married, and DiAnnie has accepted Thomas's proposal for marriage. Thomas feels it necessary to humbly ask DiAnnie's mother, Anna, for her daughter's hand in marriage.

Ephesians 5: 23. *For the husband is head of the wife, even as Christ is the head of the church, and he is the Savior of the body.* Ephesians 5: 28. *So you men to love their wives as their bodies. He that loves his wife loves himself.* Ephesians 5: 31. *For this, the cause shall a man leave his father and mother and join his wife, and they two shall be one flesh.* Ephesians 5: 33. *Nevertheless, let every one of you in particular so love his wife even as himself; and the wife see that she reverence her husband.*

And I look at the emails, before and after we met, my fiancé here in our home when you surprised me. You wrote so many emails, and we were so in love, and our passion has only grown stronger and can never be taken apart no matter what. This love came from God, and I have remained spotless for this many years for one of God's fatherless and the widow.

Thomas and DiAnnie, not going into detail about their parting from one another on the way to the airport. DiAnnie surprise Thomas and they came together with tears of joy and happiness. They separate from one another with tears and pain in their hearts for not letting go of one another. The loneliness they will experience being separated and alone will bring pain to their heart that God's children should not experience.

Knowing with their unshakable faith, the prayers that brought them together, and over time they have mended and bonded their hearts so tightly woven together, nothing can separate this love. They consume each other's thoughts continuously, and when they think of one another, they also pray and give thanks to God for this miraculous love with gracious kindness. And the love that

Thomas feels for Anna is equal to the love he feels for his fiancée DiAnnie. Although different love equally and miraculously missed when they are apart. Psalms 34: 18. *The Lord is close to the broken hearted, and saves those who are crushed in spirit.*

God brought this love together with so many similarities it defies imagination. DiAnnie's birthdate is the exact birthdate of Thomas's dad. DiAnnie's father and Thomas and his father have the same first name, only spelled differently. Each of their mothers gave birth to them at 20 years of age. DiAnnie removes pornography from Thomas's life. Thomas now finds it repulsive to even think about it. Thomas has remodeled a three-bedroom, two-bath home into a very comfortable humble abode for DiAnnie and her mother, Anna. Thomas remains spotless for many years to care for a beautiful fatherless fiancé and the mother. Thomas wants to show the love that he could have shown more of to his mother.

Both Thomas and Diane Annie complement one another. They teach one another continuously, in their love is a love they came from the Angels enter God's grace, God had to come here in the flesh as Jesus Christ our Lord, to shed his precious blood for our wretched sins. Jesus Christ, our Lord, as Jesus ascended into heaven, left us with the Holy Spirit that moves throughout the earth answering prayers. And between us to help one another. Jesus also left us with a gift of casting out evil spirits in his name. In the gift of hands-on healing. Of which Thomas is studying in the Bible. The anointing oils are very pleasing to the Lord. Thomas and DiAnnie, their calling together, God willing, while saving many hundreds of thousands of lives, shining the light in front of these lost souls, and showing the way for their soul's journey to heaven.

Be nice to yourself because you're worth it, and I'm proud of you. No worry, no stress; that is a moment of happiness and faith you will not get back. God's gift to us is life; what we do with his life is our gift to God. We cannot turn the clock backward; all we can do is move forward, grow along spiritual lines, and try to do the next right thing. God does not make junk. As divine children of God, we have been created with God's love walking through this life with our soul's journey, everything matters. God did not go on vacation, and leave any of us in charge, thank God. If Thomas thinks it's about him, he is in big trouble.

Thomas being an avid theologian in studying the word of God, prophecy is undisputed. Daniel 12: 4. *But thou, oh Daniel, shut up the words, and seal the book, even to the time of the end; many shall run to and fro, and knowledge shall be increased.* The 19th century after riding horses for thousands of years prior. We can observe the increase in knowledge today where people are running two and fro, just looking at the freeways and cities.

Thomas and DiAnnie thank God through the Holy Spirit, that they have had the opportunity to at least have come together, even though miraculously thanks to DiAnnie, and they are both aware through their unshakable faith, that the next time they come together it may be in heaven, when Jesus Christ comes to rapture his people and his church. Ephesians 2; 6. And has raised us together and made us sit together in heavenly places in Christ Jesus. Mark 10; 9. What therefore

God has joined together let not man put asunder. Psalms 55; 14. We took sweet counsel together and walked unto the house of God in company.

Romans 8: 28. *And we know that all things work together for good to them that love God, to them who are the called according to his purpose.*

And supernaturally, with my unshakable faith and a strong miraculous feeling, your dad is bringing us together.

Your dad is proud of you.

CHAPTER 4

Romantic Memoirs From Heaven, March 2019

4 March 2019

DiAnnie wrote;

Hey My love,

Sorry for the silence. It was never intentional at all, and thanks for always being an understanding person with me. It was a hectic week but good it has come to an end, and I can have some time to message you now. You sound like things have been busy as well down there.

Oh yes, when you snore, that would be the consequence, to put a nice cigar to your mouth. You enjoy it while snoring..lol but I don't think you'll, so it might be me falling into my wicked little trap, this Marine does not snore, and he might do that to me.. lol I snore sometimes. Still, I guess I must be on my guard not to snore because if I ever did, I would be the one enjoying that cigar while snoring..lol.

I'm doing very well, and it's a miracle because normally, during such cold weather, I get a lot of pain in my knees, but I haven't experienced that much this time, so I thank God so much. I just got a few more messages from you so I know we are back to communicating once more. You are always on my mind, even if I do not reply right away.

Sounds great, and I can imagine you guys did a huge work on the house. Sure now the fixes plus us coming over would make the house a home. So I guess there's still a little more work that needs to be done on the house, too. I will do some finishing touches, so look up to that. It would be so much fun..lol.

I realize God works in mysterious ways, and it is only people that truly understand the things of God that can relate well. The electricity experience you had while going out and coming back is just so amazing. If it's not a miracle, then what would we call that? When we as people of God can acknowledge the simple things, we can get the bigger ones. I just admire your understanding of things we think so much alike. I know it was never perchance God brought us together. I can see now. Thanks for asking about my Mom each time. Whenever I tell her about you, she gets so excited that this man is so much fun to be with, and we can't wait to visit.

Wow, all these dreams in a short time make you the best dreamer in the world! Lol, I must borrow that gift of dreaming from you for sure..lol, on a serious note, when you catch a fish in your dream, be it a man or a woman, it's a sign of having a child children. This interpretation is from the first national Canadian here. I can see that you caught a smaller fish and use it as bait and gave me, and then I used it to catch a bigger fish is a clear sign of having children. Sometimes I do not want to believe in the locals' traditions, but their interpretations of dreams are always precise. So we will see when the time is right. You make me want to start sleeping in the position that you sleep so I would have dreams. I enjoyed all your dreams, and the one that we went to France and I didn't want to come back is imagination to the highest degree of you, not all dreams have meaning, maybe you are afraid to lose your girl to a French guy? hahaha. No worries, Zoro, I am all yours..lol. I'm so tired, so I'll try to get something to eat later and get rest. I am looking forward to hearing from you.

Hugs and kisses from me. The love of your life.

Thomas wrote;

Beautiful, how is that for an introduction? LOL, smile with love and compassion just feeling that way today. You see a small portion of these pictures. You would have to be here to get the full impact and beauty. The laundry room, your mother's restroom, the library, the living room, dining room kitchen, and a long hallway. One thing we did not take pictures of is the back bedroom or our bathroom. Or the walk-in closet.

This house is very, very spacious now. Because of the curtains that are extra thick and insulated, we cannot hear the echo anymore. LOL smile. It's more like an empty sound with nothing in the drawers or closets.

Other than the outside, that needs a good overhaul and painting. The inside needs a lady's touch. I pray to God when your mother and you ourselves should decide to arrive in Arizona. It will be everything you have expected and more. I believe you and your mother will get busy right away and know exactly what you want to do and how you want to arrange things. The man junk is gone. LOL, a smile, I think.

Of course, you and your mother are going to beat Brian like a redheaded stepchild. I feel my heart. The first thing is going to save for is a car. I have a feeling I'm not going to see much of Brian after that. I cannot deprive him of the life of a lady if he should choose to have one. I have a feeling he does. Brian knows how much time I spend on the computer with you, and he knows how much I love you and how you have changed my life like the guardian angel you are.

And when he first moved in here, I informed him that if he brought a lady with him, he might as well plan on moving out immediately. Because where he lives would be unfair for any lady of worth or of moral standards to want to move into that 12 x 12 shack he lives in. It might even be smaller than that. It does have a shower. It does have a toilet. It does have a sink and a single bed. And it is tiny. Our walk-in closet, I would say about half the size of Brian's shack.

I was thinking about that day, and believe me, sweetheart, that was a complete miracle day as crazy as it was. Either you are praying to God, and your mother may have been too, and I was as well. God was listening to somebody that day. If you remember, I had no oil in my automobile. You were wondering how I was going to get to Berkeley with Brian gone. My nephew came with 5 quarts of oil at my request and put them in the car. I thought for sure the car was no good, and the motor was blowing up after placing the oil in the car. It sounded great.

I was then curious as to who I was going to get to go with me to Berkeley. I know I mentioned to you that I was going by myself. And I was going to. Because I go everywhere by myself if I can't find anyone to go with me to push my chair. I have never had a problem asking some unsuspecting gentlemen if he would not mind getting the chair to the back of my car and pushing me wherever I needed to go. Everyone has been more than accommodating.

I even had a couple of ladies. They were accommodating and did not mind at all. And I said to. Them, I can wait for a man to come along, please. One lady said, "you can't depend on a man." LOL :-) she was an older lady very funny. It made me laugh. The other lady was a nurse at the VA hospital. She was young and came right up to the car and asked me if I needed any help. And I said I'm just waiting for a gentleman to come along so I can have him help me. She said, don't be silly.

This is what I get for thinking. Prayers matter. All of a sudden, he walked into the house. And I have not seen or heard from him in a few months. He was already half-drunk. And I said to myself, thank you, God. And why we did not get arrested, God only knows.

Anyway, beautiful, I pray to God you and your mother are doing okay. And I pray to God you can look at the pictures I sent. And there are some sheer red curtains that I have not received that I will drape on each side of the picture over your mother's bed and pull them back in the middle. And you are teaching me to be a moral man with the integrity of noble stature. And a gentleman. I just smile about that. I want to be a well-spoken gentleman.

Although I feel that is not my character. Others like me for who I. am and my sense of humor. That comes to the Holy Spirit through me. Because I do not know what I will say until it comes from my mouth, sometimes I surprise myself. For the most part, I take other's minds out there trials and tribulations. And that is a characteristic of God. Because I know the devil wants people to taste stuck in their trials and tribulations and be depressed. Depression is not even in my thought. Has no room in my life. LOL smile what matters most in my life right now is thinking about you and your mother getting together. And down the road, at some point in time looking forward to you and your mother coming to Arizona at your convenience, God willing. No pressure. Do not worry, sweetheart or stress. I know you mentioned it's hard to do. For me, it is not. I am very blessed.

Now that I'm thinking about it, there is no reason why I cannot teach English. On the other hand, I do not know any different language other than Spanish. And not that well enough to teach. You could make a small fortune, sweetheart. And have your hours and teach as many students as you would care to. I'm curious to know what your mother would like to do and make a lot of money doing it.? That will give me ideas, or I should say God will provide me with views through the Holy Spirit. I'm a tired sweetheart. I am dead dog tired. Hugs and kisses, I love you.

Protector Provider And The Promise Keeper Of The Household

Ephesians – six-four – fathers bring them up in the theater and admonition of the Lord. How to pray, how to read the of God the father's responsibility.

Genesis 3 – 16 – your desires shall be unto your husband. The husband shall rule over you. Foreign women shall manipulate or dominate in a marriage. Every physical body has one head. If it has two leaders, it's a freak. The husband is the head of the wife. Ovulation is 14 days of wine and roses for the woman and 14 days of thunder and lightning. A new beginning depends on the total forgiveness of the married couple. There is no alternative if you're not praying with your wife start. Ephesians 5; 21 – submitting yourselves one to another. Husbands do not submit to her lead but surrender to her needs. Ephesians 6 – four – provoke not your children to wrath. Train them in the fear and admonition of God.

5 March 2019

DiAnnie wrote;

How's your night going, my love? I hope you're having a lovely evening. My night is going great, and I'm going to bed shortly. I was so exhausted last night so forgive my delay. Wow, I love all those pictures! Gives me an idea of everything there.. you think I'm going to hang you with what you use to work and use the block under your bed? .. well, thank you for showing the easiest way to tie you up. Lol, please don't change the positions of those things. I'll need them sometime..lol. All those rooms are so lovely, and I'm so surprised that you two are so good at interior decorating!

The house is empty but immaculate, and that's what matters. Honey, you guys aren't going for an award for photo-shot.. lol the pictures look nice, and I think Brian got them right. He's not so perfect, but I appreciate the views very much. I know, right.. lol when you mix these sweet words like scrumptious, beautiful, and guardian angel, they make me smile, and I appreciate you so much for being so sweet. These names make me feel special. In the French The north country society, we refer to a man that is special in our love life as Lion 🐾 or any wild animal that is protective.. reason Lion is preferred because it's the king of the forest. And I added Zorro, so you're both lion and Zorro.. lol.

I like how you connected those sweet names, and it came to God, then everything rested on DiAnnie. Haha! I am excited about all the business ideas you're suggesting. These are things to sit and think about because, after all, I'll only need one or two business ideas. I can't do all remember, lol. Well, I'm not waiting and waiting as you may think.

Anyway, my love, enjoy the rest of your time. I'll get some rest now. I am looking forward to hearing from you. All my love and regards to you. Kisses and hugs from me. Your girl.

Thomas wrote;

Sweetheart, it's not that we are alike. We complement each other through the grace of God, like placing the perfect hand inside the perfect glove, two of God's children out of 7 billion. I feel blessed that you have changed my life for the better, and more shall be revealed in that area. Once again, God's gift to us is life. What we do with this life is our gift to God. We only come this way once. One moment of worry or stress is a moment of happiness we will never get back. God does not make junk. And we do not live our life through the rearview mirror. To create a strong relationship or friendship or marriage, it takes continuous forgiveness of one another at all times. And I find prayer through fasting is powerful medicine.

What is a family? A roof over your head will keep out the rain, four walls will keep out the wind, a floor will support the tottering steps of an infant, or give comfort to aging parents, a door will welcome friends, and it will keep the enemies out. A fireplace will worm those who nestle on a cold night, and there is a family.

What is a family? A mother cooking dinner for the ones she loves, the laugh of a baby, it is the strength of the father, it is the warmth of loving hearts, it is life for happy eyes, it is kindness on parade, it is loyalty one for the other, it is covenant love, it is the first church in the first school that I ever attended. I learned from my parents what was right and what was wrong. When I attended college, I did not argue with the guy in front of me who I disagreed with. I knew in my heart he was an educated moron as far as God was concerned For not having God in his heart.

Family is where you go for comfort. When you're hungry or sick or when the world has beaten you up, they can wrap their arms around you and hug you and make the world go away. When you have been battered or bruised by the world, the family will open the very door of heaven and heal you. They will anoint your wounds with the oil of gladness. They will wrap their arms around you and make you feel like you are the most important person in the world.

A family where joy is shared and trouble is Eased. They will be glad of your success. They will be excited about your promotion. They will be proud of. You for making the honor roll at school. They will buy every newspaper on the rack because you are the high school football hero. Or you made the honor roll, or you are the businessman of the year or you with the mother of the year.

Families, where fathers and mothers are respected and loved are never addressed as older men or older women. Names of parents are used in hushed tones of respect and reverence. In advancing years, they are not shuffled off to the sidelines and forgotten. Whether they are in a wheelchair or recliner or too feeble to sit up straightly, they are there because they belong to be there. They are your flesh and blood. They are your family.

Families are where children are considered to be a blessing of the Lord. They are not looked at as being an inconvenience to my career. They are not contestable because they will destroy the schoolgirl that worked for a figure to attain, they are angels unaware that God has given to you, for a few days until they are released into society, to make America a great nation again once unless you have not taught them well they will be the reason for the loss of life liberty and the pursuit of happiness.

Families are where the most uncomplicated food is good enough for teens because it was earned by an honest day's work and sweat. It's where money is not nearly as important as loving one another and being loyal to one another. Family is. Where the teakettle even sings for joy, it's where one man loves one woman, and the angels of heaven descend from the balconies of that celestial city to enjoy the beauty of that family. That father that mother those children love that man and that woman this is family. This is heaven on earth. May God bless it, and may God preserve it. In the United States of America, is there a family in your house?

What does God expect from the father? It reflects God, Ephesians 5; 25 – Husbands love your wives, Even as Christ also loved the church And gave himself for it. No verse in the Bible says to treat your wife like the oldest child of the family. You love your wife even as Christ loved the church when the church did not even deserve to be loved,

Peace and grace of the Lord be with you and your mother through Jesus Christ our Lord's name amen I'm in love with you honey. You have to remind me once in a while, that's all, LOL LOL smile maybe tie me up, gag me put tape over my mouth, LOL LOL smile whatever it takes, you're making me laugh I am making myself laugh.

I went to get a life insurance policy, and the insurance agent said, do you participate in dangerous sports? And I said, "well, I talk back to my wife once in a while" smile one husband said to his marriage counselor, my wife and I get along very well, and then we met. Smile LOL. I pray to God you're not taking me seriously. These are jokes,

Thomas wrote;

Good afternoon, my love.

Beautiful, thank you so very much for the long email, and I know you are a very busy, beautiful young lady, my girl from The north country. And you and I think exactly alike your letter brought out the exact response I thought my soulmate would give to me. And please, whatever you do, do not worry about Satan entering into my space with other ladies. Because before we met, I have asked many ladies to leave my home or not contact me anymore, for their intentions were all wrong, and we were far apart spiritually as heaven is from hell. So I never want you to be concerned, it hurts my heart that Satan would use God's children to perform his deeds, so I pray.

This is why you are my better half and 1/2 that God has put into our lives together to make a whole family together with your mother and our children. And I'm so happy that you stipulated about foreign women and relationships it gave me a better understanding and just the understanding that I would expect for my girl. Once again, you have made me a better man because you are so intelligent with knowledge and wisdom.

That is my heart. I know you and I were meant for each other because it was God's will for us to be together, not ours. And I thank you once again for forgiving me. Please realize, sweetheart, that we are not here to communicate with one another one-on-one at present.

I am looking forward to communicating with my wife every day, all the time listening to her. This is one place in our relationship that I miss is our not being able to communicate face-to-face.

I keep going through this house, and it is becoming a project of biblical proportion, LOL smile, I think I'm going to end up throwing everything away in this house. LOL, a smile that's what it appears to be; I cannot believe how much junk a bachelor can save like wiring to computers and all kinds of things that would have no interest to a lady

114

or, for that matter, to me either. Like plug-ins to computers and wires and headphones, I have been collecting just man stuff for years and years. That I never realized until I started getting into my drawers. Not my underwear LOL LOL smile, like the kitchen drawers right now and under the covers are empty as well as above the kitchen sink I have a few dishes, and above the kitchen counter by the refrigerator, I have some lovely flower vases that very rarely get flowers put into them. But they are beautiful vases, and I have a stunning red flower vase that I will put into your mother's bedroom.

And one thing I find that should be revealed is that you and your mother will not arrive here until after I get new towels, new bedding, new comforters and new curtains, new rugs and get the house painted with new decks and a new roof before you get here, let us all pray for that if we are going to pray for something, LOL smile beautiful my precious girl from The north country my guardian angel our relationship is rock solid. Because the foundation was built on Christian belief that we both have and God brought us together, we had nothing to do with it.

And you're right about The north country is the same as the United States, and you are right again about drugs and alcohol playing a very evil part in marriages in the United States.

One thing about where you and I will live in this small town is very secluded from society and drugs and alcohol. The grammar school has approximately 200 children from kindergarten through the sixth grade. And all the parents are very involved with the small school for the simple reason and are very wealthy because I have mentioned that all the people here work and make a lot working, and they want the best for their children. So when it comes time for our children to go to school, they can go to the same school I went to when I was going to this grammar school.

The only difference is the teachers are a lot better today, and they take a genuine, sincere interest in the education and upbringing of children. Although, for the most part, and I'm not too sure about this, this might be my thinking, but I feel Christianity is being not practiced anywhere in this world as a whole? On the scale of 7 billion people, I do not think there are very many Christians. We will be a bright shining light was spiritual discernment in the eyes of others not only to ourselves but our children's upbringing along with your gracious mother's morality.

This is what I feel. And please do not worry about my health. That has never been an issue for me because I know God's will, not mine. I am a testimony to many others because of my happiness and joy for God the Bible, Jesus Christ, and the Holy Spirit. Most importantly, God bringing you into my life and joining us brings me happiness that could only come through the Holy Spirit from God.

Thank you once again, sweetheart, for making me a. better man and letting me know your thoughts through communication. Do not ever think that you're communicating with me that I do not trust or honor with respect because I do. You are my girl. You are my beautiful girl, and do not ever give up on me, please. And one thing that is so miraculous to me is why you have not given up on me for all the horrible things I have said to you in the past. And it is because of your forgiveness of my sins that we are still together. I have mentioned you're very similar to Jesus Christ our Lord in that respect in this man's I prayed.

I know one thing for sure, when a woman draws the line and concludes that this relationship is over, she means it, and there is no going back. And in the past, I have brought you to that point, I feel, and you have not given up on me, yet you made me understand and realize the sins that I have committed against you instead of ending this relationship. And for that, my guardian angel, it only makes the bond of my love stronger for you.

I want you to know that I am in love with you. I am so in love with you in a very Christian way. And you are my girl. You're my treasure from The north country and a God-given gift I will not defile or disrespect without you correcting me only to make me a better man than I am today because of you.

I pray that makes sense to you, God loves us so much, and I can see nothing but great things happening in our lives together. And because of our age difference, I feel that our love has matured and bonded so that no other marriage or relationship has because we have God in our lives.

And when I prayed for you and your mother and yourself and your father and my father and my mother and God through Jesus Christ and the Holy Spirit. That was miraculous beyond our comprehension or imagination, would you not agree? Beautiful, I will write more to you later. You are so precious in my eyes and the eyes of God. And I know in my heart once again just to let you know that you are my girl. I always think about you, one thing I ask of you, please do not get to this old shack before I get it ready for you and your mother, LOL smile.

Miraculously I know God will bring you and your mother to this home to your home and your mother's at the exact time it is ready. And believe me, I am throwing so much stuff away that I have collected without realizing it taking my home was clean. LOL, and because of your feminine beauty and wanting things to be nice in her home because that is her heart and where her family will be raised.

And I understand with all my heart that God will bless us abundantly. We will never have to worry about survival or taking care of one another because I feel through the Holy Spirit that God will take care of us very well with abundance and blessings from heaven above. I do not even think or even doubt that God has not brought us together for a very special reason to reach out and help many thousands of others either through our writing or traveling and just meeting people and people wanting to meet us because of who we are through Jesus Christ our Lord.

I love you, honey. You make sure to let your mother know that my prayers are with her and that I am anxiously looking forward to meeting her one day, and immediately upon your arrival with your mother starts teaching me how to speak French, smile with enthusiasm so your mother and I can have a conversation a gracious meaningful conversation. I love you, honey hugs and kisses from your Zoro

6 March 2019

Thomas wrote;

Beautiful guardian angel from The north country, my precious treasure. Please do not ever feel that I am going down the bunny trail again and realize that it is because of our lack of communication with one another face to face. And if we had that bond that we will have one day, God willing. We would not be having a lot of these harmful types of thoughts that I go through from time to time, that you do not go through from time to time. This is why I look forward to our communication, especially my listening to you inquisitively with grateful appreciation and anticipation.

Can you understand that? Should I never put it? After my questions, because you already know the answers, LOL, LOL, a smile, I'm just a man, sweetheart, and I'm not just a man. We are God's children, and he has placed it together. And that in itself is miraculous. I'm in love with you you are all I think about, and if I ever come across the dream, I have had so many dreams I dream every night I go to sleep, but if I do not write them down right away within one hour or two hours, they seem to dissipate from my subconscious mind.

And you mentioned your grandmother was great at interpreting dreams. That was so cool to hear that, and I thank you for saying that to me. Maybe that's why I dream, is because your grandmother is also with us. This, I have no doubt. I'm sure our grandparents had a great part to play in our coming together with one another spiritually.

I had a lovely dream last night, of course, you're right there with me, we were trying to find a certain place, and I'm thinking as I'm writing to you right now about what we were looking for were in a car, together. And I'm trying to think of what we were looking for together, but we were together and trying to find this place. Maybe you can help me out with what we were looking for? When I think of it, I will send you another email, smile LOL.

Remember in the Bible, Daniel, one of the greatest prophets in the Bible, could interpret dreams. There were quite a few mentioned in the Bible that could interpret dreams.

Joseph was another one, whose 11 brothers sold him to some traders who took him to Egypt where he was put to work in the pharaohs household, and the Pharaoh's wife tried to seduce Joseph, and when he would not go into her bed with her, she said that he wanted to rape her. In the Pharaoh, he had to throw Joseph into prison for three years, where he met a cupbearer who mentioned to the Pharaoh that Joseph could interpret dreams. The Pharaoh brought Joseph out of prison to interpret his dream.

And Joseph said there would be ten years of plenty, and there will be ten years of drought. Therefore in the ten years of plenty, store up all the grain in your storage bins and save everything you can for the ten years of drought coming. The Pharaoh did so and made Joseph second in command. And if you remember the story, Joseph's father sent his 11 brothers to Egypt to get grain from the Pharaoh. And Joseph recognized his brothers who were speaking Hebrew, that Joseph could speak and understand, and Egyptian.

Sent his brothers back to their father without their youngest brother, and they begged Joseph not to keep the most immature brother because Joseph being the youngest brother of the other brothers, was making them feel the guilt of what they had done to him by selling him off when he was a small child. Finally, when the brothers came back with their father and the 70 other members of Abraham's extended Jewish family. But before they left to get their father, Joseph brought them into a room, knowing that the

Egyptians were not circumcised, and Joseph showed his brothers his circumcision and then revealed that he was their brother.

Joseph also predicted that the Jewish people would be in. captivity and bondage for 400 years, and after 430 years, he missed the interpretation of that dream by 30 years. Maybe I doubt it personally. Smile Joseph said not to leave him in Egypt to take his bones with them when they went after 400 years of bondage, and they did. And then Moses led them out of the land of bondage with over 2 million people. And the Egyptians gave the Israelites gold and silver and everything they needed. They could not give them enough to leave Egypt after killing all the firstborn with the Angel of death. And this is why we celebrate the Passover because the Israelite's put sacrifice Lamb blood over their doorpost, so the Angel of. Death would pass them.

Anyway, sweetheart, I cannot get enough of reading the Bible or studying the word of God because more shall be revealed, and no one knows the full mind of God, and not many people, if any, know the exact word of God that he left this through the Bible. The stories are interesting. The meanings are profound and teach us spiritual discernment, and gives us knowledge and wisdom. I love you, honey I am. in love with you.

Make sure and let your mother know that my prayers are with her. I pray for both of your safety and health and security, do not forget Jesus Christ and casting out any evil before you through Jesus Christ our Lord's name, and it will be done for your security or your mother's. I have heard too many testimonies about casting out evil spirits in the name of Jesus Christ. I love you. I love you. I love you too. Have a good day. I pray you are doing well and feeling well. Hugs and kisses

DiAnnie wrote;

Hello, my love,

I hope you're having a lovely time and you're feeling great on this day. Mine is going great as well, and it's always lovely to hear from you. I'm glad that I can take some more time to write you back. I wanted to do that yesterday, but I had some errands, so I could not.

Sure the description of Christ and the church is exactly how a man and a woman suppose to be like in a given relationship. That's what I pray for to be in our case, loving and respecting one another. Without love and respect for one another in a relationship, nothing can work out between the two involved. I think the research you made concerning foreign men or women having control over American men or women may be right but one-sided, and I see it has taken over your whole thought, so then it makes you feel insecure once again.

First, providing for the home isn't only by the man. Women are also good providers for the home. If a woman has a good job and doesn't have you think the woman will sit there and let her husband and kids suffer? No, she'll provide knowing her husband doesn't have, so when you only focus on the biblical side of men being the home's overseer, it doesn't necessarily mean provision-wise. A man can also protect his family even if he does not have much.

Men being the head of the home, cover many other things apart from him providing. If men's statistic in the leaving their wives and stepfathers raping their girl children, it's because of the freedom and drug abuse in the US. No man in their right mind would do that. So with that being said, if a relationship between an American and a foreigner does not work, it's not because the person who isn't American dominates or has any cultural effects. It depends on individual attitude.

Many foreign people have a relationship with American that is going well. It is some evidence of marriages not working right with foreigners and American, but let us are real, it's not really about money sometimes that is the root causes of marriages not working between foreigners and American.

I'm not taking sides because I'm a lady, but most marriages sometimes end up for silly reasons. Because of the research, you made you think this Canadian girl would be like everyone else, no Sir, everyone has their attitude. I pray our story wouldn't be like others, you know The north country is a lovely country and has similar opportunities to the US, so I don't see why someone from here would want to give their heart to a man because of money.

If we were not equally yoked I don't think we would be here going this smooth path, I wanted the same things as you and God brought us each other's ways and here we are, you know from the beginning you have done more negative things and I always forgive you even till now, so this must tell you how much God has being guarding my heart to love you, if I decided to follow self or my own desires which are mostly not of God then the very first time we met I was to put stop to communication because to be honest you were not a nice person at all, if it wasn't for God through my mother to love and be respectful to you then we were done a long time ago, with all the rough times here we are happy more than before, so never try to put yourself in other people shoes because they got their own share base on their choices they made even if it was your relatives. I'm glad that till now you can admit the fact that I have changed your life, I still want to do more and by the help of God I'll continue to stand by you to make you the man I have prayed for all the time.

Thanks very much for being honest with me concerning your health issue. Nothing is impossible, and I would never be so mean to be angry because I get to know about something you have struggled with so long, be faithful and the rest will be fine, I would never go away from you, I have promised you that we will be together till the end of times. So never think negatively.

You mean those pictures were drawn by Sam with his hands? he a perfect artist from what I see! But why only women he draws? Lol, I guess he misses his ex and wants a real hot young girl from those pics. You were smart to know what was running in his mind, my Zoro..lol you are just as innovative as me..lol.

Oh really, you have someone in your family who is native Indian, and I see that you have a link of family all the way here, so we are connected in many ways, from Europe and North America. God has a reason for bringing us together. Good, you got that interpretation about that dream of us fishing. I wish I were much closer to my grandma. She knew so much about dreams.

It is when we let Satan enter our lives that He does His will and destroys our lives. It is left with you not to be tempted by those ladies around you. If you ever get involved with them, knowing that they do not have good intentions, then for sure you will fall, and what we started will be ruined. We will continue to pray for you but be mindful as well not to get involved with them.

No worries about all the empty spaces in the house, when we come, and I start to live with you, they will be filled..lol because I'll have so many things to get in them, I'll bring my items as well. I think the idea of writing a simple book withdrawing Sam sounds like a good idea.

You're right. I missed my Mom so much, and she does the same, and she told me she is looking forward to visiting. She's still in Belgium. Anyway, my love, you have a nice day, and I look forward to hearing from you again All my love and regards to you.

Kisses and hugs from me.

DiAnnie wrote;

Hello, my love,

It has been a while since you have not heard from me, I have been real busy, plus with all the messages you sent, I thought it was not convenient to write back with a short message knowing I hate to ignore any of your messages, so I had to take my time to message you right now.

How have you been keeping? I know you have been busy as well cleaning along with brother Brian in our home. Well, concerning Satan using other ladies coming to you, it is something I think I must be concerned about because I do not want to hurt later, knowing full well I have given all my heart for you. So don't dare allow Satan to come closer to you all.

Good, you understood my thinking toward's Sam's drawings. Most of the time, when an artist draws something from their hearts, it is what goes on in their hearts that reflects from their work. Good, you confronted him about that. He must use his energy for God so that the kids growing up will benefit from his career instead. You brought up a good idea, you think very fast, and that's why I like you very much. You're a positive thinker. If our works will bring others to Christ and help lessen privilege, then we are fulfilling God's words right there. Thanks for being real for telling me I have made you a better man. I want you to be fully in the eyes of God and to be a better man that will please me and me in return. I love! Oh, no worries, I will always forgive you no matter what. I know we do not communicate face- to-face for now, but you will realize that I am just the same, never change when I am there. I know soon we will.

You're so funny, my love, how did you manage in the first place to take all these junks in your house? Lol, I guess a bachelor life isn't that easy sometimes. If you had a lady who was a wife, you wouldn't have taken all these things in your home, good you are getting them away, and please promise not to bring some more when I start to live there, okay? Lol. I pray too not to bring some as well. You never know because junks do not come by themselves..lol.

But the cultural difference can also affect people's social lives. I don't think you and I would have so much difference as the Canadian culture is similar to that of the US as we all are North American. Sad that the United States claims this heritage for them alone..lol but we are all American. Good, your environment is a clean one with no crime and drugs, so I'm happy because I want to bring up my kids in an excellent environment to grow up with no stress.

Well, I know you are a positive individual. Still, in the case of having a health issue, one must sometimes worry because no one would be happy when they lost a loved one, and I do not want you gone right now, I want many years with you, I know it's not a big health issue, and we have God so everything will be fine with faith.

I know when a lady draws a line, she means what she says. Still, when you love someone as well, it is not easy drawing that line because you care for that person, so even though from the start I have thought about that but true love exists between us. It is difficult to resist, and when God plans something, it is not easily broken. I think this has been our secret of enduring till now. We are in love with one another. That is what important. Sure, you do make a lot of sense, God will indeed bless a union that has a strong bond, and with our age difference and still flowing so smooth, then for sure we have matured. Our parents are connected spiritually, and it also makes us stronger. I do agree with you. As long we pray and believe there's nothing God can not do for us, so I know we will have a financial blessing. We both are hard-working people, so I do not doubt anything you tell me. Lol, I look forward to you speaking French someday. It would be fun, lol.

You're always dreaming. I think in your dream that we were in a car looking for someplace that would be our home. I'm not a good dream interpreter, but I believe it's that..lol. Yes, a lot of prophets in the Bible would interpret dreams. Most of the visions were like dreams. Even the kings did. Joseph's story is very touching in the Bible. I like to read that very much. Thanks for the reminder. You are so right again! when the perfect hand fits in a glove, there's no need to need another, and that is what we are! I can relate to this perfectly as well. I love all the meaning of family you wrote. You are so good, and how amazing it is to connect all that! Wow, you are such a great writer, and you don't know how much I learn from you.

Oh, honey, I can't stop laughing so hard..lol all those jokes made my day after so much work. I like it when you make me laugh so hard.

I love all those hard jokes you and brother Brian have most of the time. Men are very good with jokes to compare to ladies. I don't mind jokes because I am also a fun-loving person to get along very well. When I read about you and Brian, I laugh so hard.

Yes, I remember my Mom did talk to you once, we talk alike, but she has a deeper voice. Most people think we speak the same, but I know the difference, though. When we come, you will see the difference.

Your health does not bother me at all. I think you got me wrong in my last email. When I ask about your health, I didn't ask to mean I'm embarrassed about your health. I was just concern about how you feel about it. When someone isn't in good health, they think to discourage sometimes, and as love ones, we worry for them. That was the manner I was asking. I love you the way you are but would not be happy to see you suffer. I hope you understand what I mean; also, what you explain above to not worry made me feel relief.

You and Brian must be working so hard for us. I appreciate that and all the work. I think putting a computer in Mom's room would be a great idea she likes movies. You guys have done a lot of cleaning. I wish I were there to work alongside you two. Anyway, some more work will be available, so I'll still get busy.

I will try to get some rest now. Thanks for all the messages. They were so much, and I try to respond to each other. It is so difficult to ignore your messages. They mean so much to me. Enjoy your time, handsome man, till I hear from you again. All my love to you.

Your wife to be.

8 March 2019

DiAnnie wrote;

Hi, my love,

Always a pleasure hearing from you and to know you are doing great as well. You're always on my mind, and I think about you often. How's your day going? I hope that you are having a lovely day full of joy. Mine is going great just supposed to send you a message so you know I'm not ignoring you. I'm at work right now.

I'm here smiling to hear that you didn't make Satan win over you just because of our prayers. Prayer is the only way to get to our creator, and when we do that honestly, He's always preparing to hear us.

Do you think I'll be a better dream interpreter? I hope my granny gift of dream interpretation is not coming after me. I remember my Mom told me she was almost like a Medium, not sure you know what that is. They are like spiritual people that even go as far as predicting what will happen in a person's life; I don't want to be that ever..lol. Would you be happy with a wife that is a Medium? Not think you would, and if you ever say yes, no, I wouldn't accept..lol. I wish I dream just like you, but what I have mostly isn't dreams. They are thoughts of us together each time because not a day that goes by that I don't think about you.

You make me feel like I have not appreciated God. When I see how positive you are even with your health and having that accident with the bike, I feel like the issue with my knees is just a minor issue, and I shouldn't be sad. You make me appreciate life even with health issues. You are also an encouragement to me. I am so much in love with your sense of humor and purpose of positivity. I love you so much, my Zoro. You made my day! I know I got a crazy Marine full of life. I do get crazy, too, so we are just the best match. It is better to make others happy and make them sad, so I know being with you would mean making others smile, not looking so much at our problems. These never really go away once a person is still alive. So why not just be happy!

Well, my Mom and I have some more time to arrive at you because me having to travel to her and other places and coming back with her to you would take a few time so no worries, but we never know if we must get back soon, then you will have no choice but to have us there even if the house is not yet finished, so lets Sam try as fast to finish the house and let's brother Brian stop sleeping till noon..lol you guys must hurry! Just kidding about brother Brian, I have a lot of respect for him as well.

Getting back to work now, and I look forward to hearing from you soon. Lunch break is over now.

Gros Bisous Mon Amour.

9 March 2019

Thomas wrote;

You are beautiful and a guardian angel and the messenger sent from God to me, for our love together has no end. Our lives are shaped by those who love us and by those who refuse to love us. The sweetest music that reaches the highest heaven is the beating of two hearts that truly love each other. To live abundantly is to live abundantly, and to love forever is to live forever. Love is the doorway through which the human soul passes from selfishness to service love does that. The three profound words in human history are, God is love. The Bible says it is beyond human comprehension.

Love is beyond human characteristics because God is love. He does not try to love you. You cannot help but love you because that's what he is.

John 3; 16 – For God so loved the world that he gave his only begotten Son that whoever should believe in him should not perish but have everlasting life. It is a concert that surpasses the knowledge of man. No man can adequately describe it. No man can't sufficiently understand it because the Bible says it surpasses understanding. God's love is one of the most profound statements and one of the most misunderstood.

1 John 4;7 – Beloved, let us love one another, for love is of God, and everyone who loves is born of God and knows God. 1 John 4; 8 – for he who does not love does not know God, for God is love. 1 John 4;9- in this the love of God was manifested towards us, that God has sent his only begotten Son into the world so that we might Live through him. 1 John 4; 10 – in this is love, not that we loved God, but that he loved us and sent his Son, To be the propitiation for our sins. 1 John 4; 11 – beloved, if God so loved us, we also ought to love one another. Let the love of God shed from us and explode from heaven, and reach the world for a living Christ, who gave his life for us. In Jesus Christ, we pray, amen.

I pray things are going well for you today, sweetheart, and you're feeling well. Keep in mind everything is okay, no negativity, worry, or stress, and everything will be okay. Because you are my girl from The north country, my treasure, and I give God the great chef an abundance of love with compliments and appreciation for you in my life. Peace, grace, and joy with happiness be with you and your mother through Jesus Christ our Lord's name and that he watches over you and protects you and your mother through his holy name.

But by the righteous the ungodly do not hold the love of God today, I am going to give you a portrait of God's low seeing others through the eyes of God's. Love three kinds of love, many practices all three of God's love in the divine flow, to shed abroad in our heart that brings spiritual and personal prosperity. Listen to this how for in this life would you go, it depends upon your willingness to love the people who do well. How much do you love them? Are you willing to show them that you love them? Can you love people who don't love you? And that's the question Jesus asked his audience. He looked at his audience and said to the Pharisees.

They love those who loved them, can you love those who don't love you, and then suddenly, Jesus said concerning the Pharisees, that prostitutes would go to heaven before the Pharisees if they love one another. Can you as a Christian love the unlovable? That's the love of God, and you can't do that unless the love of God is in you. Love is not what you say, love is what you do. A song is not a song until you sing it. A spell is not a bell until you ring it. Place this in your heart to stay, love is not loving until you give it away.

Concerning the love with the young, be compassionate, with the aged be sympathetic, with the poor, or be tolerant of the week to help those in trouble because it's unfolding in your life. One day you are going to need that someday in your life. The first principle of God's love sees others through the eyes of love.

Until you learn to see other people through the eyes of love, life will never have absolute joy. Through love's eyes, the Bible says God is Love, and they that have not to love have not God. I would think our lives are shaped by those who love and by those who refused to understand the love of God. in the Bible is found in the one verse for God so love the world that he gave his only begotten Son that whosoever believes in him should not perish but have everlasting life.

He loved the golden key to understanding the love of God. God looked over the balconies of heaven and looked at you and me through the eyes of love. And said, I'll take that one, that has been crippled, That one whose dreams have been crushed, the one who's going through a bitter divorce, one who's in the midst of a business deal and his partners have betrayed him—the one who's going through the death of a dear spouse or suffering from sickness and disease. I'll be their great physician to the one with a broken heart. The one who's been rejected, God sees you lift your heads and rejoice the best is yet to be.

13 March 2019

DiAnnie wrote;

Good evening my love,

Sorry, it has been a few days since you heard from me, it's not because your dream made me angry, but I have been busy in recent days, but that's not a big excuse at all for the one that I love. I was a little mad when I read your dream. I feel funny. Then I thought again and said to myself, maybe he's just saying his heart of what he dreamed about. No one controls dreams. I had a space to stop thinking negatively about you. I know you are a mature person and would never come so low, so rest assure that there's nothing harmful going on in my heart about the dream, OK?

I think people there stick their noses in other people's affairs..lol. Anyway, I look forward to hearing from you soon.

Love you very much. I must get some rest now. Kisses and hugs from your girl.

14 March 2019

Thomas wrote;

The most important thing a father can do for his children is to love their mother. God wants in a father, to his wife, to let her do what she wants. The second thing God wants from a husband is to be a good listener. God is a father who listens because it takes love to listen. Speak, and you hear what you know, listen, and you learn as you grow.

According to a UCLA study in America, the average Father listens to his children two minutes a day. And when you don't listen to your wife or your children, they go into the bedroom and turn on the television, and she watches something like desperate homemakers. Or listens to someone like Roseanne Barr, who tells you where to go and how to get there. Your child listens to a rock star who holds a seminar on how to do drugs and how to have love and commit suicide. Some of you are letting people into your home to train your children. You would not allow in your home without a shotgun in their face if you answered the front door. Here's something to say, when you're wrong, promptly admit it and say I'm sorry. Can you please forgive me?

God is looking for a lover and a husband, a man of faith, and then God wants a man who speaks blessings over his children and his wife. Father's, you are the spiritual authority in your children's lives. You're the priest profit provider protector over your home. God does not place spiritual authority on your wife. It's the husband's and father's responsibility. Ephesians. 6; 4 – Fathers, do not exasperate your children; instead, bring them up in the training and instruction of the Lord.

Proverbs 18; 21 –The tongue has the power of life and death, and those who love it will eat its fruit. An example in the Bible of a father who spoke prophetic blessings over his

12 sons came exactly true. His name is Joseph. If you read when he prayed over those 12 sons, each of them came exactly true as he spoke them.

80% of the Pulitzer Prize winners are Jewish. You may ask why because her Father, every Friday night at the Sabbath meal, speaks a prophetic blessing over each one of their sons. And those blessings come true. Because God and Jesus Christ are taught in those families as children, that child is then free to go out to complete that prophetic blessing that has been prayed over them by the Father.

And across the street, the Gentile father is saying, "you act just like your mother's relatives. You're never going to amount to anything". So you have a son over here going daaa, and you have a son over here becoming the boss of the plant.

Fathers bless your children in your home. You are the spiritual authority in your home and responsible for not only the actions of yourself, your families as well. God will honor that prophetic blessing that you spoke over that son or the daughter. If you do not control your son's life, or if you do not control the life of your daughter, someone else will.

Father says, my son is a strong-willed child. He will not do what I say wrong. If they can teach a porpoise at Sea world to put a ball through a basket, you can teach your child to take out the garbage and to mind you. Warm-up his gluteus Maximus until his cerebral cortex gets a brand-new revelation about who you are. I can assure you. There is a direct connection between his rear end and his Brian.

17 March 2019

DiAnnie wrote;

Good morning honey,

It's nice hearing from you, and I hope you will have a good Sunday today. I'm trying to get ready for church, and I thought to message you before I leave. Oh, you were home when I called? I felt so too because it was early, and I didn't know you were out at that time. Good, you were able to hear my voice again, but I'm glad you heard my voice again..lol.

I can understand Brian's heart, not easy to do physical work, tell him my Mom, and I will be on our way soon, and I hope he's going to get along well with us. You two are very interesting with all those tough jokes. I guess it's a men thing..lol.

You're right, something one wonders how come there are so many junks in the house, but mind you, it's not the devil at all. Still, we do not walk. We bring them little by little, not even knowing, and before you know it, junk has taken over the room, and you move in the living room. If not taken care of fast, you may want to move outside.. lol. Good, you got rid of those mountains of junks. I do clean my place everything and not much junk here, maybe because I'm new here?

It makes me feel good when I hear from you too, I want to be in touch all the time, and I wish I were not so busy the way it is right now. I'm glad you are such an understanding person. Oh yes, I'll bring a lot of things. Most of my items are in Calgary. My first visit wouldn't be one big shot, though.

I'll get my things to you bit by bit before it looks like I'm going to pack the house as you did over the years. We need air to breathe..lol. As a Marine, there are many documents or things that are important to you reason you made the place like a museum.

Wow, just your description of the rooms and the curtains' designs tells me that you guys are doing an excellent job. A Canadian flag would have my Mom falls in love with her room! Wow, I'll let her know.

Hahaha, you're so funny honey, I know you carried out a major cleaning up exercise, so I wouldn't be surprised at all why the house is empty. The junk that you are throwing out is the main reason anyone would think you're a poor soul but good you did clean, or we would say what kind of man is this with so much junk! Is he a mad man or what? So you already did the right thing..lol.

Since the check-up with Dr. Heinz poses no threat, then it is good, sure he does not have your testicles, so may not see what you see, but if none is giving pain, then no need to worry, promising that he is giving a positive result at least we can have some hope.

Nice hearing from you once again, my love, and you enjoy the rest of your day. I'm here thinking about you, and I hope you're doing the same. Have a nice Lord's day.

Hugs and kisses from your wife-to-be.

19 March 2019

Thomas wrote;

> *Beautiful,*
>
> *Most unhappiness within a marriage is due to illness. It is because they are sick of each other. LOL, smile with prayer. This is not you and I by any stretch of the imagination. We will not find happiness in marriage unless we each bring joy into the marriage. One lady said, what do I need with a man? I have a stove that smokes, a parakeet that swears, and a cat that stays out all night. Another lady said that as her minister asked her, the minister said, what you would like in a marriage? She said I want a man, who can dance, looks good, and eats everything I prepare for him. And the minister said as he clapped his hands, "congratulations, you have just described trigger. Right, Rogers horse that was the greatest source who has ever lived. Five unfair questions that a lady should never ask the husband, what are you thinking? Do you love me? Do you think I'm beautiful? How do I look? Men do not like tattletale wives. smile, what you can walk away from will determine what God will bring you too.*
>
> *Samson and Delilah were a great example of that in the Bible. Sampson received a cheap haircut, his eyes Burned out, and he lost his soul because Delilah was an unbeliever. After burning his eyes out to grind grain in the city square the rest of the days of his life, he was forced by the Philistines, where people mocked him and spat on him because he fell for a beautiful nonbeliever.*
>
> *When the anointing comes, We will know it. When it leaves, we will not know it. King David and Beersheba are other examples in the Bible. David had his general Uriah sent to the front of the battle lines to get killed because he would not sleep with his wife Beersheba when she was pregnant with David's child. And God said to the prophet Nathan came and said to David the sword shall never leave your household All the days of your life. Absalom David son had love with his wife and lost the battle he should not have lost. David's wife was raped on Amnon's rooftop, one of David's sons, while all of Israel laughed. David paid all the days of his life for having love with Beersheba, A beautiful nonbeliever.*
>
> *Some of the wrong responses to these questions are, who me? As compared to who? The wife has cellulite dimples that Ray Charles can see. These are inappropriate questions for sure. And you would never have to ask them to me, Sweetheart, you will never have*

to ask these questions because I will continuously let you know how much I love you and how beautiful you are and how gorgeous you look, and I. will praise you publicly and graciously with respect.

Please do not let me intimidate you by saying to others like there are a thousand people just waiting to defile our relationship. This is not true for the only one that knows of you. I am brother Brian, and when and if God willing your mother and yourself decide to come into our lives together and meet one another through the Holy Spirit and God's grace, no one may know that your mother and yourself as not come to visit, only the ones that come into our home will learn. I will always praise you publicly and treat you with great respect.

God help me if I ever should not because you are my girl from The north country, my precious Guardian Angel through the Holy Spirit. God has brought us together for the reason of happiness and heaven on earth, the joy we will experience together. Everything is OK. Everything will be OK, and we insist on enjoying life. We refuse to have one negative moment of worry or stress because it will be a moment of happiness we will never get back together. I do not get many visitors in this house, just a few, and please take this over. I'm not sure how I feel about committing fornication? I'm not real keen on the idea. Possibly we should get to know one another face-to-face and see how things go together and take it from there. How does that sound to you? We have developed a strong relationship on the telephone and in writing.

I pray everything is going well for you today and your mother through Jesus Christ the Lord's name, and you are both feeling well and are happy this is what I pray. God the Father through Jesus Christ our Lord's name, I know that you love Us and sent your son to the cross. To redeem us together, and we come before you, God the Father. And I confess that I am willing to praise my wife as God has commanded, and I'm willing not to be a controlling person in our marriage. And I am willing to release every person in our lives together that is not Godly.

And now, Father, in the name of Jesus, let happiness invade our hearts, let it invade our mind, let us release all regret. We remove all bitterness and every bit of un-forgiveness, we release it, we let it go, and the authority of Jesus name we receive joy and happiness, we received piece together we receive the love of God together. And from this day forward, our home together is going to be like heaven on earth. In Jesus's name, this and my wife DiAnnie and I receive his blessings graciously through the Holy Spirit and God the Father through Jesus Christ our Lord's name amen. You are my precious girl from The north country with whom I am in love with hugs and kisses.

21 March 2019

DiAnnie wrote;

Hello My Love,

I realized it had been a few days since you heard from me. Know that it's nothing intentional as you know I do all my best to keep in touch, so I'll see how you are saving as well. How is your day going, and how have you been? I hope everything is going great, I'm always thinking about you, and it makes me feel relief when you write to me. This way, I know my Zoro is doing great. I'm feeling very great health and spiritually, and thanks for always asking about Mom and me. She's doing great and still in Belgium, you know they speak French there, so she's more relaxed than Malta. I guess that's why she likes it there..lol. Thanks always for your compliments. They mean so much to me.

I'm not sure why is it so difficult to have Brian believe that we are coming? He acts like we are coming to him. We are not his guest, so let's stop worrying about my Mom and dream about her and is impatient? I guess that's why he's doubting, don't you think? If it's not for the delays from me by now, I am in Europe and make a few trips to other places with Mom and have been on our way to Arizona. Brian does not understand what's going on over here, that's why, but I don't think I have to prove anything to him neither you.

Do you think God is mad at Brian? I don't think so; I believe in his head he can't get Anna out of his mind..lol don't think Brian can't be thinking that way..lol. Are you still having these dreams? I wish I had the gift of interpretation of dreams. I'll pray about it, and who knows, I can just have my grand Mom gift! You may be a good prophet, with all these dreams all the time, I think you are right, Brian may not believe Christ is coming reason he is not having faith and doubt so much, I wish he had Christ in him, his mind about things would change. We have a patient with him. If you want to change someone, all you need is patience.

Well, my love, I know there is so much between us that would've not been by accident. For me, I don't even count the amount of messages and calls because I know I have to do these things because I love you truly. I wish I were in touch more if it weren't because I would stay in touch more because of my job. I'm glad that you understand the situation. As long someone can understand me, it is not so hard to please me. It's the love, care, and respect every right-thinking lady wants. I know what you mean.

In life is the continued building of reputation that can have others change their perspectives about you. Right now, no one knows and understands the confidence we have been building between us, which has our relationship going from steps to steps. It wasn't built on a smooth beginning. It was a continuous fight but was there in the heat and you too, and here we are now. I'm still looking forward to meeting to prove those who do not believe God's miracles wrong to see that with Christ, nothing is impossible. I know when we start to live together, there will be people who will not believe or trust but will surely do and be happy with us at the end because I know myself and not afraid because my upbringing was built on a solid foundation, my parents didn't give me gold and diamonds like other kids. Still, their teachings made me who I am today. I agree with all you said, and that is just the truth.

You're right. Most unhappiness in some relationships or marriages is people being sick of each other. If someone is sick of another, that person isn't ready to accept the other the way they're. If I must be a best friend with someone, I must be willing to take their negativities and same with them to do same with me. Most of the time, friendships and marriages are the wrong reason people get sick with others in their relationship. God forbid it's not going to be that way with us because we are going along well. You're so funny, my love, with all these jokes, I sit and laugh as I read your messages, when someone is next to me and see me smiling they asked I'm I smiling at the computer? I say yes, my husband-to-be is a big comedian, his sense of humor is beyond.

Oh, all along, I thought Christine was still around. No wonder you don't talk much about her anymore, so she went to live with her Mom? If it's the situation, you can find someone to rent the place she was, not sure finding rentals there is that easy. Concerning dividing our home, I think you will have to wait till we get there and I start to live with you. I hope I'm making sense. You seem to be worrying about our survival, if there are opportunities for jobs or me teaching French, there then no need to worry because I'll work and we can use my income with what you get from the social security, in the meantime, you can find a rental for where Christine was living. Let me know if my suggestion is OK.

I have been reading your books, my love, but I haven't read this part that you explained. You are right. A house is never a house when the lady isn't in it. It will be complete when we start to love together. I can imagine how much you and brother Brian have been working to make it a better home. Back to your book, it is interesting to know you know someone back then whose parents owned half of Silicon Valley and what happened between the two of you. Getting drunk has its negative part on a person's life.

I thought drinking glass isn't bad but too much. If I get what you wrote correctly, you mean the check that the guy signed those days of $250,000 check that put you in debt of

$400,000? not sure I got you right, I can imagine what you mean of missing the touch of a lady, and not being able to pray with two arms, it's something heartbreaking, but I'm not going to sound like I'm sad because you don't like people feeling sorry for you. Still, it touches me reading about all you have to go through till now. We can't change the situation but praise God for having you alive using your testimony to bring others to Christ.

Thanks for telling me all these things honey, you do because you love me and believe me, it's better I know, so when I get there, I will see the situation, for me, I do not see you as handicapped because you are energetic and do not behave like others who feel sorry for themselves, you are a brave person, and I like that you and I will live normal and no bad day. I like you for who you are. That is what matters. Honey, no need to ask for forgiveness, you are always forgiven, you don't do wrong here you only tell me the truth and who and what you are, no worries, OK? I look at the qualities that made us unique, not outwardly.

We hope for the best from what Dr. Heinz will say. I know it's hard,

but all this isn't your fault. We all have a shortcoming in life. That's why love is the best medicine to bring others closer and have a smile. You are vital to me no matter what. I know you are just that handsome man God has created in His image, just like me. What is important here is the fact that you love me, and I love you.

Know that you are always in my heart, and thanks for always being honest. This is one reason I love you very much. I'll get back to work; I came home to get some rest since it was my break time. I have to hurry back to work. All my love and regards to you.

Tu est mon vrai amour mon Zorro.

Hugs and kisses from your girl.

22 March 2019

DiAnnie wrote;

I just got done reading your lengthy message and all the romantic things said. You're my kind of man to admit, you sound young at heart, and I can't resist you!

How are you doing? I hope you're doing great and safe. By the Lord's grace, I'm fine and thank Him for the opportunity given us to grow together.

I am always on the lookout waiting on your messages, and whenever I hear from you, I am so excited. Good that you thought about our privacy. I have no problem with you telling people about us or our happiness, but some people are so fast in sticking their noses in other people's affairs sometimes not because they care but to know about your personal life. If you face an unfortunate situation, they laugh at your back. Most women do that. That's why I felt somehow said about the judgment your lady friend tried to judge me on. Even my girlfriend who lives with me here, not all that we tell each other, has our limit. I also feel we are connected spiritually and are mature enough to control our destiny. I am getting to pour my trust in you, and I do not want any interruption. I hope you feel the same as well.

Well, I don't think it is unfair to love someone older, as long that person is understanding why would there be an issue with loving them, once you are an honest heart that wants a lady to be happy and that lady also wanting the same things then I believe they both should be important to each other, I have been in a relationship with a young person like myself before. I saw hell and trying an older person who can treat me better than in my previous relationship. Then no need not be happy or to be scary. One person I look up to as my role model is Celine Dion, she did marry an older man, and they loved each other till the end, so the same can go for you and me, only I want you to live longer so we can enjoy each other..lol I need you to live another more 50 years..lol.

It amazes me that you are such a kind person, one that is not controlling, one thing most men miss out that they want to control. In doing that, ladies look for ways to trick them. As long you are accessible in the heart and trust a lady, she can have the conscience and, in return, love you and treat you sound like a man. It's like having a child with you. You as a parent being so harsh on the child, it makes a child get worse than just being cool hoping to see if they have the will power to be good not necessarily having to take a rod, such child becomes a good person naturally, it's the same with women.

With all you mentioned to admit and hope it's only you and me, it makes me horny. It wants you so much, causes me to want to love you more because the difference between an older man and a young man is so if my man got the same reason to think about someone younger. You're just so sweet and amazes me. I can't wait to feel you inside me. I would want to hold you tight and scream in your name several times because you make me think, lovey. I will give you myself, you can have me all to yourself and we enough quality love, all I'm hoping is to not go against my faith, as long everything is on the right path there's nothing I can't do for you. I know you're going to be my man, and me your wife. I have included a picture for you.

I was thinking so much about you today. Be safe, and I look forward to hearing from you. I wanted to tell you to sign in to your Yahoo messenger since we both have the app. I did message you there.

Yours truly.

DiAnnie.

23 March 2019

DiAnnie wrote;

Good morning my handsome man,

Thank God it's the weekend! I'm glad to be sending you a message since I missed out for a day since you wrote me last. How are you doing today, honey? I hope that everything is going great. I'm thankful for life and feel relief today since there's no work till Monday. At least I can get some rest today and tomorrow. I thought it was better to first message you before looking forward to the rest of the day.

I understand, my love, you are not the problem, but I think those around you, such as Brian, believe it is expected the way he feels because he's not the one in touch with me, and after all, it's not him. In the picture! I believe he wished it was him involved with such a nice-looking girl from The north country; men are also jealous just like any other human being, so I can see where he's coming from..lol. Even if I said Brian, I got a friend for you right now.

It is not possible for him because he can not care for that person. I know he seems a nice person, and I truly understand him. He will understand when he sees me in person and talks to him about why you and I are connected, not just worldly but spiritually. Others wouldn't be difficult to understand. First, they would be hoping that I'll dash you, but if they start to see how much we live and our love increases daily, they will change their mindsets. So you don't have to prove to anyone or have to praise me publicly. God knows our hearts.

I can't believe it. Your friend signed that check just like that especially being drunk. That amount was huge. I'll check for that chapter in your first book. I have those books in my drawer. I think it's not a bad idea to put things in my name, but you'll wait till I get there. We have so many things to arrange, and it takes one at a time to see about that. With this, things can get in shape before thinking about the rest, we have so many things ahead, but God will work in our favor. I always smile when you tell me that I do make you happy. I want to see you happy as well, my love.

My prayers all the time is to never change from the person I am right now, I have also danced with the devil in the past, and it was not good at all, so for God bringing me to Himself is something to never forget about, so I ask Him to bring me close to him all the time. We have more to know to promote the kingdom of God and get help to others who are lost spiritually and physically.

God ask us Christian to help the poor both in spirit and flesh, so it's such work that my Mom and I are planning to travel and tell me about Jesus, be kind to them, see about my Dad's properties outside The north country,

so there so much ahead, we don't plan to travel much after this trip as I am making up my mind to stay in Arizona and hopefully my Mom. We can help others in North America, the three of us.

Thanks for getting back to me, and you enjoy the rest of your day.

All my love and regards to the best man, tus est mon Zorro!

Thomas wrote;

Thank you, this is good for the both of us that I did some research and read the attachments below, please, at my age and with multiple sclerosis primary progressives I've had for 68 years. I will more than likely outlive that, and that God wants me to write more I feel spiritually with spiritual discernment. I do not have any feeling, and the only hand I have that had taken away the feeling of touch, the one thing I missed when I lost my arm, was putting my hands together to pray.

The thing I miss is a feeling of touch was the touch of a lady. Therefore, when I go to buy a pair of shoes, I do not try them on. First, I have faith after I buy them that they will fit. And that would go for a marriage. The cherry on the cake is not even in my thoughts. We have already talked about my main concern for your welfare and well-being as a young lady of Christian inspiration and faith. You may feel deprived if we cannot have children, and I would feel equally at fault if I could not provide or take care of the children if it is even possible?

I was physically capable, I would not have any problems, and I do not consider anything a problem anyway. I turn my will on life over to the care of God. There is so much life that you have to live that I have already lived, you would be depriving yourself of the life and that our age difference is horrendous. 4 April young, and I have edema in my one leg that swells up I have to lay down in bed and rest and elevate my leg otherwise it will swell up like it is doing right now when my foot starts throbbing I have to go lay down the Veterans Administration had purchased me a wheelchair because $20,000 and electric leg compression machine that cost $7500 I do not have to pay for anything.

I'm not feeling comfortable, although my faith is unshakable, and you would be the soulmate reunited in heaven. This lifetime is like a blink of an eye, as compared to eternity. And are we be gossip and mean people, and Satan would be at her heels continuously working to destroy our relationship. This does not mean we cannot be friends, as we are becoming right now without a real commitment just to a spiritual discernment that we are equally yoked. That is the strongest and most powerful love we have going for us besides prayer and our faith and our trust or more another. I would not want to destroy that trust because of my and capabilities.

I am a good Christian man, and I intend to keep working hard at writing to help others with the knowledge and wisdom that the Holy Spirit working through me will reveal to others to help them. I would love to say yes and devote my life to you. I feel that it would not be fair for you to get married in my heart of hearts because it would break my heart.

Do you have any income? Or what do you do for a living? Do you have any skills? In that, I could or would not be able to provide for you. I would feel like Satan is drawing us together for the simple reason that people will gossip and would both have to go through a lot of trials and tribulations to reconcile with that, thinking over sweetheart, God blessed with love and prayers my beautiful young soulmate who I will be with someday Thomas for eternity, get married live your life have fun and please write me back this is not the end of our communication, I learned a lot about myself doing the research and praying to God, so that was all good.

Thomas 'n DiAnnie

25 March 2019

DiAnnie wrote;

Hey Thomas,

Sorry for my delay. I guess you have been wondering why hasn't she written! I haven't forgotten you at all; you are in my heart and prayers each day. I went over to my friend Nicole, and we had a lovely time together. We went out, had fun and met a few people. I got back home early this morning to attend church. I just got back home and relaxing reading and writing you back. I hope your day is going great.

I enjoy your messages, especially the one you wrote the other day with so much information. You are someone that has excellent qualities, Thomas. I feel you have more potential than many people who have all their parts correct, so I don't think you should feel sad about anything. After all, as a Christian, God allows everything that happens in our lives is God that would enable, including positive and negative things.

I agree faith is all we have, and as you rightly put it with buying your pair of shoes not trying till you get home with the faith that they will fit is a practical example of a true believer. It is how I think about life, so the cherry on the cake you talked about, for me, I believe it is possible. I don't think I have much doubt. My real welfare has a loving man not going to describe or choose the exact type of person as in life your expectations never really come to past as you want, it happens in many people's lives. It is rare for the exact things to flow in a person's life.

Thinking about heart desires if fleshly thinking, you allow God to give you what He wants for you even if that isn't what your heart desires. As long you learn to love what is given to you by God, then you are a whole new person after God's heart. Concerning having children, it is mostly women that worry the most when they are getting older, men can have children no matter what age, that's the grace God gave men that women do not have, so I don't see why you must worry if it turns out that you can not have kids, it is something both you and me can sit and decided upon of what to do. There would be many options.

I do not think you are depriving me of anything. Suppose you truly love me and I love you and decide to consider not continuing with you because of your shortcomings. In that case, it means I'm the one depriving you of the love you have for me, so the same way you accepted me in your heart, as a person, I should do the same, that is the true love God is asking of us all.

I read carefully all you mentioned concerning your health and all the expenses you go through. I can tell you that you have had so much, and there is so much you endure, and I will also say you're lucky even though you are going through all this. The fact here is that you are alive, and that is what counts. After all, you have a place to live, you are well taken care of, your health challenges are hard, but you still manage to live that alone must tell you that God has an excellent plan for your life. Another that hurt me is you having to live all by yourself. I want to be able to come over there and take care of you. It must be difficult because, with your challenges, you're all alone, loneliness is a disease all by itself, no matter you are healthy or not healthy, and everyone needs somebody to have companionship with. I see that you need that right now.

Well, as I said before, age is just a number. I'm not saying I do not consider the age difference. People would want to ask, why is a young girl like me doing with such an old guy? their question may sound right but is not a fact why because no one knows precisely what the other person has been through and why they are making the choice they make, what you and I would share in common may not be understood by anyone else except you and me, I do not know God's plan, I do not know if I am getting you right, it is true you have children older than grandchild and me close to my age. Still, my question here is, what do you think? Are these things able to stop us?

I do not mind being your friend if you feel it's not right to continue. I'm a lady. I do not think it would make any sense to force myself into a person's life. That's the first thing I would never do ever. I must allow someone to want to love me. I am from a home where my parents taught me morals and treat people with care but not to make myself cheap. I do consider your thoughts, and I look up to knowing where we stand. I have developed a strong feeling for you, a feeling of going the extra mile to be yours and living happily, not just the love. Still, a genuine affection of someone my heart goes to so much, looking and thinking about your disability, I feel so close to you to be closer to you and care and give you the love you have not had over the years.

I was studying linguistics, and I wish to continue, but for now, I can not allow myself to sit there, so I needed a job. I am starting up a mini-store where I want to sell electronics of all kinds, it's not easy, but I have the faith that I can achieve my goal little by little.

I don't think Satan has control over us as people that I saved. Those that Satan would use to spread gossips between you and me would only win over us when we buy into their gossips. For me, I have no fear. I do not live to please human beings; I live to please

God as much as possible. Living for others is total hypocrisy, so I do not do my best not to hurt others, but I wouldn't want to live at the pleasure or of how people judge me.

Know that if you love me in my world, it is you and me and not having people stick their nose in anything we do. I am just me and not going to change for anyone. I have decided to love you as long your heart is open. If not, God is good to make the impossible possible. Thanks so much for all you said, and I pray that you are having a nice day. May you have a nice day till I hear from you once again.

My regards to you today. DiAnnie.

26 March 2019

Thomas wrote;

Beautiful Guardian Angel, just thinking about you, sweetheart, not just thinking about you, always thinking about you. Smile with compassion. You're my girl; you're my beautiful treasure of the scrumptious delicious tasty little morsel that I would savor with all the delicacies of refined cuisine. Smile lovingly. I'm in love with your beautiful soul, you will forever be inside of my heart, and I will carry you wherever ago. You consume my every thought of the love that I have never experienced.

A love that God could have only put into our lives together with honored trust, loyalty, compassion, every positive emotion of love you can imagine or that is even beyond our comprehension that will be revealed to the both of us. And for that, I thank God for you in my life who has maybe the man I am today, who has brought my soul with her as we enter the gates of heaven and welcomed by the Angels above with God's gracious love. I'm so in love with you, my precious Guardian Angel.

I just wanted to drop you a short note before I go to lay down and say my prayers that God will watch over you and your mother with care, compassion, and kindness that only God our Father can show through Jesus Christ our Lord, his only son who died and carried our sins to the cross. We can connect through the Holy Spirit through the holy bond of matrimony in spirit. We are connected, never to come apart a solid bond condoned by the angels in heaven.

And for this love, that neither of us has experienced before, we can thank God for our Father and pray for his love for us to guide us to protect this and to keep a low strong no matter the circumstances they may come into our lives and revealed to us. We know together we can fight Satan's forces that will be put before us like landmines, and we will sidestep them through the guidance of God our Father and the Angels.

God, please watch over my sweet, beautiful DiAnnie and her mother Anna as they go through this life, walking their soul journey at separate times. We pray for your safety and protection, and love and care. And that we know through your holy grace that we are protected and meant to be together. To carry your message of Christianity through prayer and witnessing others, and letting others know your children may bring light into others' lives with the abundance of joy and happiness. That DiAnnie Anna and Thomas, you have so graciously and upon us, and we thank you, God, our Father through our Lord Jesus Christ for all the blessings you have brought to us in our lives.

And we are so blessed God our Father to have got all of us together with your grace and compassion and care and protection and that we may witness to others in a godly way and bring your love into their lives with abundance as we know your love has no beginning your love has no end. Peace and grace of the Lord be with you and your mother sweetheart through Jesus Christ the Lord's name amen xoxox your Zorro

27 March 2019

DiAnnie wrote;

I got your message yesterday and thought to reply today since I was busy. It makes me so happy to hear from you each day. I hope you're having a nice day. Mine is going slow here and quiet but writing back to you makes it better for me.

I agree love cannot go without trust. The two go in parallel. Saying goodbye sometimes in a relationship can be sad and cannot be sad, depending on the situation. When leaving a hurtful relationship, you do not get that sad. It is when you cherished and love that person that goodbyes become a burden. You're right. Loving another person is the best one can do.

Life is too short to be alone, so when you meet someone deserving you, it is good to hold that person tight and not let them go. It's the situation that we are in right now, letting me go and not letting you go because the two spirits are flowing so smoothly. Sure, when we follow Jesus Christ, we are never in Darkness. We get into the light. No one in the light would have a sad life. The light is a total joy.

Wow, how sweet you are dear, the sentence is so touching! I wish many people knew this, that the will of God would not take you where the grace of God can not protect you. You are so right, I can feel it, and I have experienced it in my life. When I fell in love with my high school boyfriend, it was my will, but I knew deep in my heart it was God's will, and then though my will took me into his life, God's grace would not protect me, so the relationship failed! I'm a witness to this exact sentence you mentioned.

Well, yes, you never know what's next in life, and I never knew I would have fallen in love with someone older. I didn't believe that I would develop a feeling for an older person or having someone like you pouring out so much love, we called this destiny, I can see the right purpose of my life now, and what I thought wasn't God's plan for my life, I can feel the deep happiness in my heart since I met you, Thomas. That is true. The six things you listed are from the book of Proverbs are so true, these are common among people, and if you are not strong in the Lord, you would see yourself doing such. It would be the worst thing to do what the Lord hates! If people ceased all these things, life would have been so happy on earth.

Wow, that's a very simple way to tell if a man loves. From the German Shepard story, you can see even animals know the male is supposed to look after his female partner. If men had such characteristics as that dog, then there's no reason why their females wouldn't love them back. I hope you're like that German Shepard! my heart tells me you have excellent quality, and you are truly the man of my dream.

You touch essential points, and I sit here to take my time and reading and taking in so much then you think, you are full of wisdom, and those that read your books would save their lives, you make touching points that would bring a dying person back to life, I'm so blessed having such a person in my life, at least I wouldn't be a reader but hearing from you directly as we live together.

I do not think you have any limitations that would be selfish to me. The saddest limitation that would stop me from loving you is when you do not love me, I do not look much at the physical look of a person, I am mostly concern with the heart and the inner part of a person, you are a unique person, and I appreciate you as you are. True enjoyment is when you have someone that pours out their heart to you. Good to hear that you love my picture, can you send me some of yours again? I did save the one you sent, and you are a fine gentleman more than you know.

I am thinking about you and hope your day is going great. I am so proud of you to know that you love me, and all the descriptions make me want to live day today, you are getting deeper in my heart, and I can tell that we are just the best life can offer. I promise to love you till the end and hope you will do the same. I will get busy now, forgive me if I leave out some things you expected me to say, ask me, and I am willing to answer you anytime. You are so sweet, Thomas, and know I love you so much and wanting you so much. Have a nice day, and I look to hearing from you once again.

You're my king!

Yours DiAnnie.

28 March 2019

Thomas wrote;

Beautiful, my guardian angel, with all your infinite wisdom, smile Before I move forward, beautiful. How are you doing? How are you feeling? You are the busiest little kid I know. Because you are my girl from The north country, my precious treasure, And I pray to God with all my love for being the chef of this one and 7 billion creation that he has brought into my life.

That being said, since I am the lover of your soul and carry you in my heart 24 seven and consuming my thoughts 24 seven. What may I do for you? LOL smile

You know I am not a controlling person. And you know how much I am in love with you. Thank you, beautiful peace and grace of the Lord be with you and your mother through Jesus Christ our Lord's name amen. I love you. I'm in love with you from your ZORO.

Thomas wrote;

My humble's apology, beautiful, you are right as usual I just woke up. I have more questions, sweetheart, but I will get this off to you for now. God bless with love and prayers.

I refuse to argue or be angry or any negative thought you can think of. There's no reason why two adults in love, children of God, cannot have a Godly conversation. Double smile. How are you doing today, scrumptious? How are you feeling? I may have a few other questions for you, and I'm not, and I do not want you to feel like you are being intimidated or interrogated.

Please, these are not my intentions. Only inquiring minds would love to know. And I am proclaiming to be husband and wife to one another. That has been brought to gather through the Holy Spirit and God our Father through Jesus Christ his Son our Lord. This is who brought us both together, as well as spiritually our fathers through prayer our mothers. And our guardian angels who guide us and protect us. I am just curious because I am kind and want your advice. I would desire to have your advice because you are my girl, my precious treasure from The north country. So there.

Take that. Put it in your pipe. And smoke it. Triple smile with a double backflip

Do you feel it is none of my business? Or do you think it is something I should not know for whatever reason? You know, beautiful, my life is an open book. There is nothing I have held back from you. Only unless you have asked me to. And I refuse refuse refuse to have any negative feedback from either one of us—a Godly manner like God's children.

Peace and grace of the Lord be with you your mother through Jesus Christ the Lord's name amen. Please let your mother know that my prayers are with her and give her my best manner of character.1 Thessalonians 4; 6 – and no one should ever exploit or take advantage of his brother in this regard because the Lord will avenge all such acts, as we have already told you and solemnly warned you.

Proverbs 14; 31 – he who oppresses the poor taunts the maker. But he who is gracious to the needy honors him.1 Samuel 12; 24 – only fear the Lord, and serve him in truth with all your heart.

Have a good evening, sweetheart, to my beautiful, scrumptious precious treasure of a girl from The north country who I'm in love with. And I will give my life for this lady. Without question, without a doubt. Hugs and kisses from your ZORO

29 March 2019

Thomas wrote;

My beautiful Guardian Angel, my scrumptious treasure from The north country, my precious Savior of this man's major soul. Who needs to be tied up occasionally and reminded that because of my wife's intuition, feelings, and emotions, I am who I am today. With God as my witness has brought my wife and me together to save souls and help others through Jesus Christ our Lord's name this I pray amen.

Jesus Christ came from the splendor of heaven. Into a stinky cave of animals, cold and dreary for the redemption of our souls. Jesus came to seek and save what was lost. Jesus did not come to this earth to keep 285 squabbling denominations. The essence of the word of God is, "do you know Christ Savior and Lord." the last command Jesus came to the church, going to the world and preach the gospel. He was talking about the 12 apostles.

Go and preach the gospel casting out of evil spirits and the hands-on healing to the lesser than thou. Do not ask people to believe in what you think. Ask them to believe in Jesus Christ. He is the shepherd. We are the sheep. He is the potter. We are the clay.

He is the create tour. We are the created. He is the master of winds and waves. He is a master of Judah. He has the light of the world. He is the Lamb of God That takes away the sins of the world for your redemption. Only Christ can save your soul. The purpose of the church is not a humanistic social gospel Psychobabble sermon. To pacify hot tub Christianity, we hear about feel-good Christianity. When you are saved, you will feel good about Christianity.

You can think positive thoughts about yourself and go straight to hell. Good thoughts do not make a good person. The only thing that makes you a good Christian is the blood of Jesus Christ has washed your sins. And you are saved by that redemption, not your psychobabble. Jesus would beat with the cat of nine tails while worlds conditions showered us. Shall Jesus wears a crown of thorns, and we were roses.? Shall he be spit upon, and a humanistic non-God loving society shall socially accept us.

The Bible says beware of all men who speak good of you. One of the Democratic leaders of America stated that he was afraid that the pulpit was influencing America. Finally, we are on the map. Thank you, God, for the recognition of a Democratic politician. Smile the gospel of Jesus Christ demands that every man and woman submit their will to the will of God. You pray that in the Lord's prayer, but you probably do not mean that. Thy will be done, how can that be, only when you let his will rule your life.

Every habit every desire must be submitted to the will of Jesus Christ. Every dream, every goal should be submitted to the blood of the cross, Or not at all. Mentioned the word trial or tribulation in America or adversity and the average audience in the pulpit. Wants to hear preacher we want to hear something bright, something uplifting, something like if it feels good does it.

Not from the word of God, there is no high higher than the spiritual high of being saved through the blood on the cross of Jesus Christ, our Lord who died for our sins and suffered. Timothy writes, all those who live right in Jesus will suffer tribulation. If you're not suffering tribulation, the world cannot know that you are saved. Peter said, think it not strange that we should suffer the trials.

Do we know Christ, do we believe him, do we obey him, do we love him, is the Lord of our lives, or is he your religious Butler.? That you are sent running in your day of the crisis, he is Lord all the time, or he has nothing in your life. Are you saved? When did you make that decision? Going to church does not make you a Christian any more than pushing a wheelbarrow to the general motor assembly line will make you a Cadillac.

You are remade and renewed by the hand of God. The church is the house of the saved. It is not the source of salvation. Jesus is the Savior. The church is where the saved to meet. People say I go to church, well woo-pee, I'm glad you are here, but until you receive Jesus as your Lord, you are going nowhere. Your decisions determine your destiny. There was a day when you were not, but there will never be a day where you will not be. Do you know Jesus Christ as your lighted Lord and Savior?

Do you truly know the Lord Jesus Christ as the Lord of your life?. If you stepped from where you are and got called into eternity, would you know without a doubt where you would go? There are only two destinations, the glory of heaven only through Jesus Christ our Lord or the depths of hell. It's an eternal question, not for a secular humanist. Or the anti-Semitism. Or the atheist. And I doubt in my heart of hearts that they are not crying out for some miraculous parting of the Red Sea was walking on water was calming the water and storms. It's called faith. You either believe in Jesus Christ, our Lord and Savior of all, or you go to the depths of hell gnashing and grinding of teeth where your soul parishes.

We have decisions. John 3; 16 — for God so loved the world, that he gave his only begotten son, that whoever should believe in him should not perish but have everlasting life. Our father who art in heaven hallowed be the name, thy kingdom to come thy will be done, on this earth as it is in heaven, give us this day our daily bread and forgive us our trespasses, as we forgive those who trespass against us, and lead us not into temptation, but deliver us from evil amen.

My wife DiAnnie and I believe in one God, the Father Almighty Creator of heaven and earth. In Jesus Christ, his only son, our Lord, born of the Virgin Mary, Suffered under *Pontus Pilate was crucified, died, and was buried. He descended into hell to get the keys to hell from Satan. On the third day, he rose again from the dead and is now seated at the right hand of God the Father, waiting to judge the living and the dead.*

My wife DiAnnie and I believe in the communion of saints, the forgiveness of sins, life everlasting amen my wife and I believe in miracles. We certainly know without unshakable faith that Jesus Christ came into this world suffered emotionally and physically more than any man ever recorded. From the splendor of heaven, Jesus descended into the depths of hell for our sins and salvation. I love you, sweetheart. Take your time. I'm just so awake because I slept so many hours yesterday now I am getting tired. I pray to God that I do not go to sleep.

I love my girl from The north country, my sweet delight, and I should know better than question your ability. I do not mean to use or make you sound Deacon sending or make you feel like you're some little child who does not know what she is doing. These are not my intentions, beautiful, because you know that I know you are far better than that, and I would not be where I am at right at this very moment if it were not for you—continuously growing along spiritual lines trying to do the best I can. And everything I can do for my beautiful sweetheart and Guardian Angel.

This I pray through Jesus Christ our Lord's name and please watch over DiAnnie's mother and protector with health and abundance in all her ways through her path. I'm in love with you, sweetheart. You are my girl. Hugs and kisses from your Zorro

29 March 2019

DiAnnie wrote;

Good morning my love,

Thanks for all your messages and questions. First, I'll tell you that I have no reason to be angry with you just because you need to understand a few things that you don't understand.

Thanks for asking me how I'm doing; I am great, just getting stressed with all these questions and having to check back and for on email while working, but it's all good. I'll be fine.

These people are only assisting, so stop this silly jealousy because they are males! What are you thinking, Zorro?

You sure bombard me with emails, and you know it, and you know I hate to ignore any of your messages, especially when you have so many doubts. If I didn't sit to write such a long message this early morning, you would have so much going on in your heart. Learn how to believe your girl and trust her, we all have a terrible past, but when someone gives their life to God, they become new people. I have no mindset to mess around any other man but you. So let's not go into a state of confusion. I'm not telling you not to ask me what you don't understand.

All my love and regards to you.

You are just that old tough Zorro..lol.

Say hi to brother Brian, and I can't stop laughing at all the silly things you two do. You know how to handle Brian, and I believe his mother thought you are his Dad even though he's older. His family will be proud of you for making him a strong guy, not the lazy chair he is..lol. Don't put me in Brian's shoes because you would be in ropes, and you will know this Zorrowess does not take nonsense..lol.

Hugs, my sweetheart.

Hey, my Love! I'm having a busy day here so tomorrow I'll be able to reply to all your lovely messages. How's it going? I hope you're having a nice day, mine is great, just busy right now, but I thought it was right to send a short note so you know I'm thinking about you. I love you so much, my love. Back to work now.

29 March 2019

Thomas wrote;

My beautiful precious Guardian Angel scrumptious treasure from The north country. How are you, today sweetheart? How are you doing, and how are you feeling? I apologize for bombarding you with emails. I do realize that you are a very busy, beautiful young lady. Talking about temptations, smile LOL also, I would have to be very ignorant, selfish and inconsiderate controlling, and jealous if I did not think that you did not have friends of the opposite love. That would be little real thinking on my part.

And if you didn't, I feel there would be something wrong with your Brian, something similar to what you used to think about me being a Marine in the situations I encounter. A smile we just choose not to rub those situations or conversations into each other's face or ears or eyes. That's not our style or character,

We are moral, godly people to respect one another. And I know the men that you know that are your friends are just that you're friends. Not to think that you do not communicate with men would be mundane and immature on my part. I noticed they are males, and I realize that men have the money as opposed to ladies. There have so many things going on within the last 24 hours you would not believe it. I'm going to try to make it one email when you get time to read this. Please do.

You are my precious girl from The north country. You and I have over one year and communicating and strengthening a God-given relationship that any two people would love and enjoy experiencing in their life. We have been chosen. By God, it's not about you or me. It's about God's will for us.

Yesterday while driving around all over God's creation, smile well, maybe not that far. It allowed me to let Brian know how I felt about his lacksidazial attitude. And I was right. There are a time and a place to be in the mood of un-forgiveness and directional training. Mentioning to Brian, do you think I OU for the menial tasks you perform at your discretion around the house? And if you do, when you go flying to see your mother on 16 April in Palm Springs, why don't you stay there.

Because I have two men from Alcoholics Anonymous who would be more than pleased to have a place to stay, please do not let it stop you or interfere with your life. Just move out when you get the opportunity as soon as possible. I do not mean to be mean. I have been such a hard worker in the past, such as yourself. That I cannot stand lazy people or people that do not pick up after themselves. So Brian is a lazy chair. And that I cannot tolerate. So today, to my surprise. He woke up early way before I did because I was just a sponge that was wrung out. I mean, I was exhausted. I did all of the driving. And talk to all of the people. With professionalism.

Back to Brian, it was up early this morning went and got the mail. And when I go out after being exhausted, you could put a bomb off next to me, and I would not flinch. I'm sure you can understand the feeling. He started cleaning the kitchen, cleaned the beautiful china cabinet, clean the tables and chairs, dining room table, and chairs six wooden chairs with three leaves that go into the dining room table. Wash the windows

151

and the huge mirrors in the living room and dining room. And I mean to tell you the dining room and the living room are cleaner than I have ever witnessed them before. We have a beautiful hand-built couch, a piano, and a piano bench with an antique rocking chair. Those are just stunning. I'm telling you, beautiful this place is empty. The echo went away because of the beautiful drapes in your mother's room and our room.

I do not want you to do. Sweetheart is to worry or stress and feel loved and respected. That was not my dad's request, or it was not in his will that was the family living trust. My dad stated in his will and family living trust that we children cannot sell. The grandchildren have to. And children means our children. Honey, you are my girl. And with patience

Please, please, please, everything is okay right now. Everything is going to be okay. Okay? It looks like things are coming together really rapidly. When Brian and I say Brian and I, I mean my guidance skills over Brian to straighten his house. For you and your mother, and it is coming together rapidly. Give me a couple of more weeks, sweetheart. Don't give me a couple more weeks. I think I will take pictures of this house right now. And then I will take pictures of it when I feel we are finished. LOL, smile this out to be a good one. Keep in mind it is empty drawers cabinets closet space empty empty empty. I pray to God that you have a lot of things you can bring into our home.? It's still a house. I have two. I have three, and we have our fourth book, "soulmates from heaven" or "soulmates to heaven," and that my change whatever you decide, sweetheart. Our book.

One more thing I should mention, and I may have already. Is that I went to the hospital. They have been monitoring a tiny nodule on the top of my left lung for about four years. And I have had one biopsy already that was inconclusive. So all of a sudden, they decide they want to do another biopsy, and they did. My doctor called me yesterday and said that there was nonmalignant noncancerous, nothing to worry about. I had a feeling, but these doctors are always looking for work. And I cannot. I should say I am very appreciative of the way they take care of me.

I brought a lot of joy and laughter and happiness into about 300 people's lives the other day when I went into the hospital. And that may be putting it lightly. All the doctors and nurses enjoy my sense of humor in making people laugh to take their minds off their physical or mental limitations. Patiently I have been waiting for this love for over 20 years now. and patients. It's a virtue. So please, honey, please do not feel rushed or pressured. That you have to get here any sooner than you are going to. Smile LOL, you're not getting here one second before or one second after you and your mother are supposed to be here. So get that through your pretty little beautiful head. LOL, smile.

You and I are going through some rough times right now together, and God only knows why? We can handle it together, though. This is who we are. Would you like to hear a prediction? Lol smile let me meditate and think and pray to God. This is my prediction God will get mad at me if I bring him into this one. God says, in the beginning, we shall multiply and make the earth plentiful. To multiply? For any two people to multiply, they have to have more than two children. Do you agree? What you think about three children.?

I'm only asking beautiful, because you are the one who will note the pains of bearing children. And the decision for how many children we will have will be entirely for my beautiful way from The north country, my precious treasure. I was thinking the other night, and you know me? It is dangerous sometimes for me to think. LOL, smile now there are grandchildren. Your birthday is on the same day as my father's birthday. Your father's first name and my father's first name are sounded the same. Therefore our fathers condone our union with one another.

This is what I get for thinking. If we had children in the family. And our children are going to be God's children. Taking care of you and your mother with an abundance of blessings will never have to worry or stress or work so hard you can, sweetheart. I'm not going anywhere until the great-grandchild is born. Peace and grace of the Lord be with you and your mother through Jesus Christ our Lord's name amen. Please let your mother know that my prayers are with her for her happiness and well-being. Hugs and kisses from your Zorro.

I beautiful precious treasure from The north country. You know I'm in love with you, and God loves us both. Answer me one question please, would I be your husband if I did not ask these questions? Or would I be a milquetoast, a limp wristed, not a man but a coward? Would I not care about your welfare and well-being? If I did not ask these questions? And with spiritual discernment to the Holy Spirit, I asked these questions.

Because you're my girl, I'm not a rich man beautiful, but I am a man and a Marine and one of God's children. We have too many some people might call him coincidental. I call them miracles that brought us together. Too many things through the Holy Spirit that God has brought into our lives together and strengthened our love that has no beginning or no End. I love the way you care for me. And we have trust between the two of us. Suppose we do not have trust between the two of us over the last year. We may as well go our separate ways.

Only you can answer how you feel. I do not walk in your shoe, sweetheart. I know when God connects to people out of 7 billion. That's not perchance. And if you are going to be angry with me, over telephones,? Please explain the questions that I have to ask you. They are not unreasonable questions there only questions that only you can answer.

Let me repeat that without being mad. Smile with joy, laughter, compassion, love, care, consideration, honor, trustworthiness, a God-given passion. And for that love that God has given us, I will not defile it or abuse it or misuse it or defile it in any way. If I do, God will not answer my prayers. Not an unreasonable request. Peace and grace of the Lord be with you and your mother through Jesus Christ our Lord's name amen I'm in love with you I would give my life for you. Xoxox from your Zorro

30 March 2019

Thomas wrote;

How is my girl doing this morning? How are you feeling, beautiful? I pray things are going well for you. I realize you are very busy. And for that, I am kind of jealous; LOL, smile, not. I'm proud of you, sweetheart. You are my girl from The north country, my precious treasure. To give us a little hope.

I do not want you to worry or stress about anything at the end of your life. Or I should say at the beginning of your life. Smile with compassion for my wife. God willing. It's not my will. It will be God's will. Because I praise God through Jesus Christ the Lord's name, and every time I send an email to you, I'm so in love with God that he has shown me a passion that I have never experienced before in my life. And it's all because of you, sweetheart, my guardian angel, my precious girl from The north country. And God willing, you and your mother and I will meet someday.

When God's timing is just right, until then, beautiful, you take care of yourself. Remember that God gave the angels charge over us. That means we each have two guardian angels with this at all times. I love you and think about you continuously; back to cleaning today with Brother Brian. I had no clue how unorganized a bachelor can be. LOL, smile, and it will take a beautiful lady to make this old house a warm home. In the meantime, I'm excited that you are preparing for your trip to meet up with your mother.

And I realize that when you are reunited with your mother, it will be the happiest, joyous time in both of your lives, I'm sure. I cannot keep my mouth off of you. LOL, a smile. I will always pray for you and your mother. For your health, happiness, faith, joy with peace of mind through the grace of God and his only son, our Lord Jesus Christ that the Holy Spirit works for your life guiding and protecting you and giving you the knowledge and wisdom that I realize you already have more so than myself. Please be nice yourself. Smile once again, may I remind you that if it were not for you, I would not be the man I am today, and you have completed my journey to heaven as I grow along spiritual lines and become a better man because of you, beautiful girl from The north country.

I talked to a lady from North Carolina yesterday that I used to go to grammar school with many moons ago. Smile, and I mentioned to her about you, and I said, "if I never meet this girl from The north country, she has changed my life in a very profound spiritual way that I thank God for that came into my life as an angel. So remember, sweetheart, be kind to strangers, for we may never know when we are in the presence of angels. Smile prayerfully with appreciation and love of God

You're a brilliant, beautiful young lady. And I'm not going to pressure you anymore, sweetheart, about being my wife. I just want you to be happy and free and keep in mind that this Marine is thinking about you in love with your soul. I will always be a piece of my heart, no matter where you are or who. You're with her what you are doing. I'm in love with the love I have never experienced before. Hugs and kisses from your Zorro.

CHAPTER 5

Romantic Memoirs From Heaven, April 2019

1 April 2019

DiAnnie wrote;

Hi My Love,

Good, I can message you now after getting some quality rest. How is your day going? I hope that everything is going great today and that you and brother Brian are not working too hard. I really needed rest, and thank God I got some, and I'm having less stress now.

Well, like I always tell you, honey, I'll always be truthful to you because you are also to me, so believe me, whatever you don't understand, I'll be there to clear things up all the time. I know where we came from till now, and we are better people who have gotten along compare to months back. All this is because our both hearts are after God because we have been with the devil or, like you always say, dance with Him. Well, I know you're not jealous of me, it is easily said, but when a situation arises such can show naturally, I try not to be jealous of you. Still, I do control so hard when you talk about meeting those girls in the Motor vehicles department or the hospital that looks like me and that you wish they were me, makes my heart wants to feel jealous because it's natural, so I know you do same like I do. No one agrees on a negative thing; that's human nature..lol. I knew right you we're concerned about where those valuable items were heading and to whom it is normal, and believe me, I wasn't mad at all about the questions. *If I decided to fight instead of telling you, then you know something wasn't right.*

Well, sometimes I feel like just tying you up, but then you are such an understanding person who realizes his errors and never too big to say you're sorry. It would be one reason if I had to tie you up that I'll always forgive you. If you were a controlling person, believe me, we wouldn't be here still in touch, we disagree to agree that's life. So know that your girl isn't going to punish you unnecessarily unless you cross that line..lol. I'm not a marine, but I think I got some of the qualities of a Marine..lol. You are such a fun guy, and hurting you would be the last I'll do. Know also that doesn't mean Thomas is perfect as an angel, don't be too excited..lol. Sure, you can't be a preacher because, at this point, you're still being molded to be the person after God's heart. We all no one is 100% holy. It's only by the works of Christ. I won't give up on you. We all will get better; Christ didn't give up on us, so why me? You will be the love of my life, and I love you just the way you're.

I know you have these dreams, and I sometimes do, I do too, but a lady's way of imagining isn't precisely the same as a man, so even if I have a love dream, I better keep it to myself till we meet because that will help me to focus and prepare to make being with you possible. I'm more interested in coming over there to have the best of times with such a romantic and fun-loving man, someone may ask. He's older! But I'll tell them that I can not see it in a young man what he is made up! So now that you're a better man, more than many young guys are there. I agree. Love wasn't made by anyone else unless by the creator. All living things do it. It is natural. Wow, you nailed it with the Songs of Solomon. It explains why love is more profound than we see.

Well, I know the running around did not kill you or brother Brian, but the fact that it was your first time and all the pressure from me made me sad, but you as an understanding person didn't get mad, and you did just what I asked, which made me very excited because I know that it is a vast process but not huge to God. With God, our future will be fine, I too want to be a blessing to you and brother Brian, but I'll let you know, let me see how things start to work from my side. With each other, none of us is supposed to lack, so I told my Mom that you are a part of our family and when God starts to bless us, to share what we have with you. Two hearts will love when both of them care for each other and those around them. I do not only think about you alone being there for me but also being there for you. So let's pray for each other, OK, my love. Oh yes, up until now, I can't just understand how God made your dad and me have the same birthdays and our background coming from Europe and America. There is so much miracle when I sit and think about all we share.

You're so right. I know the story too of the man who said he was the brother of his wife, sometimes you must accept certain things to save your life, we have a lot of things right now, but we will get through, thank God you are not going to be my brother, no one is after your life..lol.

I understand that our relationship belongs to us, not others, for I have no issue with how others feel about us. My only problem, for now, is that why me still being here and haven't met yet. If we tell people about us, they will have all reason to stick their noses in our affairs because the one thing they will stick on is, do you trust him? Do you trust her? But me being there, I will have nothing to fear because nothing anyone will say would hurt me because they'll see that we love each other, even brother Brian will be surprised, for now, he too still has his doubts about us. I'm aware, but I'm not mad because he thinks like any normal human being. The degree of our understanding will never be like the rest apart from my Mom because she knows me well, you me more than anyone there. You know yourself well, and I know you for the time we have been communicating almost every day, but will the rest agree with us? a big NO because they are not us.

I know and have heard of all the sinful things in Arizona, God's children will always remain, it happens in Noah's time, but the family of the righteous did stay, it's not only Arizona but the rest of the world is polluted with evil, we have some things here as well, the society is rotten to the core believe me.

Oh yes, God will come like a thief, just like the time of Noah. No one believes it, but it came to pass. My love pregnancy with no pregnancy all I want is that we will not have to care about what others will think when I come. Love is difficult to be in hidden reason I hate to cheat on my partner because whenever you're in love with someone and try to hide it at the end or not too long people will know so we shouldn't think about them like I say, as long Mom and I come over all will start to go in place. I know you will put the house in my name, but the rightful owners will be your children because our last name will be apart from my Mom, so it's their home. Do you get my idea?..lol.

Sure, I know what you're saying honey, our love is a warm God-given one, and I know many will envy it because it does not resemble their earthly kind of love, we have worked so hard to make this relationship what it is and God who started this will make it work in His timing, sometimes our own time isn't precisely His time, we can put in the effort though. So as we put in the time to meet, God will work out the rest. All we need is to keep praying and believing that it'll be fine. If Satan was to have His will over us by now, we are not getting along; it's because we have won over Him. It's the reason we are still here going strong.

I know the feeling, my love, when I think, wow he has written long messages and I'll end here it's the more interesting it gets, no one in their right mind would want to ignore all these lovely words, I just can not ignore as I learn so much reading your messages, know that you have so much experience in life than me and no matter how much intelligence I have the older ones are the best because they are ahead before, the smaller ones came..lol, right?

Hahaha, Brian is right. Why didn't you tell him ever since that I am also called DiAnnie? DiAnnie is my name, but I just like that name Ann Maria which is DiAnnie today..lol so he is right to think you have another girl on the side who is DiAnnie and not DiAnnie, maybe those girls that looks like me at the motor department or the hospital? I'll tell brother Brian that girls easily admire you, you have that gift of taking girls attention from other men, if I look at your pictures and I see those eyes, especially when you were much younger, I can tell that it wasn't a soft Thomas, an adamant Zorro even at this time some ladies are still contacting you, but tell them that a very rough girl will soon be here and she's not going to take any nonsense from anyone..lol.

Anyway, my love, I'll try to do a few things around here, and I am here thinking about you. Enjoy the rest of the day.

All my regards to you guys. Mrs.

Thomas wrote;

Sweetheart, I did not get any quality rest LOL I'm exhausted spending most of my time on the telephone with technical gurus of Google and Yahoo who don't know absolutely anything, first of all, I would have to speak in the Indian language in the country of India to understand what they're trying to say, I came to pay attention, but now my riches are stored in your heart. Let me read your email, and I will send you another one. You must be exhausted yourself. Get some rest, sweetheart, and I will send you a long email that you can read in the morning, my precious Guardian Angel treasure from North country. Was I your mother doing? I'm you may have already answered the question in your email; I have not read it as of yet. The love of the heart grows stronger when it is a part. And makes you appreciate and realize and take nothing for granted. Peace and grace of the Lord be with you and your mother through Jesus resolute's name from your Zorro

I will give you a minute by minute account of what I have been doing since the last time I emailed you you would not believe it, and Brian has this house in an almost tiptop shape. I cannot even list everything that Brian had done with my expertise instructions and overseeing although he did sneak behind my back and put a brand-new shower-head and wanted on the shower while I was not looking, I could not believe my eyeballs this morning when I went to take a shower it was like heaven. He did it without even letting me know what he was doing. I usually beat him like a redheaded stepchild and hold his head underwater and not let him up for air, and I'll be darned if I know how he had the time to do the shower-head, LOL smile, I love you.

Thomas wrote;

Sweetheart, I just love you so much after reading that long email. You are so precious, and God loves us both as we love God. This is why we are together is because of the love that God has for us. And that is so powerful and miraculous. I would say just heartbroken; I felt like I had lost my best friend when I was unable to email you the last three days. I soon then realized how strong our love is for one another. And please, sweetheart, do not worry about those other ladies. Are you kidding me? I realize it is a natural human emotion to be jealous. Believe me when I tell you this I'm only in love with you and on the first one to let the slings know that I am in a committed relationship. I went to the doctor this morning, as I had mentioned earlier, and talked to my female Dr. Joyce. And she asked me how our relationship was going? And I feel since she took an oath with confidentiality of doctor-patient privacy and protection. I spoke for my heart, and I said we communicate daily, and I really touched her heart when I mentioned to her about letting you know That I would never deprive you of life that would be inhumane on my part to not let you go dancing with another man. Swimming hiking physical things that you may like to do that I will not be able to participate in with you. And the doctor looked at me with astonishment. I also mentioned to the good doctor that the key to a successful marriage is the forgiveness of one another continuously. And as a husband to let his wife do just exactly what she wants to do without question. And she said yes, I wish it was that way with everybody. I just had a spiritual feeling that her husband is not the kind of a husband. And I also mentioned to the good doctor about how we are equally yoked spiritually, and then that was another key to a successful marriage, and it is a priority. I explained that I read the Bible continuously and that the Bible and prophecy are beyond miraculous. I just love you, honey.

You are not going to believe this leverage Brian and I almost and I mean a long way but almost getting this house, so it looks I cannot explain the words for the with this house looks now compared to what it used to look like a while back. We most certainly have more to do, and we will be working right up until the day you and your mother decide to come here. One more thing, sweetheart, this house is going into your name.

And it's one child at a time. So please do not let me project 12 boys into our lives like the 12 tribes of Israel. LOL smile LOL and you are right, sweetheart. Just being together with you and being with us together with your mother, we will have fun and enjoy one another's company. Through prayer, prayer is powerful medicine. And I'm so in love with you.

In this old house, we have one more room to go through and throw things away, and that is our bathroom. It is clean. And always has been. It's just the three medicine cabinets and the two drawers below, and the two long medicine cabinets, or should I say cupboards on the side, are full of things that I have been just pushing in their over 20 years. LOL, and some of the stuff I have in throwing weight you would not even believe I could not even imagine that it was even in my presence. Then we rearranged pictures to where all I have on the walls is religious pictures and crosses, and I never realized I had that many spread out throughout the house. It looks pretty nice. According to my standards as a man. LOL LOL, and I know for a fact according to your standards, as a beautiful young wife and your mother will have a whole different outlook and perspective on the way things should be—double smile.

Anyway, my children are doing fine, and they would never if anything ever should happen to me would just expect you to leave. I raise my children with moral standards to a certain degree. And the children love me so much and when they see how much I love this beautiful young lady from North country. Sweetheart, I'm having a hard time thinking of how to explain our love for one another for the simple reason the love we have between us that we have developed through the Holy Spirit over the last year has been through the grace of God. And how it's used to explain miracles? I'm still in love with you, and I love your soul. Our souls were meant to be blended. I chair you always in my heart with love and overabundance of love that phone could have come from God, for the simple reason I never have in my life experience this love that I always had a feeling was there.

Sweetheart, I can't keep my mouth off of you. You are so precious. Are you getting rest, sweetheart? How are you feeling? And thank you so very much for that one long email. Gorgeous beautiful treasure from North country, you're my girl.

Just have you consumed my thoughts was all well worth the effort. Another thing I meant to inform you of that I mentioned to the doctor. "I said to the doctor" "you realize Dr. if I never meet this beautiful young lady, she has come into my life like a guardian angel that was sent from God and changed me." Until my girl from the North country came along, I do not even think about it or even want it in my life anymore. Another thing I'll be honest with you, quitting smoking is very difficult, and I'm down to just a couple of cigarettes a day now, and I'm sure when she and her mother arrived, I will quit, God willing. And also, I'm not surfing around the web talking to ladies like they used to.

Sweetheart, realize that talking to a lady online, in my mind, is like committing adultery—the seventh commandment. I know for a fact, and I have no intentions of going there that if you did not troll the line, I would. Fidelity, adultery, and fornication are nowhere in our lives. What do you think? These are not godly qualities. Let's portray a scenario, "first of all, let me say this, that we are going to be judged on our words, what we think, what we do, and what we fail to do." As I had mentioned, if you were ever to draw the line with our love for one another, that is the only thing I can think of within this guide-given miraculous relationship. The devil may try, when I tell you this beautiful, I mean this you are my girl I have never experienced this God-given love ever. I would not jeopardize it for anything, any thought, any word, or any action. I'm so in love with you with this godly love. All my life, I have wanted this love. I always had a feeling with my unshakable faith that it was obtainable only through the grace of God. I'm so excited every day about crowing and love and become a better person because of you coming into my life, in continuously changing me for the better as we grow together in this bond of love. There is no way to explain this love we have between us two any other people. It's called faith with works. And please, sweetheart, do not worry, stress, or go down the negative bunny trail.

Just having this house getting to where it is from where it came from. As given me a lot of energy. I should be dead tired, exhausted right now, and I am. Peace in the grace of the Lord is with you and your mother to Jesus Christ the Lord's name amen. One small question beautiful, in your heart of hearts, and be honest with me I can handle it, what do you feel your mother thinks about me? And about our relationship of this God-given love? Smile with compassion and care, and kindness. I love you, honey. You are my precious Guardian Angel treasure from North country, and I'm your Zorro.

Thomas wrote;

Sweetheart, my delicious little beautiful treasure, my God-given child sweet tasty little morsel elegant cuisine and praying prayerfully with love for the creator God our father for being a chef. Now tell me, could God have put together two of the most exemplary representation of God's love together out of 7 billion people.?

So be prayerfully in the lovingkindness of God God's gift to us his life what we do with this life is our gift to God.

I'm just letting you know that we have available because we live in this great state of Arizona. Immensely wealthy, possibly not all of them, but Arizona has more millionaires and billionaires. And for all of the social sicknesses to ease their conscience, these people with a lot are more than happy to provide for the lesson than thou.

They think they are getting to heaven by doing so wrong. That's where we come in, and you are such a delicious, precious beautiful god-given miracle. I love you, honey. You're my girl. We will have to live our lives one moment at a time and do the best we can do at the moment. In the meantime, everything is going to be OK, and everything is OK, alright? No worry, no stress, no negative thinking thoughts.

We cannot change the past. There's no sense in living our lives through the rearview mirror.

So let us pray to God that he answers your prayer and our prayer along with your mother, in Jesus Christ's name we pray and God our father that somehow. She needs. And thank you, father. We love everything you do in our lives, and we appreciate this life that has been so graciously and miraculously provided for us.

And we pray for health, happiness, and please let my wife DiAnnie and her mother realize with unshakable faith that at the moment, everything is OK. Our human nature will take us to a place in our minds we do not want to go although living in the moment, and everything is OK right this very moment. And we thank you for that Lord Jesus Christ. I just love my wife, and I thank you miraculously for this lady in my life for the rest of our lives. Even though she will tie me up, LOL smile, and only God knows what else my Marine Corps wife is capable of doing. LOL smile, I love you, honey, you're my girl

Beautiful, please use this email address; for now, I indeed miss not being able to communicate with you.

And time will tell not to trust or believe you we been together too long for that.

I realize you are a busy, beautiful young lady, my precious, gorgeous, delicious treasure from North country. And you very well may not have time to have replied or had even sent me an email. Only God knows. Smile LOL. They gave me shingles shot for prevention this morning. I believe it is it to series one now and one six months from now. I never even heard of a shingle shot.? Peace and grace of the Lord be with you and your mother to just same resolute amen.

Sweetheart, I love you so much after reading that long email. You are so precious, and God loves us both as we love God. This is why we are together is because of the love that God has for us. And that is so powerful and miraculous. I would feel just heartbroken, and I felt like I had lost my best friend when I was unable to email you the last three days. I soon then realized how strong our love is for one another. And please, sweetheart, do not worry about those other ladies. Are you kidding me? I know it is a natural human emotion to be jealous. Believe me when I tell you this I'm only in love with you and on the first one to let the slings know that I am in a committed relationship. I went to the doctor this morning, as I had mentioned earlier, and talked to my female Dr. Joyce. And she asked me how our relationship was going? And I feel since she took an oath with confidentiality of doctor-patient privacy and protection.

I spoke for my heart, and I said we communicate daily, and I touched her heart when I mentioned to her about letting you know That I would never deprive you of life that would be inhumane on my part not to let you go dancing with another man. Swimming hiking material things that you may like to do that I will not participate in with you. And the doctor looked at me with astonishment. I also mentioned to the good doctor that the key to a successful marriage is the forgiveness of one another continuously. And as a husband to let his wife do just exactly what she wants to do without question. And she said yes, I wish it was that way with everybody. I just had a spiritual feeling that her husband is not the kind of a husband. And I also mentioned to the good doctor how we are equally yoked spiritually, and then that was another key to a successful marriage, and it is a priority. I explained to her that I read the Bible continuously and that the Bible and prophecy are beyond miraculous. I love you, honey. I

You will not believe this leverage Brian and I almost and I mean a long way but almost getting this house, so it looks like I cannot explain the words for them with this house seems now compared to what it used to look like a while back. We most certainly have more to do, and we will be working right up until the day you and your mother decide to come here. One more thing, sweetheart, this house is going into your name. Please do not be concerned that my children are all doing very well. And once they witnessed our love for one another, they would not take anything from you, only help you in any way they can. And it's one child at a time. So please do not let me project 12 boys into our lives like the 12 tribes of Israel. LOL smile LOL, and you are right, sweetheart, just being together with you and being with us along with your mother, we are going to have fun and enjoy one another's company. Prayer is powerful medicine. And I'm so in love with you.

In this old house, we have one more room to go through and throw things away, and that is our bathroom. It is clean. And always has been. It's just the three medicine cabinets, and the two drawers below, and the two long medicine offices, or should I say cupboards on the side, are full of things that I have been just pushing in there over 20 years. LOL, and some of the stuff I have in throwing weight you would not even believe I could not even imagine it was also in my presence. Then we rearranged pictures to where all I have on the walls is religious pictures and crosses, and I never realized I had that many spreads out throughout the house; it looks pretty nice. According to my standards as a man. LOL LOL, and I know for a fact according to your standards, as a beautiful young wife, your mother will have a whole different outlook and perspective on the way things should be—double smile.

Anyway, my children are doing fine, and they would never expect you to leave if anything ever should happen to me. I raise my children with moral standards to a certain degree. And the children love me so much and when they see how much I love this beautiful young lady from North country. Sweetheart, I'm having a hard time thinking of how to explain our love for one another for the simple reason the love we have between us that we have developed through the Holy Spirit over the last year has been through the grace of God. And how it's used to explain miracles? I'm still in love with you, and I love your soul. Our souls were meant to be blended. I chair you always in my heart with love and overabundance of love that phone could have come from God, for the simple reason I never have in my life experience this love that I always had a feeling was there.

Beautiful, You will have to admit, sweetheart, and I'm sure this is true that our cultures and lifestyles from North country to the United States is not all that different. But there are differences. Do we disagree? I could be wrong, and I usually am. LOL, I'm only a man; I keep telling myself that I am just a man. LOL LOL

A lady came on Facebook who lives about two blocks up the road and around a couple of corners. I sold chicken eggs and just came on and asked me if I knew Tina, my former sister-in-law who lives next door. I said, of course, I do. Anyway, we did not communicate back and forth that long. Maybe I should not have mentioned it to her, but I did. Let me say this first, she is living with a man who just had a stroke and just had a heart attack and has a daughter that's 21 and a four-year-old child that I think he and her head together not sure. I mentioned to her everything about you, will not everything that I did suggest is that you and I were equally oak spiritually and that we have been communicating for well over a year.

And that you were planning a trip to Arizona with your mother. And I asked her, you and this man you are living with, are you married? She said no, and I said, don't you think it would strengthen the relationship and make the children feel good about having an unstable family? So she came down yesterday afternoon and dropped off one dozen eggs. I mentioned to her that I did not have any money to pay for them, but I would swap my latest book for a few dozen eggs. And she agreed. After I mentioned to her about being married, yesterday afternoon was the first time I had met her, and it turns out she and her live-in boyfriend are driving to Reno, Nevada, today to get married. That's pretty cool, I think.

This is how we are going to help others, sweetheart. She mentioned something to me I never knew, and I feel it is a great idea. You cannot go into the courthouse and get married in one day. The county was having a lot of problems with people matching too fast. So they put a three-month waiting period on marriages. And, of course, you have to get a blood test. I will find out the information in detail, talk to my Baptist minister, and update you beautifully. peace and grace of the Lord be with you and your mother through Jesus Christ our Lord's name amen I'm so in love with you, Ms. PostScript; I feel the most romantic thoughts and feelings that I have had in the last three days, without contacting my beautiful girl from North country. It has made me realize just how much our love has strengthened and grown over the previous year. And it took just a break, like three days, to have an impact of appreciation for the love that we have for each other only through the grace of God. I do not want to lose this email, sweetheart, so that I will pick up where my thoughts leave off. I love you so much.

Thomas wrote;

Sweetheart, I can't keep my mouth off of you-you are so precious. Are you getting rest, sweetheart? How are you feeling? And thank you so very much for that one long email. A gorgeous, beautiful treasure from North country, you're my girl.

Another thing I meant to inform you of that I mentioned to the doctor. "I said to the doctor" "you realize Dr. if I never meet this beautiful young lady, she has come into my life like a guardian angel that was sent from God and changed me." Another thing I'll be honest with you, quitting smoking is, and I'm down to just a couple of cigarettes a day now, and I'm sure when she and her mother arrived, I will quit, God willing. And also, I'm not surfing around the web talking to ladies like they used to.

In my mind, sweetheart realizes that talking to a lady online is like committing adultery — the seventh commandment. I know for a fact, and I have no intentions of going there that if you did not troll the line, I would.

Fidelity, adultery, and fornication are nowhere in our lives. What do you think? These are not godly qualities. Let's portray a scenario, "first of all, let me say this, that we are going to be judged on our words, what we think, what we do, and what we fail to do." As I had mentioned, if you were ever to draw the line with our love for one another, that is the only thing I can think of within this guide-given miraculous relationship.

The devil may try when I tell you this beautiful. I mean this, you are my girl. I have never experienced this God-given love ever. I would not jeopardize it for anything, any thought, any word, or any action. I'm so in love with you with this godly love. All my life, I have wanted this love. I always had a feeling with my unshakable faith that it was obtainable only through the grace of God. I'm so excited every day about crowing and love and become a better person because of you coming into my life, in continuously changing me for the better as we grow together in this bond of love.

There is no way to explain this love we have between us two any other people. It's called faith with works. And please, sweetheart, does not worry about stress or go down the negative bunny trail. Just having this house getting to where it is from where it came from. As given me a lot of energy.

I should be dead tired, exhausted right now, and I am. Peace in the grace of the Lord is with you and your mother to Jesus Christ the Lord's name amen. One small question beautiful, in your heart of hearts, and be honest with me I can handle it, what do you feel your mother thinks about me? And about our relationship with this God-given love? Smile with compassion and care, and kindness. I love you, honey, you are my precious Guardian Angel treasure from North country, and I'm your Zorro.

DiAnnie wrote;

Hi My Love,

Good, I can message you now after getting some quality rest. How is your day going? I hope that everything is going great today and that you and brother Brian are not working too hard. I really needed rest, and thank God I got some, and I'm having less stress now.

Well, like I always tell you, honey, I'll always be truthful to you because you are also to me, so believe me, whatever you don't understand, I'll be there to clear things up all the time. I know where we came from till now, and we are better people who have gotten along compare to months back. All this is because our both hearts are after God because we have been with the devil or, like you always say, dance with Him. Well, I know you're not jealous of me, it is easily said, but when a situation arises such can show naturally, I try not to be jealous of you. Still, I do control so hard when you talk about meeting those girls in the Motor vehicles department or the hospital that looks like me and that you wish they were me, makes my heart wants to feel ealous because it's natural, so I know you do same like I do. No one agrees on a negative thing. That's human nature..lol. I knew right you were concerned about where those valuable items were heading and to whom it is normal, and believe me, I wasn't mad at all about the questions. If I decided to fight instead of telling you, then you know something wasn't right.

Well, sometimes I feel like just tying you up, but then you are such an understanding person who realizes his errors and never too big to say you're sorry. It would be one reason if I had to tie you up that I'll always forgive you. If you were a controlling person, we wouldn't be here still in touch, and we disagree to agree that's life. So know that your girl isn't going to punish you unnecessarily unless you cross that line..lol. I'm not a marine, but I think I got some of the qualities of a Marine..lol. You are such a fun guy, and hurting you would be the last I'll do. Know also that doesn't mean Thomas is perfect as an angel, don't be too excited..lol. Sure, you can't be a preacher because, at this point, you're still being molded to be the person after God's heart. We all no one is 100% holy. It's only by the works of Christ. I won't give up on you. We all will get better. Christ didn't give up on us, so why me? You will be the love of my life, and I love you just the way you're.

I know you have these dreams, and I sometimes do, I do too, but a lady's way of imagining isn't precisely the same as a man, so even if I have a love dream, I better keep it to myself till we meet, because that will help me to focus and prepare to make being with you possible. I'm more interested in coming over there to have the best of times with such a romantic and fun-loving man, someone may ask. He's older! But I'll tell them that I can not see what he is made up in a young man! So now that you're a better man, more than many young guys are there. I agree. Love wasn't made by anyone else unless, by the creator, all living things do it. It is natural. Wow, you nailed it with the Songs of Solomon. It explains why love is more profound than we see.

Well, I know the running around did not kill you or brother Brian, but the fact that it was your first time and all the pressure from me made me sad, but you as an understanding person didn't get mad, and you did just what I asked, which made me very excited because I know that it is a vast process but not huge to God. With God, our future will be fine, he too wants to be a blessing to you and brother Brian, but I'll let you know. Let me see how things start to work from my side. With we having each other, none of us is supposed to lack, so I told my Mom that you are a part of our family and when God starts to bless us to share what we have with you. Two hearts will love when both of them care for each other and those around them. I do not only think about you alone being there for me but also being there for you. So let's pray for each other, OK, my love.

Oh yes, up until now, I can't just understand how God made your dad and me have the same birthdays and our background coming from Europe and America. There is so much miracle when I sit and think about all we share.

You're so right. I know the story too of the man who said he was the brother of his wife, sometimes you must accept certain things to save your life, we have a lot of things right now, but we will get through, thank God you are not going to be my brother, no one is after your life..lol.

I understand that our relationship belongs to us, not to others. I have no issue with how others would feel about us. My only problem, for now, is that why me still being here and haven't met yet. If we tell people about us, they will have all reason to stick their noses in our affairs because the one thing they will stick on is, do you trust him? Do you trust her? But me being there, I will have nothing to fear because nothing anyone will say would hurt me because they'll see that we love each other, even brother Brian will be surprised, for now, he too still has his doubts about us. I'm aware, but I'm not mad because he thinks like any normal human being. The degree of our understanding will never be like the rest apart from my Mom because she knows me well, you me more than anyone there, and you know yourself well. I know for the time we have to stay in touch communicating almost every day, but will the rest agree with us? a big NO because they are not us.

I know and have heard of all the sinful things in Arizona, God's children will always remain, it happens in Noah's time, but the family of the righteous did stay, it's not only Arizona but the rest of the world is polluted with evil, we have some things here as well, the society is rotten to the core believe me.

Oh yes, God will come like a thief, just like the time of Noah no one believes, but it came to past. My love pregnancy with no pregnancy all I want is that we will not have to care about what others will think when I come. Love is difficult to be in hidden reason I hate to cheat on my partner because whenever you're in love with someone and try to hide it at the end or not too long people will know so we shouldn't think about them like I say, as long Mom and I come over all will start to go in place. I know you will put the house in my name, but the rightful owners will be your children because our last name will be apart from my Mom, so it's their home. Do you get my idea?..lol.

Sure, I know what you're saying honey, our love is a warm God-given one, and I know many will envy it because it does not resemble their earthly kind of love. We have worked so hard to make this relationship what it is. God who started this will make it work in His timing. Sometimes our own time isn't precisely His time. We can put in the effort, though. So as we put in the time to meet, God will work out the rest. All we need is to keep praying and believing that it'll be fine. If Satan was to have His will over us by now, we are not getting along; it's because we have won over Him. It's the reason we are still here going strong.

I know the feeling, my love, when I think, wow, he has written long messages. I'll end here it's the more interesting it gets, no one in their right mind would want to ignore all these lovely words, I just can not forget as I learn so much reading your messages, know that you have so much experience in life than me and no matter how much intelligence I have the older ones are the best because they are ahead, the smaller ones came..lol, right?

Hahaha, Brian is correct. Why didn't you tell him ever since that I am also called DiAnnie, DiAnnie is my name, but I just like that name Ann Maria which is DiAnnie today..lol so he is right to think you have another girl on the side who is DiAnnie and not DiAnnie, maybe those girls that looks like me at the motor department or the hospital? I'll tell brother Brian that girls easily admire you. You have that gift of taking a girl's attention from other men if I look at your pictures. I see those eyes, especially when you were much younger. I can tell that it wasn't a soft Thomas, an adamant Zorro. Even at this time, some ladies are still contacting you, but tell them that a very rough girl will soon be here. She's not going to take any nonsense from anyone..lol.

Anyway, my love, I'll try to do a few things around here, and I am here thinking about you. Enjoy the rest of the day.

All my regards to you guys. Mrs.

Thomas wrote;

Sweetheart, I did not get any quality rest LOL I'm exhausted spending most of my time on the telephone with technical gurus of Google and Yahoo who don't know absolutely anything, first of all, I would have to speak in the Indian language in the country of India to understand what they're trying to say,

I came to pay attention, but now my riches are stored in your heart. Let me read your email, and I will send you another one. You must be exhausted yourself. Get some rest, sweetheart, and I will send you a long email that you can read in the morning, my precious Guardian Angel treasure from North country. Was I your mother doing? I'm you may have already answered the question in your email; I have not read it as of yet. The love of the heart grows stronger when it is a part. And makes you appreciate and realize and take nothing for granted. Peace and grace of the Lord be with you and your mother through Jesus resolute's name from your Zorro

I will give you a minute by minute account of what I have been doing since the last time I emailed you you would not believe it, and Brian has this house in an almost tiptop shape. I cannot even list everything that Brian had done with my expertise, instructions, and overseeing. However, he did sneak behind my back, put a brand-new shower-head, and wanted on the shower while I was not looking. I could not believe my eyeballs this morning. When I went to take a shower, it was like heaven. He did it without even letting me know what he was doing. I usually beat him like a redheaded stepchild and hold his head underwater and not let him up for air, and I'll be darned if I know how he had the time to do the shower-head, LOL smile, I love you.

Thomas wrote;

Sweetheart, I just love you so much after reading that long email. You are so precious, and God loves us both as we love God. This is why we are together is because of the love that God has for us. And that is so powerful and miraculous. I would say just heartbroken; I felt like I had lost my best friend when I could not email you the last three days. I soon then realized how strong our love is for one another. And please, sweetheart, do not worry about those other ladies. Are you kidding me? I know it is a natural human emotion to be jealous. Believe me when I tell you this I'm only in love with you and on the first one to let the slings know that I am in a committed relationship. As I had mentioned earlier, I went to the doctor this morning and talked to my female Dr. Joyce. And she asked me how our relationship was going? And I feel since she took an oath with confidentiality of doctor- patient privacy and protection. I spoke for my heart, and I said we communicate daily, and I touched her heart when I mentioned to her about letting you know That I would never deprive you of life that would be inhumane on my part not to let you go dancing with another man.

Swimming hiking material things that you may like to do that I will not participate with you. And the doctor looked at me with astonishment. I also mentioned to the good doctor that the key to a successful marriage is the forgiveness of one another continuously. And as a husband to let his wife do just exactly what she wants to do without question. And she said yes, I wish it was that way with everybody. I just had a spiritual feeling that her husband is not the kind of a husband. And I also mentioned to the good doctor how we are equally yoked spiritually, and then that was another key to a successful marriage, and it is a priority. I explained that I read the Bible continuously and that the Bible and prophecy are beyond miraculous. I love you, honey.

You are not going to believe this leverage Brian and I almost and I mean a long way but almost getting this house, so it looks I cannot explain the words for the with this house looks now compared to what it used to look like a while back. We most certainly have more to do, and we will be working right up until the day you and your mother decide to come here. One more thing, sweetheart, this house is going into your name.

And it's one child at a time. So please do not let me project 12 boys into our lives like the 12 tribes of Israel. LOL, smile LOL, and you are right, sweetheart. Just being together with you and being with us together with your mother, we will have fun and enjoy one another's company. Through prayer, prayer is powerful medicine. And I'm so in love with you.

In this old house, we have one more room to go through and throw things away, and that is our bathroom. It is clean. And always has been. It's just the three medicine cabinets, and the two drawers below, and the two long medicine cabinets, or should I say cupboards on the side, are full of things that I have been just pushing in there over 20 years. LOL, and some of the stuff I have in throwing weight you would not even believe I could not even imagine that it was even in my presence. Then we rearranged pictures to where all I have on the walls is religious pictures and crosses, and I never realized I had that many spread out throughout the house. It looks pretty nice. According to my standards as a man. LOL LOL, and I know for a fact according to your standards, as a beautiful young wife and your mother will have a whole different outlook and perspective on the way things should be—double smile.

Anyway, my children are doing fine, and they would never if anything ever should happen to me would just expect you to leave. I raise my children with moral standards to a certain degree. And the children love me so much and when they see how much I love this beautiful young lady from North country. Sweetheart, I'm having a hard time thinking of how to explain our love for one another for the simple reason the love we have between us that we have developed through the Holy Spirit over the last year has been through the grace of God. And how it's used to explain miracles? I'm still in love with you, and I love your soul. Our souls were meant to be blended. I chair you always in my heart with love and overabundance of love that phone could have come from God, for the simple reason I never have in my life experience this love that I always had a feeling was there.

Sweetheart, I can't keep my mouth off of you. You are so precious. Are you getting rest, sweetheart? How are you feeling? And thank you so very much for that one long email. Gorgeous beautiful treasure from North country, you're my girl.

Just have you consumed my thoughts was all well worth the effort—another thing I meant to inform you of that I mentioned to the doctor. "I said to the doctor" "you realize Dr. if I never meet this beautiful young lady, she has come into my life like a guardian angel that was sent from God and changed me." Until my girl from the North country came along, I do not even think about it or even want it in my life anymore. Another thing I'll be honest with you, quitting smoking is very difficult, and I'm down to just a couple of cigarettes a day now, and I'm sure when she and her mother arrived, I will quit, God willing. And also, I'm not surfing around the web talking to ladies like they used to.

Sweetheart, realize that talking to a lady online, in my mind, is like committing adultery—the seventh commandment. I know for a fact, and I have no intentions of going there that I would if you did not troll the line. Fidelity, adultery, and fornication are nowhere in our lives. What do you think? These are not godly qualities. Let's portray a scenario, "first of all, let me say this, that we are going to be judged on our words, what we think, what we do, and what we fail to do." As I had mentioned, if you were ever to draw the line with our love for one another, that is the only thing I can think of within this God-given miraculous relationship. The devil may try, when I tell you this beautiful, I mean this you are my girl I have never experienced this God-given love ever. I would not jeopardize it for anything, any thought, any word, or any action. I'm so in love with you with this godly love. All my life, I have wanted this love. I always had a feeling with my unshakable faith that it was obtainable only through the grace of God. I'm so excited every day about crowing and love and become a better person because of you coming into my life, in continuously changing me for the better as we grow together in this bond of love. There is no way to explain this love we have between us two any other people. It's called faith with works. And please, sweetheart, do not worry, stress, or go down the negative bunny trail.

Just having this house getting to where it is from where it came from. As given me a lot of energy. I should be dead tired, exhausted right now, and I am. Peace in the grace of the Lord is with you and your mother to Jesus Christ the Lord's name amen. One small question beautiful, in your heart of hearts, and be honest with me I can handle it, what do you feel your mother thinks about me? And about our relationship of this God-given love? Smile with compassion and care, and kindness. I love you, honey. You are my precious Guardian Angel treasure from North country, and I'm your Zorro.

Thomas wrote;

Sweetheart, my delicious little beautiful treasure, my God-given child sweet tasty little morsel elegant cuisine and praying prayerfully with love for the creator God our father for being a chef. Now tell me, could God have put together two of the most acceptable representation of God's love together out of 7 billion people.?

So be prayerfully in the lovingkindness of God God's gift to us his life what we do with this life is our gift to God.

I'm just letting you know that we have available because we live in this great state of Arizona. Immensely wealthy, possibly not all of them, but Arizona has more millionaires and billionaires. And for all of the social sicknesses to ease their conscience, these people with a lot are more than happy to provide for the lesson than thou.

They think they are getting to heaven by doing so wrong. That's where we come in, and you are such a delicious, precious beautiful god-given miracle. I love you, honey. You're my girl. We will have to live our lives one moment at a time and do the best we can do at the moment. In the meantime, everything is going to be OK, and everything is OK, alright? No worry, no stress, no negative thinking thoughts.

We cannot change the past. There's no sense in living our lives through the rearview mirror.

So let us pray to God that he answers your prayer and our prayer along with your mother. In Jesus Christ's name, we pray and God, our father, that somehow. She needs. And thank you, father. We love everything you do in our lives, and we do appreciate this life that has been so graciously and miraculously provided for us.

And we pray for health, happiness and please let my wife DiAnnie and her mother realize with unshakable faith that at the moment, everything is OK. Our human nature will take us to a place in our minds we do not want to go although living in the moment, and everything is OK right this very moment. And we thank you for that Lord Jesus Christ. I just love my wife, and I thank you miraculously for this lady in my life for the rest of our lives. Even though she will tie me up, LOL smile, and only God knows what else my Marine Corps wife is capable of doing. LOL smile, I love you, honey, you're my girl

Beautiful, please use this email address; for now, I indeed miss not being able to communicate with you.

And time will tell not to trust or believe you we been together too long for that.

I realize you are a busy, beautiful young lady, my precious, gorgeous, delicious treasure from North country. And you very well may not have time to have replied or had even sent me an email. Only God knows. Smile, LOL; they gave me shingles shot for prevention this morning. I believe it is it to series one now and one six months from now. I never even heard of a shingle shot.? Peace and grace of the Lord be with you and your mother to just same resolute amendment.

Sweetheart, I love you so much after reading that long email. You are so precious, and God loves us both as we love God. This is why we are together is because of the love that God has for us. And that is so powerful and miraculous. I would feel just heartbroken, and I felt like I had l36ost my best friend when I could not email you the last three days. I soon then realized how strong our love is for one another. And please, sweetheart, do not worry about those other ladies. Are you kidding me? I know it is a natural human emotion to be jealous. Believe me when I tell you this I'm only in love with you and on the first one to let the slings know that I am in a committed relationship. As I had mentioned earlier, I went to the doctor this morning and talked to my female Dr. Joyce. And she asked me how our relationship was going? And I feel since she took an oath with confidentiality of doctor- patient privacy and protection.

I spoke for my heart, and I said we communicate daily, and I touched her heart when I mentioned to her about letting you know That I would never deprive you of life that would be inhumane on my part not to let you go dancing with another man. Swimming hiking material things that you may like to do that I will not participate with you. And the doctor looked at me with astonishment. I also mentioned to the good doctor that the key to a successful marriage is the forgiveness of one another continuously. And as a husband to let his wife do just exactly what she wants to do without question. And she said yes, I wish it was that way with everybody. I just had a spiritual feeling that her husband is not the kind of a husband. And I also mentioned to the good doctor how we are equally yoked spiritually, and then that was another key to a successful marriage, and it is a priority. I explained that I read the Bible continuously and that the Bible and prophecy are beyond miraculous. I love you, honey. I

You will not believe this leverage Brian and I almost and I mean a long way but almost getting this house, so it looks like I cannot explain the words for them with this house seems now compared to what it used to look like a while back. We most certainly have more to do, and we will be working right up until the day you and your mother decide to come here. One more thing, sweetheart, this house is going into your name. Do not be concerned that my children are all doing very well. And once they witnessed our love for one another, they would not take anything from you, only help you in any way they can. And it's one child at a time. So please do not let me project 12 boys into our lives like the 12 tribes of Israel. LOL smile LOL, and you are right, sweetheart, just being together with you and being with us along with your mother, we are going to have fun and enjoy one another's company. Prayer is powerful medicine. And I'm so in love with you.

In this old house, we have one more room to go through and throw things away, and that is our bathroom. It is clean. And always has been. It's just the three medicine cabinets, and the two drawers below, and the two long medicine offices, or should I say cupboards on the side, are full of things that I have been just pushing in there over 20 years. LOL, and some of the stuff I have in throwing weight you would not even believe I could not even imagine it was also in my presence. Then we rearranged pictures to where all I have on the walls is religious pictures and crosses, and I never realized I had that many spreads out throughout the house; it looks pretty nice. According to my standards as a man. LOL LOL, and I know for a fact according to your standards, as a beautiful young wife, your mother will have a whole different outlook and perspective on the way things should be —double smile.

Anyway, my children are doing fine, and they would never expect you to leave if anything ever should happen to me. I raise my children with moral standards to a certain degree. And the children love me so much and when they see how much I love this beautiful young lady from North country. Sweetheart, I'm having a hard time thinking of how to explain our love for one another for the simple reason the love we have between us that we have developed through the Holy Spirit over the last year has been through the grace of God. And how it's used to explain miracles? I'm still in love with you, and I love your soul. Our souls were meant to be blended. I chair you always in my heart with love and overabundance of love that phone could have come from God, for the simple reason I never have in my life experience this love that I always had a feeling was there.

Beautiful, You will have to admit, sweetheart, and I'm sure this is true that our cultures and lifestyles from North country to the United States is not all that different. But there are differences. Do we disagree? I could be wrong, and I usually am; LOL I'm only a man; I keep telling myself that I am just a man. LOL LOL

A lady came on Facebook who lives about two blocks up the road and around a couple of corners. I sold chicken eggs and just came on and asked me if I knew Tina, my former sister-in-law who lives next door. I said, of course, I do. Anyway, we did not communicate back and forth that long. Maybe I should not have mentioned it to her, but I did. Let me say this first, she is living with a man who just had a stroke and just had a heart attack and has a daughter that's 21 and a four-year-old child that I think he and her head together not sure. I mentioned to her everything about you, will not everything that I did suggest is that you and I were equally oak spiritually and that we have been communicating for well over a year.

And that you were planning a trip to Arizona with your mother. And I asked her, you and this man you are living with, are you married? She said no, and I said, don't you think it would strengthen the relationship and make the children feel good about having an unstable family? So she came down yesterday afternoon and dropped off one dozen eggs. I mentioned to her that I did not have any money to pay for them, but I would swap my latest book for a few dozen eggs. And she agreed. After I mentioned to her about being married, yesterday afternoon was the first time I had met her, and it turns out she and her live-in boyfriend are driving to Reno, Nevada, today to get married. That's pretty cool, I think.

This is how we are going to help others, sweetheart. She mentioned something to me I never knew, and I feel it is a great idea. You cannot go into the courthouse and get married in one day. The county was having a lot of problems with people matching too fast. So they put a three-month waiting period on marriages. And, of course, you have to get a blood test. I will find out the information in detail, talk to my Baptist minister, and update you beautifully. piece and grace of the Lord be with you and your mother through Jesus Christ our Lord's name amen. I'm so in love with you, Ms.

PostScript; I feel the most romantic thoughts and feelings that I have had in the last three days, without contacting my beautiful girl from North country. It has made me realize just how much our love has strengthened and grown over the previous year. And it took just a break, like three days, to have an impact of appreciation for the love that we have for each other only through the grace of God. I do not want to lose this email, sweetheart, so that I will pick up where my thoughts leave off. I love you so much. I

Thomas wrote;

Sweetheart, I can't keep my mouth off of you-you are so precious. Are you getting rest, sweetheart? How are you feeling? And thank you so very much for that one long email. A gorgeous, beautiful treasure from North country, you're my girl.

Another thing I meant to inform you of that I mentioned to the doctor. "I said to the doctor" "you realize Dr. if I never meet this beautiful young lady, she has come into my life like a guardian angel that was sent from God and changed me." Another thing I'll be honest with you, quitting smoking is, and I'm down to just a couple of cigarettes a day now, and I'm sure when she and her mother arrived, I will quit, God willing. And also, I'm not surfing around the web talking to ladies like they used to.

In my mind, sweetheart realizes that talking to a lady online is like committing adultery — the seventh commandment. I know for a fact, and I have no intentions of going there, that if you did not troll the line, I would. Fidelity, adultery, and fornication are nowhere in our lives. What do you think? These are not godly qualities. Let's portray a scenario, "first of all, let me say this, that we are going to be judged on our words, what we think, what we do, and what we fail to do." As I had mentioned, if you were ever to draw the line with our love for one another, that is the only thing I can think of within this God-given miraculous relationship.

The devil may try when I tell you this beautiful. I mean this, you are my girl. I have never experienced this God-given love ever. I would not jeopardize it for anything, any thought, any word, or any action. I'm so in love with you with this godly love. All my life, I have wanted this love. I always had a feeling with my unshakable faith that it was obtainable only through the grace of God. I'm so excited every day about crowing and love and become a better person because of you coming into my life, in continuously changing me for the better as we grow together in this bond of love.

There is no way to explain this love we have between us two any other people. It's called faith with works. And please, sweetheart, does not worry about stress or go down the negative bunny trail. Just having this house getting to where it is from where it came from. As given me a lot of energy.

I should be dead tired, exhausted right now, and I am. Peace in the grace of the Lord is with you and your mother to Jesus Christ the Lord's name Amen. One small question beautiful, in your heart of hearts, and be honest with me I can handle it, what do you feel your mother thinks about me? And about our relationship with this God-given love? Smile with compassion and care, and kindness. I love you, honey, you are my precious Guardian Angel treasure from North country, and I'm your zero

4 April 2019

DiAnnie wrote;

Hi, my love,

Sorry it had taken me some time to get back to you. When I got back home, I ate and then took a nap, waiting to hear from you. I just woke up off to the bathroom, and then here's your message. But I'll try to figure out things and believe I'm not mad at you, and you tried your best. Have a lovely evening, and sorry for having you guys up and down again today.

Your girl.

DiAnnie wrote;

Good morning my love,

Sorry I could not get back to you yesterday due to my busy schedule. Good, I can message you now and start to get ready for work later. It is a bit early here, and I thought to write before leaving for work. How were your day yesterday and your night? I hope everything is going great. I'm doing fine here, just exhausted most of the time, especially during a weekday, but let me not complain too much as all is part of life.

Well, I agree with you, I think God knows all 7 billion people of this world can not meet at once, and there are people you will never meet or see from birth to death. Still, God has his way of bringing people to know one another according to His miracle, so yes, out of 7 billion people, He knew this girl would come to know His child Thomas and show each other true love beyond human comprehension.

If I'll have a house in my name, then the septic tank is also a part. I know it sounds funny when someone wants to take ownership of a septic tank, especially when Brian is there...LOL, I know he's a nice person, so I don't think we will have to think about putting him in there. I do not get mad when he doubts it as that is normal for the natural human being. I'm a person that welcomes other people's views.

Well, I know you have more blessings around you there, and it's the same in most developed countries, if not precisely the same. Still, closely, with all we have, not many of us appreciate such things to admit, even you and I, seeing the life status that others are living, I don't think we would want to be the ones receiving food stamps. Human wants are unlimited reasons people do not appreciate; only those who do not store their hope in this present world can understand God for the little things.

If you didn't have God and store your riches in heaven, I don't think you would appreciate the opportunities around you. Oh, I know Arizona in the US has the most wealthy people. Arizona was a gold and diamond mine before colonial times, so it attracted many rich activities, I made some history on the state of Arizona, and it is the most prosperous state with the highest GDP amongst all the conditions there, I think the more profitable a person gets, the more they add on them a useless lifestyle, one of the silliest things that I have thought about, but no answer is the act, then the use of drugs,

First, a man going to bed with another man is not natural at all. The two have the same love organs that have no means ever to produce a child. Going in bed isn't as well because the two have the same organs and have no mechanism to make a child. Still, a man and a woman have two different organs and can produce even animals, so alone should tell that God isn't stupid; He made everything perfect. Still, most of those people in such acts are wealthy, not all, though, but most and Satan should be the reason. They must be part of dangerous sects that promotes those acts. For drugs or alcohol, it is understandable in a way. Someone takes something and gets used to it when they feel high and finds it difficult to leave it like you smoking is a habit right now, I did some too, but I was never encouraged by anyone to stop. Still, I did because It made me weak, and I was not caring for myself and didn't feel beautiful as I am now, so I guess that was God that saved me because He had a plan for me.

Hey Zorro, you're not kicking that black bucket right now. God hasn't finished with you yet, so giving Brian's number isn't about giving me the news that you have kicked the bucket, you're not old at all as you think, no one in their right mind would ever believe you are old, and then you're in good health too, so I don't think what is going to push you to kick the bucket. I pray that brother Brian or all of us not kick the bucket right now. We have a lot of work to do for God. So know that my prayers and Mom are always with you and Brian, and keep us in yours.

You two are the silliest guys I know. Lol, if Brian has ever to marry my Brian, it really should be God or maybe in the next world, and then when you ask Brian if he will marry Anna, what did he say? Accept to be your stepdad? I guess he was smiling, and then the bad news pops up that he will be run in the septic tank for the whole six months, too..lol Brian would be your dad and my dad. One day, I told my Mom that there's a guy who lives with Thomas that saw your pic and said, you're beautiful, and you know what she said? She said, wow, that is kind of him. I know I'm beautiful, DiAnnie Maria! and I said I'm beautiful too! And she yep, but I'm more because I Anna blessed you with this beautiful through God..lol.

Please don't talk about us next time to the doctor because you may just be having her jealous; she wishes her husband was that nice as you, and you have her old heart getting burned..lol.

Honey, I want the same as you, romance, caressing, and kissing gently. These are experiences that a lady misses. I know we are preparing for a lasting relationship. It isn't easy getting the most incredible things in life, so we have passed the most challenging part and heading for the smooth road, so I'm also excited about all this. Before we know it, we will be right in the presence of each other, making love we started.

I saw the headlines on the news, the most exciting story is about the family that travels many miles to see and eat at the restaurant! that was funny, but I guess it is worth it because if people can come from there to see the restaurant, then all you have told me about the restaurant was true, I thought you were making a paradise to have your girl in a hurry to fly..lol I'll see if having the French classes or working at the restaurant would be the best pick, time will tell.

Anyway, my handsome man, I'll get ready now for work. I look forward to hearing from you soon. Enjoy the rest of your day.

All my love and regards to you. A big hug and a kiss from me.

I will reply to your most recent message. I was writing you when it came in, and I'll be on my way to work soon. Love you, and I'll try my best to check my message at work and reply to you back.

Thomas wrote;

Scrumptious,

I'm not sure what to say, sweetheart. I do not feel like much of a husband to his wife for not providing for her. I do not feel sorry for myself, not one minute. It just makes me think that we have a God-given love that brought us together. And God will take care of us moment by moment. Everything is okay right this very moment. So please do not be stressed or worry over everything. LOL, smile, and I have you to thank for that sweetheart because you are my girl from North country, my lovely and great compliments with love to God the chef.

I will get this off to you now, sweetheart, and wait to hear back from you. I pray to God you understand. Smile LOL. Fortunately, I left those days behind. I love you, honey

Beautiful, and I thank God for you in my life. I'm so proud of you honey, how are you feeling today? How are you doing? I pray everything is going well for you and your mother. Brian and I will continuously work on this house until you and your mother should so decide to arrive. And I thank God for you, and you should be proud of yourself. I'm very proud of you because I will keep going on this old house until it will be ready for Sunset magazine. LOL smile. We never know, do we.?

Sweetheart, I'm just projecting into the future, and I certainly would like to know your thoughts. Is that when your mother and yourself, God willing, should decide to make the trip to Arizona to our home. First of all, I would like to start by saying that I'm thinking right now.

That we lived together for three months before we get married or have intercourse with one another. Please do not tie me up for saying this, LOL smile, and I'm serious. Because we do not know spiritually until we meet and get to know one another personally in a spiritual acquaintance and getting to know one. I feel three months would give us a good foundation and stability for deciding to get married then. And God willing that our love continues to strengthen within those three months. And I can't think of any reason why it would not.

And we will take it one day at a time; these are my thoughts right now. Since God brought us together in a very holy way, we should show our love to God by refraining from intercourse with one another. Think about it we have been waiting this long, I have been waiting, I'm guessing about 20 years, and you have been waiting quite a while. I feel that three months would not be too much to ask of ourselves. That's easy for me to say is in it? Right now.t could change within one night.

I pray, and please pray with me. That we can lay together and sleep together in the same bed and hold each other and kissed each other and talk and get to know one another, I'm not sure if I can refrain from that.

Although if both of us tried and prayed, it could be possible. It would be quite a testimony to others, and you will have to admit that. Nobody would ever believe us. LOL smile, and that's on them, but in our hearts and God knows that what we say is true.

I realize you are very busy, beautiful, and exhausted when you get home from work., God willing, we get married. Do you think in your heart of hearts that you can be a stay-at-home mom? Or shall we wait and see and take one day at a time. That's something you have to decide, honey. There is a lot to do from this home. We are stuck right in the middle of multimillionaires and billionaires. As I have mentioned before a lot of opportunities. Keep in mind that I am an author, and I love to write. And that takes solitude of being by myself without interruption. I could do it when you are sleeping in a soundproof office that would not disturb you from time to time. It would not be 24 seven because I do 24 seven is thought about you and write to you at this point. Very difficult for me to get into writing books with the consumption of the love you have given to me through the grace of God.

My sweet treasure from North country. I saw a documentary on North country today, and it's another chapter I am going to do research on and write about. The people are very conscious of their elderly and take care of them very well. I believe they said about 25% of the elderly in North country are being taken care of by their family. I think the percentages were higher. Anyway, the message was that people take care of their elderly very well. In the United States, not always, but for the most part, families stick their parents in a home and very seldom go and see them.

Another story Brian had mentioned to me. His wife's sister was a nurse and met some old biker guy in the hospital who could not care for himself. And she was well aware of what was needed to take care of him. Evidently, they got married, and she took him to her home, and they still lived together to this day. And I'm not saying this because I cannot take care of myself, and that's the only reason I want you to be here with me. I feel you know that, and you know we have developed more than that; I would love no beginning our love will have no end as God has his love for us.

Think about the three months of living together before we get married. And only God knows, we may just become friends, or you might meet some other guy you would want to make a life with other than myself. God only knows beautiful. It would help if you did not feel trapped. Or make you feel like you are being forced into something that you would not want. Or feel obligated, and you may not be able to handle the trials and tribulations that I go through. I want you to be happy; I want you to feel free. I want you to be satisfied. And do whatever it is you want to do. Smile with compassionate care and kindness. As it stands now, honey, I'm in love with you. I love your soul. I will always have you in my heart, no matter where you are or who you are with. Because you can always count on me for being your guardian angel and praying to God that his will be done for the both of us. Peace and grace of the Lord be with you and your mother through Jesus Christ the Lord's name amen from your Zorro

5 April 2019

DiAnnie wrote;

Hey, my Love! I'm having a busy day here, so tomorrow I'll be able to reply to all your lovely messages. How's it going? I hope you're having a nice day, mine is great, just busy right now, but I thought it was right to send a short note so you know I'm thinking about you. I love you so much, my Love.

Back to work now.

6 April 2019

DiAnnie wrote;

Good morning hun,

I'm glad it's Saturday! I got a quality rest last night and can write you back now. I hope you had a great and peaceful night. Mine was great as well, and I am always here thinking of you but hearing from you each time brings some relief. I like that and look forward to the day that we would not need a phone call or email to communicate, it'll be the most exciting time of our lives, and I look forward to that and pray that God put everything we desire in place.

I'm sorry if I try to sound like I am stress, you know I love you very much. Nothing is going to come between us. Suppose I have the end my relationship with you today. In that case, I'll feel unfortunate knowing that I have wasted a whole year of what we started. We have been going very smoothly. However, there have been so many people sticking their noses in our lives we two think much alike, and nothing has shaken us. God brought us together because I haven't loved someone as I do you, especially our age difference, many people will not understand because our Love isn't the of this world, people would think we are both silly people, but it's only those that wear their shoes that those the position of their toes, not those who are not wearing.

I look forward to the day that we will be lying in the same bed, kissing, hugging, and having every time all to ourselves, and you think when I see the changes taking place with the house there, I don't feel like coming right away? With all the exciting things you have told me about life there and the fun with you and Brian, I want to arrive any day, but Mom and I have a few things to accomplish reason you have to be patient with us. I know you do but not easy being alone for 20 years and not wanting your girl closer, or being a year and not wanting a kiss or a hug.

I want that so much and cuddle. I wish our trip were not on hand before meeting; it's a huge family matter like I told you before, not just seeing other countries or for tourism purposes but beyond that. I tell my Mom each time you ask about her, and she says, oh poor man, he's so caring for us, God bless his heart, and I look forward to meeting him and sitting to explain much about our lives. I'll be the interpreter though, my Mom is a good talker, and she looks forward to meeting you as well, but they say you will not know a person until they are before you. When we come and spend some time and start to get used to each other, we all will have a good picture of us all. I miss you very much, especially when I am so occupied and unable to write to you.

I realize Arizona is a great place, and I will be happy having my kids grow up there, and being with such a Godly man like you, I feel honor for making you a better person that can not be denied because comparing of how you were at first till now I see that no one is evil at all, but life drives people in some ugly directions just like we all. Reconnecting with God is the best we can do for ourselves.

I'll try to feel things in place, my Love, and please get back with me, think things over, and know I have almost three weeks to travel. I have already sent my letter out to the management of where I work to replace me. So in a week, I'll not be working again. I must think about traveling to Mom and coming to be with you, and it is important than going to work each day. Our future is much important because we can have a job anywhere.

So my Zorro, thanks for all the messages and tell me what you wanted to hear that I didn't talk about. I have seen pictures of Zorro. Finally, you are so cool! LOL. Enjoy the rest of your day!

Hugs and kisses from your girl and favorite friend, a best friend too.LOL.

9 April 2019

DiAnnie wrote;

Hi, my Love,

I'm my Love recovering and missed the few time we haven't communicated; I know not very long, but when you get used to someone, even a second counts, and I know it's the same feeling going on there with you. I'm glad to be able to write you this message tonight. I hope that everything is going on well with you and brother Brian. I'm thankful to God as well for the strength. I didn't go to work till now since I last wrote you that I am ill.

It makes me feel proud to make Mr. a better man, and no sound-minded lady would want her man to be the worse. I wish that if you and I go places, people will be proud of you, we take care of each other that is what an excellent God-given relationship is all about. What we share is beyond the understanding of regular humans, so we please not them but God and what we are.

There are so many things I want to talk about in my reply to all your lovely messages, but I feel so weak, but I am getting much better, so I will have more to say later or tomorrow. It's always great to hear from you, my Love, and take this thinking from your head that I am gone forever when I do not write a day or two! I am yours, and you'll realize that soon when we come. We have gone so long to give up along the wayside. I'm not that type. So free your mind, my Zorro.

Have a lovely evening till I hear from you again.

Kisses and hugs from your girl.

P.s. I was sending you a message, and then I got your last message about the bill that AT&T sent you. I'm confused, can you tell me what I need to explain to you, my Love? I will be honest to explain anything you don't understand. Please write me back as soon as possible. Thanks.

11 April 2019

Thomas wrote;

Beautiful, Did I ever mention to you that I had a Marine Corps pilot named Jim when I was in the Marine Corps. Who flew a small C-130 aircraft. Jim was telling me the story. He had an unusual crew of only three. He was transporting Henry Kissinger, a significant, knowledgeable negotiator for human rights throughout the world. You may have heard of him many years ago. He also had a Catholic priest on board. And believe it or not, he had a hippie on board. They were flying about 20,000 feet when one of the engines had trouble, and they were going to have to bail out of the airplane with parachutes. Jim stepped out of the cockpit and said to the other three passengers that there were only three parachutes. So Jim intuitively grabbed a parachute, put it on, and jumped out of the plane. Henry Kissinger said, "since I am the most intelligent world negotiator, I will jump out next. The Catholic priest said to the hippie, oh my poor boy! And the hippie said, "do not worry, father, Henry Kissinger put on my backpack." LOL, smile. This is a joke, sweetheart.

How are you feeling today? How are you doing? Did you have a hangover? That is the reason you were sick, LOL LOL, smile. I prayed to God you have fun wherever you are and who you are with. That is the most important thing is that you are happy. I would not think of being jealous of any other guy that you happen to be with. For this reason, I know that you are my only girl from North country. My beautiful precious scrumptious delicious guardian angel of a treasure from North country. LOL smile.

Big smile Brian is leaving for Palm Springs Tuesday morning early. I'm bringing him to the San Francisco airport; we are going here at 5 AM.

Believe it or not, it is his birthday and his youngest brother's birthday on the same day. So they are all meeting at Brian's mother's home in Palm Springs, Arizona. He will be gone for about one week. To keep you, updated sweetheart. Rather than gray curtains, I feel purple would look far better.

I need to help. There is no way on God's green earth I will have this house cleaned for you and your mother. For the simple reason, there's no way a man can clean like a lady. So Brian and I will do the best we can do, and that's all we can do. And believe me when I tell you this that this house is 100% far cleaner than whenever I could remember. We are still going to keep working on it. Today we removed about eight blinds on the Windows that we pulled and threw in the garbage. Vacuumed the whole house, empty bathroom drawers out wiped counters and shelves and drawers out. I cannot even list the things we did today. I would say about 200 pounds of man garbage. What a nightmare. And I thought my house was clean. LOL, smile dreaming and laughing, not telling the truth until getting into cleaning for you and your mother and then realizing what a man I have been. Quite embarrassing, I might say. LOL smile. It's been too long, honey. God has been preparing us both to be together. I love you God, the chef. I pray every day and give him thanks for you in my life as well as your mother. Not sure what I would do without either of you. I know I would not be the man I am today if it were not for you, in this miraculous graceful gracious miracle that has been in doubt on both of us. Reflecting on where I came from and how you changed me to a path that most certainly will lead me through the gates of heaven. Not to mention what will be revealed to the both of us about a love that has no beginning nor has no end. Call me anytime, sweetheart, if the spirit moves you and if you feel like it. And you know me better than worrying or being stressed. LOL smile, I do not even go there. It is not in my character. And please do not worry or stress yourself everything is OK. One moment at a time, live in the moment and keep telling yourself everything is OK right now. Right this very moment. We are blessed; two-thirds of the world do not even know where their next meal will come from. And God loves you and I and your mother with reverence and holy grace. And God, through Jesus Christ the Lord and the Holy Spirit, has great things in front of us.

Although there will be resistance, without the resistance of water, my ship could not go forward. Without the resistance of gravity, we would not be able to walk. Without the resistance of air, a plane would not be able to fly. Without the resistance of a person, an iPhone would not be able to work.

LOL, laughing, I had to throw that in, smiling you're my girl. This I know is that you are Marine Corps Sgt. girl. And for that, I know when the going gets tough, the tough will get going. I do know you that well. The smile we could not be a family or a team without a dream. And we have been planning together for quite some time now to have a child—one at a time. Twelve boys later, LOL laughing. Just think your mother would be very happy. Smile with respect and reverence. But most importantly, to carry a very important message to the world and save many souls.

Otherwise, why would God have placed us together? There's something very spiritual of biblical proportion that will be revealed to us. This I know because the Bible tells me so. I'm in Love with your soul. You are always in my heart, never far apart. And constantly consuming my mind of every waking thought. We have a book to write together. In a. life to live together. Because you and I together are a very strong couple. Without one, the other one could not hold the weight placed on us from time to time. We will have to be a family, and we will be a strong family with the Holy Spirit working through the never-ending Love of God and us. You are precious, my guardian angel. Hugs and kisses are traveling back and forth between us for eternity. From your Zorro

DiAnnie wrote;

Good morning my Love. Sorry again for my delay. It's not intentional at all, and I hope you understand. I needed to recover, and I'm grateful for regaining my strength. So we're back to our regular communication. How are you doing? I hope everything is going great, and it was excellent hearing all the things you're doing concerning the house and all those purchases you're making for our rooms. You have a taste of good things. LOL.

Thanks for always being a nice person to my Mom and me. We appreciate you in our lives and can't wait to meet you. I believe it will be a very special day in each one of our lives. I'll tell Mom the surprise you have for her. There will be so much fun, and I look forward to that and our lives in Arizona. I know Mom will like it there as long I stay there, but mind you, she will want to fly to Calgary once in a while and even put someone in the house to look after it. I'll fly in once in a time as well. You and us would have to visit North country once in a while and back to Arizona and other places. We're not going to be stationed like that. LOL. Thanks so much for your prayers and concerns about your girl and her Mom. You're a great man Thomas. All my Love to you, and thanks so much for taking the time out for me. Love you very much, my Zorro. I'll get busy for the day now. I'll check my email later. Hugs and kisses.

Thomas 'n DiAnnie

12 April 2019

Thomas wrote;

Beautiful, LOL laughing, you make me smile all the time, you are the funniest little girl from North country I know, LOL smile as a matter fact you're the only girl from North country I know. LOL smile. Are you sure? My sweet little scrumptious tasty little morsel? One thing that will be traveling is my mouth to your mouth, LOL smile a big smile. Laughing, are you sure I do not have to worry? Double LOL smile. I have not been able to go to sleep for days. LOL, with my fingernails dug into the desk, anxiously awaiting your response. Laughing, I love you. I'm going to tickle you until you tie me up. LOL, I think I'll get back to worrying. LOL, it makes my hair turned black and makes me look ten years younger.

I could pinch your cheeks, you your mother, and I are family. We look out for each other, we take care of each other, and it will always be that way because we care about each other with kindness, consideration, and love. You're my girl, and I'm so happy to hear that you're feeling okay, honey. And I realize that I am not a beautiful young woman such as yourself, and I thank God for that. Smile with love, and sometimes it slips my mind that a lady has her menstrual cycle every month. And those are times when the lady is not feeling too well, and a man seems to forget. That may or may not be the reason you are feeling poorly or not will anyway. Also, considering that I must hide under the bed during those times of the month and make myself disappear. I'm not sure if I'm smiling. I could scream, I love you so much.

Speaking of which, this friend of mine was a trick pilot in an old dual- wing airplane. I recall one time he gave a farmer and his wife a ride in his airplane. He was going straight up in the air, doing barrel rolls, making a plane go backward in every which way. Then although a friend of mine said to the farmer, I thought you were going to scream? And the farmer said I almost did scream when you did that one barrel roll when my wife fell out. LOL, smile only a joke. This old house is starting to look well. For my life, I cannot believe how much junk one man can collect for years and think it was normal? You still have not answered my question about the drapes? What color in each room except for your mother's, of course, our beautiful royal red. Should the whole house be done in purple drapes? Personally, and what do I know about home decorating? It has taken me 20 years to make this place look like a man's clubhouse.

LOL, smile, and you're also right about it being an extraordinary time. When our small family comes together and meets for the first time, it will be a God spiritual moment of joy, happiness, and love through God's grace. It will be like Christmas morning. Or it may be like a trip to Disneyland? Regardless it will be fun, and we will most certainly enjoy each other's company companionship and communication. Like I have mentioned before, my mouth is going to be traveling to your mouth quite frequently, as well as the rest of your delicious petite body. Smile between you and me with great compassion and love and care for each other.

For this reason, you are my guardian angel who God put into my life to save my soul. And I believe you have known the change in me through our communication? And more shall be revealed. And for that, I thank God, and I pray to God daily moment by moment with every consuming thought of you, sweetheart. You are my girl, my unique treasure from North country. I do have a good feeling about your mother. When she is introduced to this area and especially our home, that will be your home and your mother's. She may want to have someone stay in her house in Calgary like you had mentioned and move in with us permanently. I just have this spiritual feeling and a warm glow that comes over me.

And I thank you for that thought once again. I'm proud of you, honey. And God only knows what I would do without you. I would be teetering on the edge of damnation and going to hell. I just have this gut feeling. Inspired by my guardian angel, this is not the case with great kindness, appreciation, consideration, and a love that only God knows between you and me. I have never experienced this love in my life. And it will be inspirational through the grace of God very holy writing our book to help many other couples in this world to know that there is a love that can be tapped in through only the grace of God.

Please pray for me; I need help. Laughing, and I'm not ready to be a minister just yet. Not with your sneaky little thoughts that bouncer my head like visions of sugar plums dancing through my head. In the theater of my mind, only God knows what goes on there.? I am a moment-by-moment child of God, and I laugh and have fun continuously making others laugh when the time is appropriate. The times I cry are when someone else is hurting. Or has a lost love one. Or when someone hurts a person unnecessarily. According to God, there's a time and place for everything under the sun, as the Bible says. And I turn my will and life for the care of God and let his Holy Spirit work through me to help others. And take their mind off the trials and tribulations, and if I can bring some joy into someone's life, that's the main spiritual character that God has given to me only through his grace. It might even travel to you very passionately. So yes, my sweet, beautiful little girl from North country, there will be some traveling going on between you and me.

I just have a feeling in my bones, and my toes are pointed in the right direction. Laughing, why did you say that? I think about that, and I laugh all the time. You are crazy. It only makes me realize even more that you are indeed a Marine Corps sergeant's wife. Peace and grace of the Lord be with you and your mother through Jesus Christ our Lord's name. I feel that your mother is going to move in with us permanently eventually. And who knows, she may decide not to go home at all. Smile respectively. It was 76° yesterday here, and the weather is starting to get nicer. The sun sure does feel good. It is just beautiful here. So I'm going out and lay back in the sun today and soak up the warmth of this miraculous life that God has so graciously given to every one of us. God's gift to us is his life. What we do with this life is our gift to God. Traveling hugs and traveling kisses back-and-forth. This I know our love will never miss because we have a passion that has been bonded from the four above. I love you honey, hugs, and kisses from your Zorro

postscript; please,! Can I worry and stress? LOL laughing hard. Because my toes are pointed in the wrong direction, laughing even harder, have a good day, honey.

Thomas wrote;

Beautiful, gray? Delicious, you have been living under the clouds too long. LOL smile, are we a little under the weather again. LOL, a smile. I believe your brain has been frozen too long. Laughing. Just so your mother will not feel lonely in her bedroom, I have received a wolf that is stuffed. Smile. This model comes with removable eyes. LOL, you can either remove one eye or the other, so it appears to be winking, and either you choose. Or, you can remove both eyes to have the appearance of being asleep. LOL, also, this model comes with a constant smile on his face. And you can either order a male or female. The mail comes with the appearance of lifting his leg on the vanity. And, of course, the female will be squatting in the middle of the bedroom floor. LOL, laughing, and may I remind you all models come without fleas. LOL, and you can order these models with teeth or without teeth. LOL, laughing, you better not tell your mother either. LOL, this is between you and me. Also, for our bedroom, we will get a stuffed elk head. You are smiling, of course, with removable eyeballs. LOL laughing hard, see what you do to me, sweetheart? You climb right into my head and make yourself right at home, don't you? LOL laughing

And I do not change diapers. I would march the boys out in the backyard and hose them off with a garden hose. LOL, you are laughing harder. I do believe your mother will enjoy the entertainment. Once again, you better not tell her this is between you and me, sweetheart. And it's all your fault. LOL laughing harder, Beautiful, and I have you to thank for all this lovely thinking that God has inspired. Smile with reverence and appreciation and thankfulness from God our Father for having a sense of humor. Have a good day, beautiful I pray you are feeling better now. And quit crawling inside of my head, LOL laughing how are you feeling? Tell all your friends at work to pull my finger. LOL, you are laughing harder. I'm only a Marine, and I love you.

13 April 2019

DiAnnie wrote;

Good morning my love. I hope you're having a great day, mine is starting well, and I look forward to the rest of the day. It is the weekend, so glad I can message you back. I'm here laughing so hard from your jokes about those pilots, and I believe when it was going on, it was no laughing matter at all, lol. It's when something has happened that we laugh. Hahaha, and since Henry Kissinger thought he was intelligent, it was wise to fly with a backpack.. lol you're so funny. Thanks for asking, I'm doing well now, and it wasn't a hangover that made me sick. I didn't go drinking, so no way a hangover would have happened. LOL. I had a migraine and then tiredness as well. Good, I'm your only girl from North country. If not, you would have gotten in serious trouble with me..LOL. Even if you say you're not jealous, I know it's in your human nature, not just you but for me as well and the whole world.. LOL, so Zorro, don't think you're not a jealous boy... LOL.

We will do our best to rearrange whatever that's not in place, Mom and I are hard workers. I appreciate you and brother Brian for working very hard on the house. You guys are hard-working people as well, or I'll say you because you told Brian was lazy as chair .. LOL. I'll see if I can give you a call today or tomorrow.

So look on the way. I missed hearing your voice. So even though I'm so tired, but the going gets tough, the tough get going. I'm a marine in the heart as well, so I always put strength in myself.LOL. What is deer head and eyes going to do in our rooms! Haha, if we get scared and start to run around the house at midnight, don't blame me, okay? It will be because of the deer head and eyes.. oh God, this man is so crazy! We are just the perfect match..lol. You need 12 boys and no girl, and you think I'll be happy? So maybe five boys and five girls.. lol we will only have to reduce that number to 4 2 girls and two boys. And my kids are not going to work for at&t, so they can't be paranoid like those silly people that tried to give you hell in Blossoms hill ..Lol. Wow, you guys are making progress on the house. I like all those dramatic changes in the place. If the jacuzzi is working it will be very relaxed, and we can spend time there the two of us.

I think Brother Brian is getting impatient, and I'm not even in a relationship with him lol he must be a jealous guy. Tell him no need to worry because our next stop will be home after my trip, and Brian shouldn't think he will have anything to do with Anna LOL.. she's very picky. Maybe it's why uncle Brian is inpatient? LOL.

I'm sorry you didn't have much time to spend with your mom. I realize you have talked more about your dad than Mom. Sure, I count myself fortunate still having my mom around, I always thank God for this, and you make me feel so proud of you willing to treat my mom like a queen. I, too, wish yours was still around, but God knows all. We will be a small happy family. Thanks so much for taking your time to write once again, my love.

It's impossible to ignore any of your messages, and you know that.. lol. Love you a million times, and I pray to God for a long life for us all. Much love, mon Zorro. Hugs and kisses from me.

14 April 2019

Thomas wrote;

Three reasons why women scientists thought a computer should be referred to as he. LOL smile. Are you ready? Number one, to get their attention, you must turn them on first. LOL smile. Number two. They are supposed to solve the problem, but half the time, they are the problem. LOL, number three. As you got one computer, you suddenly realize that if you would've waited a little longer, you could have got a better one. LOL smile The men's scientist said, here are three reasons you should name the computer she. Are you ready? LOL smile. Number one. No one but the creator understands their internal logic. Smile. Number two. Even your most minor mistakes are stored for long-term memory. Smile. Number three.

As soon as you commit to one, you find yourself spending half your paycheck on accessories.

Ladies have many faults. Men only have two: everything they say and everything they do. LOL, a smile I thought you would like that one, laughing —Ephesians chapter 5 verse 28 through 33. Husbands love your wives just as Christ loved the church And gave himself for her. so husbands ought to love their wives as Christ loved the church. So husbands ought to love their wives as their bodies. He who loves his wife loves himself.

Nevertheless, each one of you loves each other, and husbands respect your wife, as your wife respects you.

Any man who does not respect his wife, God will reprimand that man by not listening to one prayer he ever says. I'm in love with you, honey, because we love each other, and God put us together for the reason that shall be revealed that is far beyond our comprehension or imagination. Although it is all good and we both know that. Peace and grace of the Lord be with you and your mother through Jesus Christ our Lord's name. Hugs and kisses

15 April 2019

DiAnnie wrote;

Good morning honey, hope you had a great night, and you're doing well. I'm doing great, and thanks to God always for keeping us all alive. I got your messages, and you know due to today being Sunday, it took me a while to get back home from church. When I arrived, I was so exhausted and decided to do a few things like eating, and then sleep took me away. I thought I would be able to write you but see, and I slept.. lol. Well, it's not like you brought my mom into our relationship. I feel you do ask about her each time because you have great respect for her. It's only a decent man who will do that, and you don't know how much I admired that about you.

Not many guys would want to respect their mothers-in-law. You have an excellent quality that I don't see in many people. Please never change for any reason, okay? I'm not worried at all. I know life has challenges, but when we trust God, all will be fine. Worries come about when we don't seem to see things we wished for coming into place. I'll try not to worry but please never make me fall into the state of worry. We love each other, so we have to do all we can to be happy.

I know I'll do that. I know you got more free time on the computer than I do, but I'll never see your messages and ignore them as I told you before. Even if I'm busy and can't message back right away, know that I'll do. Honey, you know you're never last in my world. It's the planning of the trip that has us coming to Arizona last but not you.

It seems like you are interested in learning the French language, no worries, you will know faster as long we are together. This way, you don't need an app, but naturally. You make me laugh so much about the survey between men and women; it's so true, although it was so funny.. lol. I feel so sorry for Samuel, your nephew. Dealing with heartbreak isn't easy because it happens within the heart unless that person involved in the situation is a good listener. I'll put him in my prayers. Let's not even think of any of us going to heaven very soon. lol

I know anything can happen at any time, but we should be positive. In case it's happened to you, and I'm still around, and maybe I'll have to fall in love with someone, sure it will have to be a godly man. It'll also be difficult for me to love or develop a passion for another man like I did with you. If it's the other way around, then you must do the same. You're a great person.

It'll depend on where we are to know how much we will need. So start saving. That's a good idea. Sure, Mom and I miss each other very much. Lol, if I was still a kid, I guess I'll be here crying.. lol. I hope my Zorro is having a great day. I look forward to hearing from you. Have to get busy now. You also mean the world to me. Love you very much. All my regards to you. Hugs and kisses.

16 April 2019

DiAnnie wrote;

Good morning my love. Sorry I didn't wake up early to see all your lovely messages. I believe you have already left, taking Brother Brian to the airport. Could you get back to me when you get back home? I hope you had a great time last night. My night was very good. I slept well and didn't wake up sooner. I guess it's because I was exhausted. Another working day and here I am working and thinking about you.

My mom will be the happiest person. Having you treat her as if she's your mom will make me love you more. You are a part of us, and your right house divided among itself is not of the Lord. I think Brian will have a few issues with our relationship with you; we know how to have those that do not like us falls in love and change their ways, so by telling him more about God, I know he'll be an all-new person.

I thank God for the man you are. You have a very significant character! It's the reason I'll not stop loving you. I'll get busy now, my love, and I look forward to hearing from you later. Enjoy the rest of your day. Kisses and hugs. Your northern girl.

Hi again, my love, We will always be safe. Yes, mom is still in Belgium, and as soon as I'm ready to travel, she'll go to Malta. I'll send this off to you and wait to hear from you. Love you so much. Hugs.

Thomas wrote;

Beautiful, please do not worry or stress about gasoline or anything like that. You are my northern treasure from North country God. Just the thought of listening to you in communicating, holding you, kissing you, and very romantic situations that the Holy Spirit working through me will let you know that I love you. I'm in love with your soul, your precious heart I carry in mind, and you consume my thoughts with reverence kindness.

So if you can get that to me tomorrow, I will make that a priority. And I pray to God that will expedite your trip to your mother. You must know in your heart that I would do anything for you. Especially not seeing your mother for this time must have been hard on both of you. So let us pray together that everything will go according to God's plan.

What will always keep us young, healthy, and in love is obtaining God's love as heaven on earth between two married children of God. God wants a covenant between a man and woman. It's the blueprint of happiness that God has provided for us. God wants a man of the covenant, a promise keeper. That is what the man says he means and keeps the covenant. A man's word is his bond, is yes it is yes, and is no. We live in a world of deception and deceit, where a man's word is no longer his bond.

It's destroying the fabric of marriage. God to his men, I want men of integrity, I like men of the covenant, God is saying he wants men of integrity, men of honor. Men and women will bring fragmented marriages together with God and their wives.

The word covenant is essential in marriage because God never breaks covenants. The Lord says he shows mercy to those who show covenant to God. Covenant is When two people together with God's covenant is the secret to the abundance from God.

In the Bible, a covenant is the death of two wills and the birth of one will. When two people walk down the church aisle, that's the last time they are Individuals in the eyes of God. When they speak that covenant, they become one of the covenants with God. When two people die for their omnipotent opinion, people are willing to surrender their self-centered ego. And their desire to control the marriage or the other person. Marriage is hell on earth when two people get together that are self-serving and self- centered, and everything has to be their way or the highway. Marriage is dying of who you used to be.

Sweetheart, this is from a sermon I heard this evening I thought I would share with you. Because I care, that's why I share. Because my guardian angel brings me to a higher level of consciousness and grows continuously along spiritual lines to better a relationship between you and me and your mother, we will take care of her with respect, love, and anything she desires that we can provide for her. I'm sure we both pray to Jesus Christ, the Lord's name. Because we prayed together, we stayed together. And that includes your mother or prayers are mighty as well as yours in between the three of us we have a. lot of power to help many other souls get to where they are supposed to be going to the will of God taking them along with us.

I tried to be as honest as I can with you and everything I say and do because trust and honesty are most certainly the foundation that we have built this relationship on. If I cannot confess to you of any sins that I may have that may be forgiven by the blood of the cross that Jesus Christ died for our sins. Only if we confess one to another are we to be saved.

And I'm in love with you. You're the reason I am getting younger, smile and healthier, and our home or I should say this whole house, is coming together and will only be home with your mother and yourself here. Brian and I would continue going forward, although I feel very comfortable if your mother and yourself were to show up at this very moment. As compared to what this old hunting lodge is to be like, LOL smile. No deer heads on the walls, LOL smile all the man junk is gone. I pray to God you can bring a lot of things for the simple reason there are many empty spaces here. Drawers, closets, rooms, etc., etc., and if not, we can purchase them as we go along.

And we are the glue that will keep this covenant going because it is not a house divided. It is a good foundation of a relationship that we bring together into a home and a family. The struggles, trials, and tribulations are well worth the effort. I know and feel that we will be blessed abundantly through the grace of God once we come together as a family. Without the subdivision will flow together and become heaven on earth. How do you feel, honey? How are you doing?. God bless with love and prayers through the grace, joy, happiness, protection, care kindness of God our Father to you and your mother through Jesus Christ as Lord's name Amen. From your Zorro

17 April 2019

DiAnnie wrote;

> *Well, you are the one on the ground, so you sure know the ups and downs on that journey.. lol when I come, we will drive all to these places so I can see Arizona for myself. I'm also excited to come over to you and see my mom. We have so much fun waiting and having a great time together. I'll go back to sleep now, okay? Love you so much and sweet dreams.*

18 April 2019

DiAnnie wrote;

> *Good morning my love, Lol you have had a lot of fun guys you have moved with, and when I sit and read all these stories, I start to laugh. Coworkers want to know what makes me smile when reading my messages.. lol I tell them the one I'm in love with has me smiling because his sense of humor is beyond me lol. So chocolate brought Melvin and Sally as a couple, and what made them come here to North country?*

> *Anyway, North country is the safest place in the world.. lol. It's just a saying because I know there are many safe places in this world. Haha, you need prayers because you are so good to have everyone cracking 😁. Mom is doing great, and thanks for asking for her. She does ask about you each time she writes or calls. I think you have a special place in her heart.*

> *Anyway, I'll get busy for now and will check my message later. I hope you're doing well, my love, and that you had a great night's sleep. I love my Zorro so much! Hugs and 😮.*

Thomas wrote;

> *Beautiful, I cannot keep my mouth off of you today; smile with love, compassion and kindness, gentleness, and appreciation. You're my northern girl of a precious treasure that could only come to the miraculous miracle and grace sent from God. And for that, I thank God for you in my life and your mother. I try to imagine where I would be without you, honey. And I can't. One thing I would like your prayer for. Is that after*

putting oil in my car? All the dash lights are out now, and I have to put water in the radiator. I took it for a small test drive to Alice's restaurant about 7 miles up the hill this morning. To give a friend of mine a ride and back to his house. If I take it to the mechanic shop, it may be tied up for days.

I can hardly wait to bring our love together with your mother because I cannot see God placing us together and having you leave your home to come to our home without any security at all. Like I have met you before, it will be yours and your mother's home as soon as you get to this house.

With relief. I just have this spiritual feeling of beauty that God will bless us with an abundance we have never known before. As the same with love, we have for one another that we have never known before. It will be beyond our comprehension or imagination. This is what I feel spiritual. Our house will no longer be divided against itself. It has never been spiritually only monetarily have we had to know the trials and tribulations of being broken and struggling. And these will be good memories. I love you so much.

This friend of mine named Bob, his wife came into the house and said the car would not start, and I think there's water in the carburetor. My friend Bob said, "how do you know there is water in the carburetor?, You do not even know a carburetor from a tailpipe. Then Bob asked, "where is the car?" His wife replied, "it is at the bottom of the swimming pool." LOL, smile laughing.

Freely to new places and meet new people. And that they may enjoy their trip this I pray O God our Father. Thank you, Jesus, amen. I love you, honey xoxo

19 April 2019

DiAnnie wrote;

Oh, my love, you are still here. Are you still awake at this time? I just woke up to go to the bathroom, seeing your messages, and then here I am again. I thought that you were asleep already so, please try to get some rest. I will try to get some sleep again, so I talk to you in the morning. I love you so much, my love, sweet dreams. Hugs and kisses.

20 April 2019

DiAnnie wrote;

Hello my love, thank God I can finally get back to you at this time. I thought I was going to be less busy today as usual, but hell no! It felt like a regular working day even though It was the weekend. I didn't get enough sleep this morning as I woke up to clean this place and go downtown after getting a few things and then to the church. I got back around 5:30 pm and got some rest, and here I am writing you back. Thanks for all those lovely messages. They mean so much to me.

God had a purpose for you. Imagine most of your friends are in more strenuous situations still struggling with their past. I have had my ugly past, and I will only be thankful to God for making me the person after His heart. You and I are alike, and I know it was because God was preparing us for each other. I'm glad that the migraine went away.

Sure Easter is already here! I remember very well that you can sing, you remember when you left a voicemail with your songs when I had my phone then? You sounded like Kenny Rogers, believe me.. LOL he's Mom's favorite American singer LOL. I use to ask her, and you don't understand English, why do you like his songs and not Michel Sardou, the French singer? She tells me it's just his voice, my child but no message at all. LOL.

She and I sing Celine Dion's songs and gospel music to be a great music band, LOL. I know in my heart you'll always be okay. I can't wait to see my Zorro. Anyway, babe, I'll get some rest now and be able to gain strength for church tomorrow. Thanks for all your lovely messages. All my regards to you. You're the sweetest guy I know—hugs and kisses from me.

21 April 2019

Thomas wrote;

Beautiful, I give it all away, and being a man and not having my better half, it's just the way it is. LOL smile. Those little prayers you said? They might seem minor to you, but those are huge miracles, and God heard every thought. Because he knows you love him as much as I do. And we show our love through prayer. They might be little bits to us in our minds and seem meaningless. But believe me, sweetheart, I feel there are not many that show the love we do through prayer. Keep in mind that we will be judged, on our thoughts, words, what we have done, and what we have failed to do.

That's why I felt that you said a small prayer in my heart because I recognize them the way the circumstances fell into place yesterday.

The only reason I had that migraine for a short time. It is because of his loud, boisterous voice and the thunderous racist music he was listening to. I guess that was my penance for bringing the miracle along. Sweetheart, do not worry about how far I have to travel. I mentioned to you way early in our friendship and relationship that we have developed over the last year. I said I would give my life for you, and that's what I meant.

Because I knew in my heart, mind, soul, and spirit that you were sent from God, and to misuse or abuse a gracious miraculous gift sent from God would be the worst thing imaginable to do. And you are so unique, sweetheart. You are my girl. Now, this might seem like a small coincidence to you. Think about it. Your mother is liking Kenny Rogers and me sounding like Kenny Rogers.? LOL, smile. Let your mother know that we will be performing on stage for the three of us. LOL with great joy and fun and happiness. Big smile and laughing very kindly and appreciative. As usual. LOL with love and compassion, smiling with romance. You are my girl.

Smile miraculously, knowing that it could happen with our faith. We will travel the United States first and move up into the North country, North country. Then who knows where God will take us? Only God knows. Hugs and kisses from your Zorro

You make sure and let your mother know that my prayers are with her, and I think about her daily as I do you. However, you consume my mind 90% of the time—more than likely more than that. I'm not sure what percentage of my thoughts would go to your mother. But the thoughts that go to her are prayerful with respect and appreciation for having a daughter that God sent to me. And an opportunity for me to show your mother the love that I never show my mother.

To test the spirit of truth, the unbelievers of the fact they do not want examination. Suppose you criticize the unbelievers of reality if you endeavored to contend for the truth. And if you expose their error, they will turn it around and condemn you as the sinner.

If this is the Holy Spirit's actual work, know that they do not want examination. They would be inviting all the scrutiny they could get if they were honest and truthful. They would wish to the affirmation and the authentication.

If they were honest? Being deceitful and fraudulent in the errors of their ways. You're the one standing in their way of the truth and discernment of the Bible and Jesus' teachings.

For them to succeed, they have to turn iniquity into a transgression against Christ. Sound doctrine proves that they do not survive. Beloved, believe not every spirit, but try the spirits whether they are of God: because many false prophets are gone out into the world.

1 John 4;1-21.

Beloved, believe not every spirit, but try the spirits whether they are of God:

because many false prophets are gone out into the world.

Hereby know ye the Spirit of God: Every spirit that confesseth that Jesus

Christ comes in the flesh is of God:

> *And every spirit that confesseth not that Jesus Christ comes in the flesh is not of God: and this is that spirit of antichrist, of whom ye have heard that it should come; and even now already is it in the world.*

> *Ye are of God, little children, and have overcome them: because greater is he that is in you than he that is in the world.*

> *They are of the world: therefore speak they of the world, and the world heareth them.*

> *We are of God: he that knoweth God heareth us; he that is not of God heareth not us. At this moment, know we are the Spirit of truth and the Spirit of error.*

> *Beloved, let us love one another: for love is of God, and every one that loveth is born of God and knoweth God.*

He that loveth not knoweth not God; for God is love.

In this was manifested the love of God toward us, because that God sent his only begotten Son into the world, that we might live through him.

Herein is love, not that we loved God, but that he loved us and sent his Son to propitiate for our sins.

Beloved, if God so loved us, we ought also to love one another.

No man hath seen God at any time. If we love one another, God dwelleth in us, and his love is perfected in us.

Now know we that we dwell in him, and he in us, because he hath given us of his spirit.

And we have seen and do testify that the Father sent the Son to be the Saviour of the world.

Whosoever shall confess that Jesus is the Son of God, God dwelleth in him, and he in God.

And we have known and believed the love that God hath to us. God is love, and he that dwelleth in love dwelleth in God, and God in him.

Herein is our love made perfect, that we may have boldness in the day of judgment: because as he is, so are we in this world.

There is no fear in love, but perfect love casteth out fear: because fear hath torment. He that feareth is not made perfect in love.

We love him because he first loved us.

If a man says, I love God and hateth his brother, and he is a liar: for he that loveth not his brother whom he hath seen, how can he love God whom he hath not seen?

And this commandment has we from him, That he who loveth God love his brother also.

Thomas wrote;

Beautiful, how are you feeling? How are you doing? I'm doing very well, thank you for asking. Have I told you lately that I love you? Smile with compassion and love. I think about just holding you in my arms and romantically kissing you. With gentle hugs and soft-back massage. God willing one day.

The key to love is understanding. The ability to comprehend not only the spoken word but those unspoken gestures, the little things that say so much by themselves. The key to love is forgiveness, accepting each other's faults, and pardon mistakes Without forgetting, but remembering what you learned from them. The key to love is sharing, Facing your good fortunes and the bad, together; both conquering problems, forever searching for ways to intensify your happiness. The key to love is giving without the thought of return, but with the hope of just a simple smile, and by giving in but never giving up. The key to love is respect. Realizing that you are two separate people, with different ideas; that you don't belong to each other, that you belong with each other, and share a mutual bond. The key to love is inside us all. It takes time and patience to unlock all the ingredients that will take you to its threshold; the continual learning process demands a lot of work, but the rewards are more than worth the effort. And this is the key to our love together no beginning, no end, and revealing love.

I'm pleasantly pleased, sweetheart, that you had a great day at church and were able to see a lot of friends that you have not seen in quite some time. And you're right about me being a preacher or a minister. Not just yet. However, I appreciate how you have perceived the biblical messages that God has given through the Holy Spirit to you. Because you're worth it. You're my girl. And please let your mother know that I pray for you and her continuously because I cannot stop thinking about you or your mother.

Everything is OK. Everything has been alright; otherwise, we would not be here right now. Everything is OK right this very moment as you read these words. OK? Be nice to yourself, honey. God loves you. Your prayers are powerful. And I know your mothers are as well; otherwise, we would not be communicating or together. This I spiritually feel. Any mother would pray for a man for her daughter, such as myself. This is why I know your mother's prayers are very powerful. And your mother was to be so grateful that her daughter has brought all three of us together as a family through the Holy Spirit and prayer. I love you, honey, I love your soul, I love your mind, I love your spirit, I love your heart, I love your beautiful body, and I especially love God for bringing this guardian angel to me.

That so graciously and miraculously brought my whole soul into the kingdom of heaven with my beautiful Guardian Angel and her mother. This I know because the Bible tells me so. One day God willing, and with your approval, I will become a great minister, and you will be right by my side. You will be teaching the ladies in the church a compelling message that will also bring their souls to the gates of heaven. And your mother will also be teaching a class in our church. I feel this is God's will for us. More shall be revealed. I would never have thought that unless I did not hear it from you and how you explained how I minister the Bible to you. Once again, it is your fault. LOL smiling and laughing. From your Zorro

Thomas wrote;

Beautiful, Happy Easter scrumptious. Let us be thankful that the good Lord has risen to a higher level of consciousness in a place called heaven. As Jesus said, I go before you and prepare many mansions if it were not so I would tell you. How is my girl this morning? I pray everything is going well? We must all have dreams, they keep us young, and they keep us alive. Without goals, what do we have to live for? Going to heaven with God is about doing the right thing and not always what we want to do. It is about sacrificing obedience and appreciation, and love. Everything is OK, sweetheart. Everything is OK right this very moment.

Please keep that in your mind at all times, and everything will be OK. You are my dream. You are I love sent from heaven above. That I have never experienced before in my life. God's gift to us is his life. What we do with this life is our gift to God. Being equally out spiritually, we have everything going for us. We have too many things in common that are not just coincidental but miracles that God has put into your life for reasons that shall be revealed.

I want you always to know that I'm in love with your soul. I will always have you in my heart, and you consume my thoughts of a love that I find graciously miraculous. And for that, I thanked God and prayed to God all I can when I'm not thinking about us. And being a singer with your mother is a dream. That can be obtainable, and we can have fun with it. One thing is for sure we can always sing in church. Smile with spirituality and holy grace. Keep in mind we do have a book to write. And our story will lead us to an undefined unrevealing destiny together. Although I want you to be free. I have to let this love go and let it be free, and if it were meant to be, it would come back to me., no matter what you are doing or who you are with. I am your Zorro.

You are my guardian angel From the North country. Is there anything you need or anything you would like me to do for you? And that question always stands. Your freedom and happiness are what is essential in my eyes and the eyes of God. Through our Lord Jesus Christ and the Holy Spirit that works through us, we are aware of God's love through the miracles. No matter how small they are in our lives, we are aware of them. One year and two months a little bit over, we have been communicating continuously.

We've had our ups and downs, although you have seen a change in me that only has been brought about because of you. And I keep changing and growing along spiritual lines and thanking God daily moment by moment for such a lovely young lady coming into my life to have made it possible for me to get to heaven. And along my journey will be able to help and save a lot of others.

One thing we have to complete that I am looking forward to is our book. And I have been putting that on hold because of my continued studying the Bible, listing to my ministries, and passing what I learn on to you. And it has only strengthened our love for one another. And we must always keep in mind love of God has no beginning and has no end. And for you and I to tap into that eternal love is going to be revealing beyond our comprehension or imagination.

This I know because the Bible tells me so. Please let your mother know that my prayers are with her, and I asked about her all the time. I wish the best for her and yourself for your happiness, joy, peace of mind, safety, and love of God through Jesus Christ our Lord's name that the Holy Spirit protect you and guide you until the time comes when we meet. No matter what, that is going to happen. And I look forward to meeting your mother as well.

I also realize that you are a brilliant young beautiful lady with a lot of spiritual discernment with a smile. Your feelings, emotions, and intuition are far more intelligent than any man. This I have experienced. LOL, a smile I do not mean for this email to sound hypocritical or to make you lose any trust or feelings that I may have for you.

I would tell you the truth it would break my heart in one respect if we were not to be together again. But if I knew you were happy. That would make me happy. I know you realize and understand what I am saying?

Don't you? I certainly do not want to confuse you. Maybe I should just throw this email away. LOL :-) like the idiot man I am. Double laughing.

I love you so much, honey. Hugs and kisses

Thomas wrote;

Beautiful, my precious Guardian Angel from the North country. Now please take a spiritual journey with me.? In the theater of your mind, go back in time to 2019 years. The Virgin Mary, about 15 or 16 years old, was announced by Gabriel the Archangel that she was with child and would have the Savior of all humankind. This is the love that I have for you, is a very similar love that Joseph and Mary have for one another. Mary and Joseph were playing their bar mitzvah, and Joseph was building a home for Mary and their family. Mary came to tell Joseph the news. Can you imagine being told by your young girlfriend that you are pregnant with a child? Joseph may have been upset at the time. But later on in a dream, the voice of God our Father through the Holy Spirit came to Joseph and said that it was through the prophets that would be a seed of David that Mary was to have this child. Joseph then accepted Mary for her Immaculate Conception through the Holy Spirit. This is the love I have for you, beautiful. I accept you for who you are no matter what has ever happened in your past or will ever happen to you. My love for you is unconditional. Because our love was sent from God, the same passion that Joseph had for Mary. And keep in mind Joseph and Mary went on to have more children. One of the apostles was James, Jesus Christ, our Lord's brother from Mary and Joseph.

There was some turmoil in their town of Nazareth. With the Roman soldiers. And it was that time of the year when they had to go to Jerusalem, their birthplace, to register. Jesus was born a Nazarene because Jesus grew up in Nazareth, so his common language was Nazarene. Although Jesus Christ our Lord was born in Bethlehem in a manger. Because there was no room at the Inn, delivered in a humble surrounding of animals, the Norstar appeared in the sky to the three wise men who came to humble themselves before the king of the Jews and Savior of all humankind. These three wise men brought frankincense murre and gold as an offering. Herod, the king of Jerusalem at the time, heard through the three wise men that came to pay homage. King Herod asked the three wise men or Madge's, To please come back when they found out where Jesus was so he could also pay him homage. King Herod ordered every Male child in Bethlehem under two years old to be put to death. An angel of the Lord came to Joseph and said to take Mary and the baby Jesus to Egypt, where they fled from the carnage and escaped the death of Jesus Christ, our Lord, and Savior.

Fast-forwarding to the crucifixion of Jesus Christ, our Lord who went to the cross for the transgressions of our sins. Jesus Christ, our Lord, was 33 years old at the time. How young are you, sweetheart? Smile with great appreciation and a miraculous love that neither of us has experienced. And more shall be revealed. Would you please let your mother know that my prayers are with her and wish her a happy Easter for the Lord has risen? There's a reason for the celebration today. Jesus Christ, our Lord, appeared in 13 different locations to over 500 Christians before he ascended into heaven. There is a reason. Thank God, rejoice and be glad in it. I love you, honey. You are my girl. Xoxox from your Zorro

The Key to Love

The key to love is understanding...

The ability to comprehend not only the spoken word, but those unspoken gestures,

the little things that say so much by themselves. The key to love is forgiveness...

to accept each other's faults and pardon mistakes, without forgetting, but with remembering

what you learn from them. The key to love is sharing...

Facing your good fortunes as well as the bad, together; both conquering problems, forever searching for ways to intensify your happiness.

The key to love is giving... without thought of return,

but with the hope of just a simple smile, and by giving in but never giving up.

The key to love is respect...

realizing that you are two separate people, with different ideas;

that you don't belong to each other,

that you belong with each other and share a mutual bond. The key to love is inside us all...

It takes time and patience to unlock all the ingredients that will take you to its threshold;

it is the continual learning process that demands a lot of work... but the rewards are more than worth the effort...

and that is the key to love.

Thomas wrote;

Morning my love.

Thank you. Have a happy Easter. My prayers are with you and your mother, and I love you. Hugs and kisses have a great day. Get some rest, beautiful.

Beautiful, I love my girl from North country. How are you doing today, sweetheart? How are you feeling? How is your mother doing? Is she still in Belgium?

I just thought I would send you a short note to let you know that this house that I thought in my flawed thinking was clean. LOL, it is a nightmare. Thank God you brought me to the realization of how unfeminine it is. Brian and I are still cleaning and have a lot more to go. Throwing a lot of stuff out that a bachelor would collect a lot of clutter to old television sets, boxes, and boxes of books rearranging curtains and pictures removing a lot of stuff from the walls. This house will be empty when you arrive, God willing, if you and your mother decide to. And I pray to God I can put enough stuff in place to make it very acceptable to both you and your mother. And I have a feeling you're going to be overwhelmed with the vision of your home that I have in mind. This house is huge, and it will be empty, smile a lot of drawers are empty a lot of shelves are empty in the kitchen and the bathroom. And that I do not know what you would want to put in all of that space? But you will have a lot of space, smile. I'm not sure how you will fill everything of things that you would like to put in its place?

I'm starting on a straightforward book, and I believe it will take off. I had no idea, my nephew, Samuel, was an artist, and I believe I sent you some of the drawings. They may not seem like much to you, and I will send you more, excluding the one picture of a naked lady that he tried to draw. I informed him that our target audience was kindergartners or first-graders in school. And that I am going to contact all the school districts within the state of Arizona and extend it to other states to see if I get to school systems to buy this book. It will be a very simple book, a very simple drawing for young minds to understand, and it will be biblical. I asked Samuel to draw animals of the ones in Alaska and stay away from the so-called women he has been drawing. And try to keep it biblical and try to draw little children etc. I plan to market this myself and just go to a printer and have them print copies as the orders come in. I'm going to try to promote that book. I'm starting on it right away because I'm excited that it is very simple and get it to teach young children about the Bible etc. I think it will go with hugs and kisses

Since Samuel recently got a divorce from his wife from Nigeria, she loved going back to Nigeria. You can tell by his drawings that he would like to have a woman in his life. We are going to change his drawings for a younger Christian audience of preschoolers possibly. Maybe you have some ideas of your own that we can use what you think might sell? These are going to be abridged books, maybe 20 pages for each book. I'm going to have a friend of mine that is a graphic designer work on the cover.

I'm taking every opportunity I can to have blessings with abundance so that I can provide for my wife and our family, and your mother. So if you have any ideas, sweetheart, please do not hesitate to let me know. You are my better half. And I pray to God all the time I think about us being together that this may not be one of my dreams that just dissipates before I wake up.

Although if that should happen, for whatever reason that life happens to show up, you have shown me a path to heaven I would've never done without you and have me a greater man than I could've ever thought of being without you in my life. And that's what I think God for, all the time I think about you, I am praying, working out fasting and working on our home I should say my house until you arrive and then it is your home. A woman's home is where her heart is.

You know I'm in love with you and us. We have so many things in common that we both know that it was meant to be through the grace of God and the Holy Spirit working through both of us, especially your mother's prayers. I have a spiritual feeling was spiritual discernment that your mother was praying for a man for you that was a man of God, and a good man that would provide for you and take care of you and treat you with respect and have children that is what your mother is living for is to have grandchildren. And a man that will treat her daughter like a queen.

God will provide for us beyond our wildest comprehension. This I know for a fact because my faith is so unshakable. If we approach the friendship that we have developed over the last year and looking into the future at our marriage with our children and your mother with honesty and trust in the Lord, Jesus Christ of the Holy Spirit will provide for us beyond ours. wildest comprehension or imagination.

You also mentioned to me that you. wanted to travel across the United States or around the United States and see everything. And that brought an idea to my mind that I would like to minister to others across the United States and have revivals I would love. to speak to those Christians who need to hear a message. And we could travel from town to town, and you never know we could travel worldwide. I am a great testimony for the Lord, I lost my arm to save my soul, and I have lived the past that will eternally last, and the miraculous thing is I should not be here many many times over I should have been taken home because of the crazy things I used to do.

And thank you, sweetheart, with your knowledge, wisdom, and intelligence with intuition, feelings and emotions came into my life as a guardian angel that God sent me through his grace. How fortunate can I be, and how much love does God have for the both of us? There is no beginning to our love, and there will be no ending for our love. It will continue to grow along spiritual lines, and more shall be revealed. Just keep in mind please do not come into the United States and a relationship even if it is not with me, thinking like my brother's wife from Columbia and thinking like my nephew's wife from Algeria, that you can take advantage of the United States and the American people because of all the opportunities we have to offer here.

I offer my love to you through Jesus Christ, our Lord's name, and we have equally yoked spiritually money had nothing to do with our getting together. God will add that through his overabundance, grace, and blessings. That is what Satan would like you to do, and that is not the faith that God has for us if we have faith and trust in God moment by moment and do not go down that road of worry or stress into the future or the next five minutes.

And I know the unforgivable forgiveness that you have had for me is a spiritual gift especially sent from God, not many ladies, and I have never known a lady such as yourself to have had that spiritual gift. Do you realize how special you are because you have that gift of forgiveness.? And never looking through the rearview mirror and living your life through the rearview mirror. I love you, honey. I'm in love with you xoxo

postscript; the more I pray to God for you in my life, and I would never have thought that Satan would attack me in a way that I could never handle. And I recognize him and his evil ways when I see them or when they come into my life spiritually in a very negative evil cunning way. So please, you and your mother, keep praying for me, Satan tries to tempt me, but I am beyond temptation. I know I have a girl in North country who loves me, and we are in a committed relationship together. So it is very easy for me to say to others that I am in a committed relationship. What amazes me is, is how often they come at me and out of nowhere. The picture looks good. I know I'm going to heaven because of you, a guardian angel that was sent into my life, and I would never defile that. That would be similar to blasphemy of the Holy Spirit and unforgivable sin. And I'm not going there.

Here is one riddle I put forth to others, and no one has been able to solve this riddle. When I buy a brand-new pair of shoes, I do not try them on first before I buy them. I purchase the shoes take them home, and have the faith that they will fit. That's the riddle, and I know you know the answer.

And it amazes me no one knows the answer to that riddle. That riddle is so simple that it mystifies everyone except for my beautiful girl from North country. The answer is, you get married before you make love. Now is that simple? And to build that cake like we have been doing from scratch from day one, we will eat the cherry and share it off the top of the cake one day. And I think about that from time to time, and I have dreams about that and the two of us together making love and holding each other. And I feel it is far beyond my comprehension or imagination of the love that God has for the two of us that we have never experienced before. It will all be new, believe me, and who will be heaven-sent. Once again, I love you. Honey, has a great day.

22 April 2019

DiAnnie wrote;

How is my love doing? I hope that you had a great night. Mine was great. I have overslept, and now I'm getting ready to go to church for the Easter celebration, my love! Our Lord rose today!! Hugs, my Zorro.

Hello, my love, it was a very long day today with all the activities at the church and meeting people I know here, so it's now that I got back home, and I'm so exhausted. Not sure you're home yet, but I know much is going on there as well. Your story about Jesus got me reading along as you made it sounds very interesting. The way you put those bible stories is so different when others are explaining it. When I read what I write, it's like I'm right there. I can easily relate, and it does not sound like how some pastors explain as if it's some fictional people. You can be a great pastor if you wish to, but I like that you tell the truth, that you know yourself fully well, and you can not push yourself into something that others would expect from an angel... LOL, that's how people view those that get in the things of God. They expect no mistakes. They expect you to live like a being that isn't from this world, and it's not possible! Am I right?

Thanks so much for making me smile this evening. Tell me how much you love me. My love for you is unconditional, and you know that. I appreciate your concerns and prayers for Mom and me. We do need that very much. I hope you're having a great time, my love. Enjoy the rest of your day as it's still in the afternoon there. All my love for this great guy. Kisses and hugs, babe.

Thomas wrote;

Sweetheart, OK? Smile with gentle compassion, safety, and love. Hugs and kisses

The most crucial key to love. God through Jesus Christ, his only son, our Lord, and the Holy Spirit that works through us. The key to the poem I emailed you in the last email. I happen to get off-line and felt it was appropriate for our love for one another. It did not mention the most important to you to love, so I thought I would say that. And I pray to Jesus Christ the Lord's name that you and your mother are happy, joyous, and free with the safety and love of God our father. Now you have my mind a ministry. And I feel for a fact I would be a great minister. The Baptist Church provides for its ministers and their families. The only requirement is to move where they ask you to or where you are needed. It's something to think about anyway: most of the ministers are real Montaigne and boring, or they have their sermon on the script already prepared. I would not minister that way. I would minister with the aggressive faith believing speeches that lost souls would be sent to me in abundance. We may be in Montréal ministering as a Baptist minister. We never know. But I will be darned if I'm going to sit in a small town when God has more for me to offer through his miraculous grace to many others. Let me know what you think, sweetheart, and let me know how your mother feels about that. I love you

Thomas wrote;

Beautiful, my precious Guardian Angel, a treasure from the North country. Scrumptious delicious, delectable precious tasty little morsel simply exquisite elegant, and for this I humble myself before thee and give great compliments for the graceful miraculous union that God our Father through Jesus Christ our Lord and the Holy Spirit working through us, to God the chef. LOL smile with love, kindness appreciation of family bonding that only a mother could have prayed for her daughter that a man is brought into her life to protect and care for her mother and DiAnnie. Through the Holy Spirit, DiAnnie's father, and Thomas's father (Jean, Gene) Felipe and Eugene. Sweet precious DiAnnie, same birthday as Thomas's father, 15 January. Childhood heroes Zorro link miraculously to the grace of God to strengthen the bond over time. one year and four months of constant communication weaving a bond that only God could have brought together.

Ladies and gentlemen and children of God, please, if you would be so kind as to take a trip with me as we go back in time to when our Lord Jesus Christ was crucified, and his blood saves us at the cross. Caiaphas, the chief priest on the eve of Passover. Caiaphas a Sanhedrin and head of the Jewish Council. Had Jesus arrested just outside of Jerusalem at the garden of Gathsemane. Peter the apostle cut, and you're off of a centurion soldier, as Judas betrayed Jesus with a kiss. Jesus Christ, our Lord, immediately placed the ear back on the Roman centurion and was instantly healed. Jesus Christ, our Lord's apostles, did not just include the 12 apostles as most know of it.

Many lady apostles were with Jesus and his followers. The most renowned lady apostle was Mary Magdalene. Mary Magdalene was possessed with seven evil spirits. She kept saying to Jesus do you hear them? Do you hear them? And Jesus said yes as he hugged her and removed all of the evil spirits. From that moment on, she was a faithful follower of Jesus Christ, the Lord. At the Last Supper, Mary, the sister of Lazarus, broke a 12-ounce box of costly perfume, similar to Chanel number five. It cost one year's wages as she broke the alabaster box and washed Jesus's feet with her tears and wiped his feet dry with her hair as she anointed Jesus Christ's complete body with this expensive oil.

Judas (betrayer) was in charge of the apostle's money being a tax collector. And scoffed at Mary for using expensive perfume to anoint Jesus with. Jesus said to Judas, be quiet. You know not what she is doing? Jesus Christ, our Lord's other women apostles were, Mary his mother, Susan, and a lady called Anna. And, of course, Mary Magdalene. This costly perfume that Mary was anointing Jesus with, she had no idea why she was doing it, for the reason she was preparing his body for death.

Jesus Christ was arrested at the garden and taken to Pontus Pilate. Pontus Pilate's wife Claudius had a dream about crucifying Jesus, and she knew in her heart they were crucifying the wrong man for the wrong reasons. Pontus Pilate, for that reason, did not

217

want to crucify Jesus. And as prophesies throughout the Bible and the Old Testament. Reading chapter 53 of Isaiah, written 700 years BC. And then going into the theater of your mind back in time farther, 1400 BC and read the Psalm of David chapter 22. These two chapters in the Old Testament, along with other major and minor prophets, prophesies the death of Jesus Christ our Lord and lets us know of his coming through the seed of King David. Moses wrote the first five chapters of the Bible, which brought Israel out of bondage to the promised land as prophecies.

After Jesus was arrested, beaten with the cat of nine tails, long strips of leather with steel hooks on the ends that ripped flesh from the back of Jesus Christ our Lord. Then the Roman soldiers put a crown of thorns on Jesus Christ's head, pushing it down tightly. Punched in the face numerous times, punched in the stomach numerous times, spit on, and humiliated by crowds. Pontus Pilate was a tradition during the Passover holiday to let one prisoner go free. He put it to the crowd it was either Jesus or Robert and no one murderer, Judas Iscariot. The crowd set Judas free. As Pontus Pilate said to Caiaphas, I washed his hands of this, and it sent to man's blood Jesus Christ and Pontus Pilate told Caiaphas, you crucify him as Pontus Pilate walked away.

Jesus was carrying the cross that way between 100 pounds and 300 pounds, approximately 300 yards out of the town up and down through winding terrain with crowds mocking him. The third time Jesus fell on the cross, the Roman soldiers ordered Simon and the African-American to help Jesus carry the cross. Also, one of the 12 tribes, the tribe of Levi, was an African-American tribe that today still resides in Africa. And it is said that they guard the Ark of the covenant. The Ark of the covenant contains the 10 Commandments, In the first five books of Moses in the Bible. and the Holy Spirit dwells in its presence. To protect the Ark of the covenant.

After Jesus was crucified as prophecies, not one bone shall be broken by Isaiah and David and other prophets. It was normally the rule of the Roman soldiers after prison was hanging on the cross for some time to break their legs with a heavy sword. This way, the body could not hold up the weight, and the prison would die of suffocation. A Roman soldier pierced Jesus Christ's side with a spear when it went right between the ribs, and Jesus did not have one broken bone. After taking Jesus Christ's body down and they had to bury his body before sundown.

Joseph of Arimathea, one of the Jewish Sanhedrin that once on the Council that crucified Jesus, had his doubts about the Council voting to have Jesus crucified. He went to Pontus Pilate and asked if he could take Jesus Christ's body down and bury it in his tomb before sundown when the Sabbath and celebration of Passover began. It was against Jewish law to do any work on the Sabbath, including the burial of a family member or anyone. So Jesus Christ had to be taken off the cross from 3 PM to 5 PM when the sun went down. Pontus Pilate agreed and gave Joseph of Arimathea permission. At the cross was the apostle John, and all the women apostles were there. This is where Michelangelo, as you will see in the Vatican, the only sculpture he ever signed was the Pieta. A sculpture of mother Mary holds her son Jesus in her arms after he was taken down from the cross.

They had just enough time to get Jesus to the tomb, clean the body and wrap it in a shroud provided by Joseph of Arimathea. Pontus Pilate was afraid that robbers would rub the grave of Jesus, so after having a huge stone rolled up from the tomb entrance guarded by two Roman soldiers. Jesus was crucified on Friday, good Friday, Jewish holiday is the Sabbath is on Saturday. Then Sunday Easter morning at sunrise Mary Magdalene was allowed to go to the tomb to anoint Jesus's body. When she got to the tomb, the huge stone was rolled away, and the tomb was open, and Roman soldiers were gone. Normally the Roman soldiers would have rolled the stone away from the tomb so Mary Magdalene could have entered an anointed Jesus body with oil. She ran into the tomb, and it was empty.

All that was there with this shroud. Mary thought to herself as she cried, they have taken my Lord. It was not enough that they crucified him and humiliated him. They have taken my Lord. Mary Magdalene ran as fast as she could and went and told the apostles that Jesus's body was gone. Peter and James ran back to the tomb with Mary Magdalene, where they found Jesus's body was gone. Mary Magdalene then told the two apostles to go and leave me alone she was angry and was mourning and crying for Jesus. The two apostles left her alone in the tomb.

As Mary was leaving the tomb, a voice came to her and said, "Mary, why are you crying"? She turned around, and two angels were standing like bookends at each end of the slab, and the shroud laid. Mary said, "They have taken my Lord." She was so Griff stricken that she did not even acknowledge the two angels that said to her and didn't even recognize them as angels. She walked out of the tomb, and there standing in front of her what looks to her to be a gardener. Was Jesus Christ our Lord. And he said to her, "Mary, it is I Jesus" do not cry, go and tell the others what you have seen. This may have been the greatest eyewitness of the whole Bible that gave testimony to Jesus Christ, our Lord's resurrection. She ran and got the apostles, and they came with her, and there was nobody there. Jesus Christ, our Lord, appeared to all the apostles at once as they were leaving the tomb. And spoke with them for quite some time and asked them to go to buy and spread the gospel and what you have witnessed.

Sweetheart, peace, and grace of the Lord be with you and your mother through Jesus Christ the Lord's name. This is only one of my sermons, and I have not even started with this sermon. As of yet, there's a lot more to say about the sermon. I did not want to fry your brain with too much information. LOL smiling and laughing. You're my girl, and I'm in love with you whether you like it or not. LOL :-) xoxo from your Zorro

God has great plans for the two of us. I should say the three of us, including her mother, I will never forget your mother. She was always included in our family, and she always will be. Say your prayers, honey. Because God loves you and your mother, and I do to

Sweetheart since your favorite color is purple, I would just be wondering if you have ever heard of "a one-eyed one-horned flying purple people eater"? LOL, smile laughing. Sometimes it's not what we know. It's who we know, and the combination of the 2 Can Take us places through the Holy Spirit that we could never imagine miraculously. Another thing, honey, I would like to ask you a favor, please?. If you ever get involved with another man, could you please let me know? I would certainly appreciate it. Peace and grace of the Lord be with you and your mother through Jesus Christ the Lord's name amen xoxo beautiful I would never be who I am today if it were not for you, and I keep growing spiritually, and for that, I thank you as my guardian angel. You're a brilliant young beautiful lady, and I'm proud of you. You will always be my girl.

Beautiful public speaking is my forte. When I was writing Harley- Davidson's, I was a public speaker for the group. At different events. When I got sober in Alcoholics Anonymous, I was the secretary of many meetings in the greater San Francisco Bay Area. I have spoken at Alcoholics Anonymous meetings at Christmas time, usually a 45-minute speech and an audience of 500 a couple of times. Anonymity is our spiritual foundation. In the United States Marine Corps, I trained 200 Marines at one time. I led 32 Marines into covert operations. My records are sealed, as you will know. By the CIA and I wouldn't say I like to talk about any of my missions for apparent reasons, and I will never speak to you about them. Say your prayers I pray for your mother and yourself through Jesus Christ the Lord's name amen, xoxo how I told you I loved you lately? Smile with God's love, a guardian angel and a brilliant young lady sent to me to save my soul. If we get together one day, God willing, I want to work on a couple of books. All the emails we have compiled between us will make several books and possibly a television series. We must have these dreams, honey. God willing, some of them may come true with the Holy Spirit working through us doing the right thing. We will be blessed abundantly.

Sweetheart, please say your prayers and have your mother say hers. I love my DiAnnie, and I care for her mother, Anna. This is my calling beautiful either through books and writings about being a testimony to others about our love for one another that has no beginning or end.

I have many more sermons, and I'm studying for many, many more to come. You are my inspiration. This all could not have transpired if it were not for you. You're my girl, my precious Guardian Angel sent from God through the Holy Spirit, and here we are. LOL :-) do not worry, do not stress, everything is OK, everything is OK right now, everything has been OK, and everything is going to be OK. OK? :-) With prayers and protection with great love that we have never known, please rest when the spirit moves you. Please let me know that you are OK. How are you feeling besides exhausted? LOL :-) wishing I was there with you holding you are kissing you, giving you excellent soft massages, and whispering romantic words into your ears

DiAnnie wrote; 22 April 2019

Morning my love.

Hey Zorro, you make me laugh, lol. I'm not suspicious at all. It's only not to make my friend think I went through her accounts. If it's her brother's, boyfriend's, I don't care about that. I only want you to delete that email from your inbox and sent it so that you may not make any mistake to email there, that's all. Well, honestly, I'm not worried at all or making this an issue. I know as long you hear that it was a male account, you'll be going to tease me, and no, it's not a likely story lol, you silly man! Lol, if I was not so used to your sick sense of humor, I was going to get angry just like I always did in the past when we newly met. You were always driving me nuts, and I was always falling for it.. lol. I know, and you know, getting a boyfriend is not in my book right now. Getting a boyfriend isn't as easy as you think, knowing where you and I came from. Was it easy? So I don't think it'll go for another guy. My mind is made up right now for only this man called Thomas.

Sure I have unconditional love for you, and I know you have the same for me, and it's only the both of us that understand that through the word of God. We know all we *share in common, and it's only God would have done that. I'll send your regards to Mom. She's looking forward to hearing news about you, so for sure I'll lol. Write, and I'll check back with you later. Hugs.*

DiAnnie wrote;

Morning my love.

Hello, my dear, it was a very long day today with all the activities at the church and meeting people I know here, so it's now that I got back home, and I'm so exhausted. Not sure you're home yet, but I know much is going on there as well. Your story about Jesus got me reading along as you made it sounds very interesting. The way you put those bible stories is so different when others are explaining it. When I read what you write, it's like I'm right there, I can easily relate, and it does not sound like some pastors explain as if it's some fictional people. You can be a great pastor if you wish to, but I like that you tell the truth, that you know yourself fully well, and you can not push yourself into something that others would expect from an angel... LOL, that's how people view those that get in the things of God. They expect no mistakes. They expect you to live like a being that isn't from this world; I believe you when you describe something because you're a wise writer and explanation of things isn't difficult for you. Thanks so much for making me smile this evening. Tell me how much you love me. My love for you is unconditional, and you know that. I appreciate your concerns and prayers for Mom and me. We do need that very much. I hope you're having a great time, my love. Enjoy the rest of your day as it's still in the afternoon there. All my love for this great guy. Kisses and hugs, babe.

Thomas wrote;

Beautiful, my precious Guardian Angel treasure from the North country. Everything happens for a reason. And I have to be honest with you, that hurt my feelings. And being a man, it has taken me a while or did take me a while to figure it out. As humans, we always have to jump to conclusions, and they are usually wrong after knowing each other for over a year. And all the miracles God has worked in our lives together from the beginning. Let me know what you think or how you feel. I feel we have more than a committed relationship with one another. I consider you to be my fiancé. And wife, God willing, when we finally get together.

The way this whole house looks now as compared to what it used to look like. Even though your mother and yourself would have a little work to do here, do you know ladies and especially ladies in their own home? LOL smile with great appreciation, kindness, and care with loving consideration. To be honest with you, honey, I could not imagine you be with any other man than myself. Like I have mentioned once before, you could break my heart. And that has to be the worst feeling that I could ever imagine.

Please let me know how you feel. I am personally inspired through the Holy Spirit and God's will through Jesus Christ our Lord. There is not a doubt in my mind with my unshakable faith that we belong together forever. I will write more when I hear back from you. You are my girl. Do you know it felt good? Is when you said that I was your man. You do not say that too often or at all. Anyway, you just saying those few words, that's what turned my thinking around. And especially when you brought God into it. You are indeed my girl. And I'm in love with you. Being a man and your man is why I need my better half. That is when we will be blessed abundantly. Our home will no longer be divided amongst itself. You will have to admit, sweetheart, it has been hard on both of us because we have not been together.

And I realize you had this trip planned a long time ago. I remember when your mother was in Calgary. And I'm not sure how long that has been sent. Has she been away from you? Xoxox from your Zorro honey, you will have to admit not only your birthday being on my father's birthday but childhood heroes such as Zorro. What are the chances? And they keep piling up. This is why I know God loves both of us and has something great in mind for us. I'm going to start studying for my ministry. I have watched many, many hours of documentaries and biblical ministers and pastors that are renowned. Think about it. There is a chapter I believe I left in both of my books. Called "lost my arm to save my soul." God willing, I would not mind traveling a speaking circuit for ministry. This way, your mother, you, and I, plus many others, would be traveling together. This is what I feel the Holy Spirit has in mind for me. One thing I am not, I am not shy. Very outspoken when it comes to the Lord and the word of God, letting the Holy Spirit work through me to help others. And that has been my mission for many, many years to reach the multitudes of people to save souls. I love you, honey, and you will always be my girl.

Beautiful, you and I both know in our hearts that God put us together in a miraculous way. And let me say this to you once again, I want you to be free and want you to be happy. I do not want to own you or control you in any way. Just a quote in the Bible that says, "what God has put together let no man take apart." Thank God, hallelujah, praise the Lord, thank you, Jesus pass the blessings. LOL, smile, my girl, my precious

Guardian Angel, the treasure from the North country. It is getting to know my sick sense of humor. LOL laughing.

Scrumptious. Are you sure? Can't I send a bunch of funny emails to that email address? LOL laughing hard. OK, I will stop it. I could have more fun with this one than a double barrel of monkeys. When is the last time you heard from your mother? And how is she doing? And what has she been doing? And is she still in Belgium? You make sure every time you talk to her, do not ever forget to let her know that my prayers are with her with kindness, appreciation, consideration for her happiness, peace of mind, and safety from God our father. I love you, honey. You are my girl. You're my precious treasure from the North country. I just love writing that. Sounds pretty cool. Hugs and kisses from your Zorro

My treasure is beautiful, honey, sweetheart, delicious, tasty little morsel, a splendid little delight from the North country. I could have more fun with this one than a barrel of monkeys. LOL, smile. I could keep going on and on and on. I understand, beautiful. Remember our unconditional love? Well, with the trust and honesty issue as far as developing a relationship, that matters. Just put yourself in my shoes with your toes pointed in the wrong direction? Laughing so hard.

I love you scrumptious you're my girl, and I will stop it. I am laughing hard. I could keep going with jokes and jokes. Not my style. I just bring my mind back to my guardian angel. The reason God put you in my life, and we put each other into each other's lives as well as your mother, and the three of us are family. In this, I know because the Bible tells me so, and so does God. So please do not worry or stress I will not bring it up again. You will have to admit it was pretty funny, pretty funny. What did I stutter? I sounded just like a parrot there. LOL, smile, have a great day. Get some rest, sweetheart, peace, and grace of the Lord. Be with you and your mother through Jesus Christ the Lord's name amen. Hugs and kisses from your Zorro

Beautiful, Guardian Angel precious treasure from the North country. God loves you. I love you. Your mother loves you. Bugs Bunny loves you. The Easter Bunny loves you. LOL, smile, and most importantly, I love you. So take that. LOL smile. I could just kiss you, and I could just hold you, and I could just give you a nice massage and say romantic things to you because to the grace of God and the Holy Spirit working through me, that's what I am supposed to do. Hugs and kisses from your Zorro

Did you change your name? LOL smiling and laughing. Go back to sleep, sweetheart.

Thomas wrote;

Beautiful Guardian Angel. Thank you, I just got myself, and I am watching a ministry program constantly learning more and more.

Honey, sweetheart, scrumptious my tasty little morsel my splendid little delight from the North country my treasure. I could have more fun with this one than a barrel of monkeys. LOL, smile. I could keep going on and on and on. I understand, beautiful. Remember our unconditional love? Well, with the trust and honesty issue as far as developing a relationship, that matters.

Just put yourself in my shoes with your toes pointed in the wrong direction? Laughing so hard.

Beautiful, you and I both know in our hearts that God put us together in a miraculous way. And let me say this to you once again, I want you to be free and want you to be happy. I do not want to own you or control you in any way. Just a quote in the Bible that says, "what God has put together let no man take apart." Thank God, hallelujah, praise the Lord, thank you, Jesus pass the blessings. LOL, smile, my girl, my precious Guardian Angel, the treasure from the North country. It is getting to know my sick sense of humor. LOL laughing.

Sweetheart, Beautiful, my precious Guardian Angel treasure from the North country. Everything happens for a reason. And I have to be honest with you, that hurt my feelings. And being a man, it has taken me a while or did take me a while to figure it out. As humans, we always have to jump to conclusions, and they are usually wrong after knowing each other for over a year. And all the miracles God has worked in our lives together from the beginning.

The way this whole house looks now as compared to what it used to look like. Even though your mother and yourself would have a little work to do here, do you know ladies and especially ladies in their own homes? LOL smile with great appreciation, kindness, and care with loving consideration.

To be honest with you, honey, I could not imagine you be with any other man than myself. Like I have mentioned once before, you could break my heart. And that has to be the worst feeling that I could ever imagine. Please let me know how you feel. I am personally inspired through the Holy Spirit and God's will through Jesus Christ our Lord. There is not a doubt in my mind with my unshakable faith that we belong together forever. I will write more when I hear back from you. You are my girl. Do you know it felt good? Is when you said that I was your man. You do not say that too often or at all. Anyway, you just saying those few words, that's what turned my thinking around.

And especially when you brought God into it. You are indeed my girl. And I'm in love with you. Being a man and your man is why I need my better half. That is when we will be blessed abundantly. Our home will no longer be divided amongst itself. You will have to admit, sweetheart, it has been hard on both of us because we have not been together.

And I realize you had this trip planned a long time ago. I remember when your mother was in Calgary. And I'm not sure how long that has been sent. Has she been away from you? Xoxox from your Zorro

In Isaiah 53:9, the prophet Isaiah wrote about a sinless servant (the Messiah) being put to death with the wicked and buried with the rich. This was among the many details that Isaiah prophesied about in regards to the Messiah. About 700 years after Isaiah recorded this prophecy, Jesus was put to death along with two criminals and was buried in a tomb owned by a wealthy man, Joseph of Arimathea, as explained in Matthew 27:57-61, Mark 15:42-47, Luke 23:50:56, and John 19:38-42. Jesus was resurrected three days later.

Prophecy

"And he made his grave with the wicked, and with the rich in his death; because he had done no violence, neither was any deceit in his mouth." Isaiah 53;9.

Fulfillment

"When the even was come, there came a rich man of Arimathaea, named Joseph, who also himself was Jesus' disciple: He went to Pilate and begged the body of Jesus. Then Pilate commanded the body to be delivered. And when Joseph had taken the body, he wrapped it in a clean linen cloth, And laid it in his new tomb, which he had hewn out in the rock: and he rolled a great stone to the door of the tomb, and departed." Matthew 27; 57-60.

Joseph went boldly to Pilate and begged from him the body of Jesus. For the first time, Pilate learned that Jesus was dead. Conflicting reports had reached him regarding the events attending the crucifixion, but the knowledge of Christ's death had been purposely kept from him. Pilate had been warned by the priests and rulers against deception by Christ's disciples regarding His body. Upon hearing Joseph's request, he, therefore, sent for the centurion who had charged at the cross and learned for a certainty of the death of Jesus. He also drew from him an account of the scenes of Calvary, confirming the testimony of Joseph.

The request of Joseph was granted. While John was troubled about the burial of his Master, Joseph returned with Pilate's order for the body of Christ; and Nicodemus came bringing a costly mixture of myrrh and aloes, of about a hundred pounds weight, for His embalming. The most honored in all Jerusalem could not have been shown more respect in death. The disciples were astonished to see these wealthy rulers as much interested as they in the burial of their Lord.

Neither Joseph nor Nicodemus had openly accepted the Savior while He was living. They knew that such a step would exclude them from the Sanhedrin, and they hoped to protect Him by their influence in its councils. For a time, they had seemed to succeed; but the wily priests, seeing their favor to Christ, had thwarted their plans. In their absence, Jesus had been condemned and delivered to be crucified. Now that He was dead, they no longer concealed their attachment to Him. While the disciples feared to show themselves openly as His followers, Joseph and Nicodemus came boldly to their aid. The help of these prosperous and honored men was greatly needed at this time. They could do for their dead Master what the poor disciples couldn't do, and their wealth and influence protected them, in a great measure, from the malice of the priests and rulers.

Gently and reverently, they removed with their own hands the body of Jesus from the cross. Their tears of sympathy fell fast as they looked upon His bruised and lacerated form. Joseph owned a new tomb, hewn in a rock. He was reserving for himself, but it was near Calvary, and he now prepared it for Jesus. Together with the spices brought by Nicodemus, the body was carefully wrapped in a linen sheet, and the Redeemer was borne to the tomb. There the three disciples straightened the mangled limbs and folded the bruised hands upon the pulseless breast. The Galilean women came to see that all had been done that could be done for the lifeless form of their beloved Teacher. Then they saw the heavy stone rolled against the tomb entrance, and the Savior was left at rest. The women were last at the cross and lasted at the tomb of Christ. While the evening shades were gathering, Mary Magdalene and the other Marys lingered about the resting place of their Lord, shedding tears of sorrow over the fate of Him whom they loved. "And they returned, . . . and rested the Sabbath day according to the commandment." Luke 23; 56.

23 April 2019

Thomas wrote;

> *Morning my Love.*
>
> *I love you so much, honey. You're my girl, my precious Guardian Angel. Beautiful Guardian Angel precious treasure from the North country. There are promises that husband and wife should make to one another. This husband will make this promise to this wife, this God-given wife. That that thought will never cross my mind again, believe me when I tell you this, honey. You're my girl and your mother, Anna. I want to show the love and respect that I would have liked to give my mother when she was still alive. I just would like the opportunity to accept this Love from God graciously. This I pray for. Of course, my prayers will go unanswered. Unless my wife feels that she can forgive her husband? I love your gentle hugs and soft kisses whispering romantic words into my wife's ear.*
>
> *Beautiful, is there anything you need? I am your trusted humble servant, and I am at your beck and call. I feel so embarrassed and humiliated and heartsick. Can you please forgive me? I would like your forgiveness for God to answer my prayers. Thank you, honey, if you find it in your heart to do so. God, I love this Guardian Angel so much. Please, God, I beg for your forgiveness, and I beg for my wife's forgiveness. I pray this prayer that this husband's wife hears this prayer. I feel so bad.*

Thomas wrote;

> *Beautiful precious Guardian Angel, the God-given treasure from the North country. Sweetheart, I will never ask that question again because I know better. I knew better than to ask it. As I said, I need a good beating once in a while. Big LOL laughing hard and possibly running and jumping under the bed to hide from you. That's how embarrassed I feel. LOL laughing hard. That is insulting my wife's intelligence. That's the way I think, honey. How are you feeling today? Other than me making you feel bad.*
>
> *That does not make me much of a man for this beautiful Guardian Angel God has sent to me. I just love you. Like I have met you before, you are my better half. You are the air beneath my wings. You're my inspiration, and I could never live without you in my life. I'm so mad at myself, and I'm also angry at myself. I think I will slam myself on the*

ground, kick myself in the face taking all my teeth out, then supergluing them back in. Pick me up and looked normal. I am laughing harder. See what you do to me? It's all your fault, honey, big smile, just like a man has to blame it on his wife. I feel so foolish, and you're right. It is beyond embarrassing. Honey, if I ever asked you that question again. I do not make promises because promises are made to be broken. Because we are not perfect. But there are specific promises that a husband and wife should make to each other. In this, I promise you, honey, I will never ask you that question again.

That is disrespecting God's Love. And for this disrespect is a reason God will not answer my prayers. So I not only ask you for forgiveness, will you please ask your mother for my forgiveness and pray for me for God's forgiveness through Jesus Christ our Lord's name and the Holy Spirit that works through us. I love you so much, beautiful. Please let your mother know every time you communicate with her once again that I pray for her.

Hugs and kisses. You made my day, honey. Now let me run back and get under the bed and hide. Just in case you and your mother should walk to the front door right now. I do not want to be around. Laughing hard, I humble myself with forgiveness to you, honey.

Beautiful, it is my man thinking, can you please forgive me? And the one- horned one-eyed flying purple people eater. LOL, smile you said, where the hell did I get that? LOL, laughing, you answered the question. From hell, where else would that come from. LOL, you make me laugh. You know we were made for each other. You realize that all the time, and somehow in God only knows why. You are far more intelligent than I am, and I miss my wife's intuition. I love you so much, honey. I'm in love with your soul; I love your intuition that is your knowledge and wisdom. I'm in love with your heart; I keep it next to mine all the time. I'm drawn to your spirit with the love that has no beginning or no end. Because you are my girl, my special guardian angel girl, the treasure from the North country. And your mother is such a gracious, honorable lady to have had such a precious daughter. Our fathers drew us together. And through your mother's prayers, mine and yours. It is the only reason we came together through the Holy Spirit, and God answered all of our prayers.

I will never ask that question again, and I knew when I ask it. It was so stupid of me. I took God out of the equation. And I thank God for you in my life to slap in the face once in a while, kick me in the groins, tie me up, gag me, and whip me with the belt, and possibly put a rope around my neck, and pulled me slowly up to the ceiling, letting me direct back down when I turn purple. No wonder that is your favorite color, LOL laughing you want to watch me turn purple, don't you? This is the reason I ask stupid questions. To protect myself get tortured by his wife. And turn purple. Laughing hard, see what you do to me, sweetheart. You are so precious xoxox from your husband. You are my scrumptious wife. With a mother that is so gracious. I love you, honey

Beautiful, it hurt my feelings, and I will be honest with you when you sent me that email that said Jimmy so and so on it. I love only you, and you are all I will ever love. You are my wife for the rest of our life, and we have a long beautiful life ahead of us with your mother's hugs and kisses. I just wanted to get this off to please do not feel that I would ever think of another lady, and you're right. It is insulting to ask that question. I just had to because thinking of you with another man would break my heart to pieces hugs and kisses.

Sweetheart, since your favorite color is purple, I would wonder if you have ever heard of "a one-eyed one-horned flying purple people eater"? LOL, smile laughing. Sometimes it's not what we know. It's who we know, and the combination of the 2 Can Take us places through the Holy Spirit that we could never imagine miraculously. Another thing, honey, I would like to ask you a favor, please?. If you ever get involved with another man, could you please let me know? I would certainly appreciate it. Peace and grace of the Lord be with you and your mother through Jesus Christ the Lord's name amen xoxo beautiful I would never be who I am today if it were not for you, and I keep growing spiritually, and for that, I thank you as my guardian angel. You're a brilliant young beautiful lady, and I'm proud of you. You will always be my girl.

A man recently asked me about a troubling verse. "My wife says my prayers are hindered because I don't respect her enough." He was referring to this verse:

Husbands, in the same way, be considerate as you live with your wives and treat them with respect as the weaker partner and as heirs with you of the gracious gift of life so that nothing will hinder your prayers. (1 Peter 3:7) What does it mean to hinder your prayers? Here is the wrong answer: "God doesn't listen to jerks."

The good news is that God does hear the honest prayers of jerks and crooks and thieves and sinners (see Luke 18:14). If you see yourself as a bad husband or a bad wife, be assured your heavenly Father hears you when you call to him. How do I know? Because no one is beyond the reach of his love and grace.

So how do we hinder our prayers?

When I was asked that question, I was momentarily stumped. It wasn't a question I had thought about, but I probably should have since I am a husband. What can I do to my wife that might hinder my prayers? Immediately, the Lord brought a picture to my mind that helped me understand this verse. His revelation showed me exactly how husbands (or wives or anyone) can hinder their prayers. But before I took it any further, I wanted to check what other commentators said about hindered prayers to confirm that I was on the right track. Guess what — they say nothing. I went to all my favorite guys and found they were silent on the subject of hindered prayers.

So I feel very blessed as though the Lord has given me a little gift to share with you, a revelation you may not find anywhere else. (Of course, I could be wrong, and this verse is so apparent that you already know what I'm going to say about hindered prayers. If so, come back next week. It'll be better, I promise.)

Thomas wrote;

Beautiful, precious Guardian Angel, a treasure from the North country with whom I am in love. Thomas studied most of the day, preparing for theology classes and preparing for this Sunday's ministry. Annie was busy in the kitchen preparing Thomas's dinner. Thomas was starving, and his wife DiAnnie prepared a very eloquent meal for Thomas. Annie treated her husband Thomas like a king. And she said to her husband, please sit down. I have prepared something special for you this evening. DiAnnie said it was a special French dish of eloquent cuisine. And that it would be very pleasant to the pallet and Thomas would enjoy the meal immensely. Thomas was anxious to taste this delicious meal that DiAnnie had prepared for her husband, Thomas. Annie had spent many hours preparing these meals, especially for her loved husband. It was greamy grimy golfer guts, mutilated monkey meat, saturated chicken feet, and a great big glass of all-purpose porpoise puss. Annie made a pate, putting it all through the meat-grinder placing the ingredients on crackers to start with the hors d'oeuvres. Thomas complimented his wife DiAnnie for preparing such an elegant meal. Not knowing why DiAnnie was grinning from ear to ear, watching and pleasant delight of her husband Thomas enjoying the hors d'oeuvres. And occasionally taking a drink of the all-purpose porpoise puss. LOL laughing hard. I pray to God you enjoyed preparing this meal for me. After hors d'oeuvres, I wondered why you had me brush my teeth several times and gargle with mouthwash three or four times. Before you would come near me. LOL :-) did you enjoy preparing this meal? As much as I enjoyed eating it? I had to start with something. That was fun.

I love you, honey, you're my girl, and you always will be. As I was reading today and praying to God, I realized how strong of a bond our love is for one another through the grace of God. And if I had not asked that stupid question. I may not have known. I'm not sure you feel the same way. Or if you're ever going to speak to me again. That would break my heart to pieces.

When I was going to college, I had studied anthropology which is the study of mankind, and the human psychology and philosophy of why we are the way we are. I found it to be an exciting class. I will give you a, for instance, and I'm sure you know of a few people like this that are narcissistic. "The reflective love of self" there never has been one known cure for this psychological disorder that occurs in 1/10 people. And most of our psychology comes from Greek mythology. As strange as that might sound. Narcissus rejected the nymph, Nemeses' Love. And for doing so, the God Zeus. Made Narcissus look into a pool of water for eternity. Selfish people are very arrogant, and there's nothing you cannot tell them because they know everything. That is the main characteristic of a selfish person.

Also, and I was a little in disbelief when I first heard this in an anthropology class. The number one abuse of children is that a mother left alone with her children will inevitably hurt them. This is true. And the reason is. Usually, the husband leaves the wife for another woman or defiles their marriage in some way. And this is the mother's way of getting back with the husband, having to take care of the children with no money, no child support, no way of making a living. She hurts her children out of anger for what her husband has done to her. And subconsciously a way of possibly having the children taken away from her so that they might find a better home.

And I have said this to you before, that ladies are far more intelligent than men for the simple reason they have intuition, feelings, and emotions that men do not have. And the ladies thanks with both sides of her brain where a man only things with one side. Ladies have learned to develop that intuitive side for survival of not only themselves but also their children. if you tell, a man so-and-so died. The man usually says, oh, that's too bad. And that's that. Not a lady. They cry about it. They get their support group together and talk about it and mourn the death of a loved one or friend. The only trouble with the lady support group, which is not always true, Is that ladies will usually listen to the sickest lady in the bunch. And get some really bad advice.

I still intend on working on that book called the greatest story ever told. Because I know so much about the Bible, and that's only thanks to you. Then when I realize that you did love me. Being a man, I was still in disbelief. And you know it before I did how much love you have for me. I have to be reminded once and well, honey. And God helps me. I do not mean to hurt my wife's feelings. I love this precious Guardian Angel so much. We have love together that God has given to both of us only through his grace.

And when I mentioned to you, and I should have reworded that I said it wrong. I'm just a man, and that is no excuse for treating his wife with disrespect and hurting her feelings. You are a. great teacher, honey. God, I love this woman. When I was in the store in San Francisco, I mentioned ladies wanting to be around married men. And the reason I feel is that ladies feel safe around a married man if they know that man is not going to hit on them. In one place, I can express my love for you in public to others in such places as stores. And I always praise you highly. I set my wife was sent from God as my guardian angel. Right away, everybody's ears pick up. Nobody says that kind of thing. I praise you very highly, and I get respect for doing so.

And I say things like, God brought my wife and me together because God's Love has no beginning and God's Love has no end, and my wife and I are learning how to tap in that kind of love for our marriage. It is the only opportunity I have two talks about you like that in public. It was a great feeling, and I await not only to spread Christianity but the Love that God has for you and me together. And I find that the young saleslady's and those stores gather around me because they are curious and want to know more about that love that I have for my wife. I cannot express that love like that to my family just yet. And that was the first opportunity I had to express my love for you and public honey. It felt good. And more shall be revealed.

1 Peter 3; 7 – Husbands, in the same way, be considerate as you live with your wives and treat them with respect as the weaker partner and as errors with you of the gracious gift of life so that nothing will hinder your prayers.

Our life is a gift from God. What we do with this life is our gift to God. I thank God for this guardian angel brought into my life to have carried me through the gates into heaven as we continue to grow along spiritual lines. Please, beautiful nature, and let your mother know that my prayers are with you and her and that I need your mother's prayers as well as yours because I'm in love with you. You're my girl. Hugs and kisses from your Zorro

Genesis 1:27-28: "So God created man in his image, in the image of God he created him; male and female he created them. And God blessed them. And God said to them, 'Be fruitful and multiply and fill the earth and subdue it and have dominion over the fish of the sea and the birds of the heavens and over every living thing that moves on the earth.'"

Malachi 2:14-15: "But you say, 'Why does he not?' Because the LORD was witness between you and the wife of your youth, to whom you have been faithless, though she is your companion and your wife by covenant."

Isaiah 54:5: "For your Maker is your husband, the LORD of hosts is his name; and the Holy One of Israel is your Redeemer, the God of the whole earth he is called."

Song of Solomon 8:6-7: "Set me as a seal upon your heart, as a seal upon your arm, for love is strong as death. Jealousy is fierce as the grave. Its flashes are flashes of fire, the very flame of the LORD. Many waters cannot quench love, neither can floods drown it. If a man offered for love all the wealth of his house, he would be utterly despised."

Ephesians 4:2-3: "With all humility and gentleness, with patience, bearing with one another in love, eager to maintain the unity of the Spirit in the bond of peace."

Colossians 3:14: "And over all these virtues put on love, which binds them all together in perfect unity."

Ecclesiastes 4:9: "Two are better than one because they have a good return for their labor: If either of them falls, one can help the other up. But pity anyone who falls and has no one to help them up. Also, if two lies down together, they will keep warm. But how can one keep warm alone?" Ephesians 5:25: "For husbands, this means love your wives, just as Christ loved the church. He gave up his life for her."

Genesis 2:24: "Therefore a man shall leave his father and his mother and hold fast to his wife, and they shall become one flesh."

Ecclesiastes 4:12: "Though one may be overpowered, two can defend themselves. A cord of three strands is not quickly broken."

Mark 10:9: "Therefore what God has joined together, let no one separate." Ephesians 5:25-33: "Husbands, love your wives, as Christ loved the church and gave himself up for her, that he might sanctify her, having cleansed her by the washing of water with the word, so that he might present the church to himself in splendor, without spot or wrinkle or any such thing, that she might be holy and without blemish. In the same way, husbands should love their wives as their bodies. He who loves his wife loves himself. For no one ever hated his flesh, but nourishes and cherishes it, just as Christ does the church, ..."

Bible Verses About Love

The Bible has a lot to say about the bonds of love and devotion. Bible verses about love speak of the perfect love that everyone should have toward their friends, family, and mankind, not to mention the Lord. However, Bible verses about love also reveal the strength and hope that romantic love can provide. It can be challenging to put your feelings for one another into words, but these Bible verses about love seem to capture its essence just right.

Romans 13:8: "Owe no one anything, except to love each other, for the one who loves another has fulfilled the law."

1 Corinthians 13:4-5: "Love is patient, love is kind. It does not envy. It does not boast. It is not proud. It does not dishonor others. It is not self-seeking, it is not easily angered, it keeps no record of wrongs."

1 Corinthians 13:2: "If I have the gift of prophecy and can fathom all mysteries and all knowledge, and if I have a faith that can move mountains, but does not have love, I am nothing."

1 Corinthians 16:14: "Do everything in love."

Song of Solomon 8:7: "Many waters cannot quench love; rivers cannot wash it away. If one were to give all the wealth of his house for love, it would be utterly scorned."

Psalm 143:8: "Let the morning bring me word of your unfailing love, for I have put my trust in you. Show me the way I should go, for to you, I entrust my life."

Proverbs 3:3-4: "Let love and faithfulness never leave you; bind them around your neck, write them on the tablet of your heart. Then you will win favor and a good name in the sight of God and man."

1 John 4:16: "And so we know and rely on the Love God has for us. God is Love. Whoever lives in love lives in God, and God in them."

Ephesians 4:2: "Be completely humble and gentle; be patient, bearing with one another in love."

1 Peter 4:8: "Above all, love each other deeply because love covers over a multitude of sins."

John 15:12: "My command is this: Love each other as I have loved you."

1 Corinthians 13:13: "And now these three remain: faith, hope, and love. But the greatest of these is love."

Song of Solomon 4:9: "You have captivated my heart, my sister, my bride; you have captivated my heart with one glance of your eyes, with one jewel of your necklace."

Bible Verses About Relationships

No relationship manual tells you how to overcome obstacles and strengthen your ties with your loved ones (but Lasting can help). Thankfully, Bible verses about love serve as excellent guides; these scriptures offer jewels of wisdom that can help you navigate the ups and downs of love, as well as convey your heartfelt thoughts to your future spouse. There are a number of wedding scriptures and Bible verses about love that touch on the subject of relationships that you may want to mention on your wedding day. Hebrews 10:24-25: "And let us consider how we may spur one another on toward love and good deeds, not giving up meeting together, as some are in the habit of doing, but encouraging one another—and all the more as you see the Day approaching."

Proverbs 30:18-19: "There are three things that amaze me—no, four things that I don't understand: how an eagle glides through the sky, how a snake slithers on a rock, how a ship navigates the ocean, how a man loves a woman."

1 John 4:12: "No one has ever seen God; but if we love one another, God lives in us, and his love is made complete in us."

Proverbs 31:10: "Who can find a virtuous woman? for her price is far above rubies."

Ruth 1:16-17: "Entreat me not to leave you, Or to turn back from following after you; For wherever you go, I will go; And wherever you lodge, I will lodge; Your people shall be my people, And your God, my God. Where you die, I will die, And there will I be buried. The Lord do so to me, and more also, If anything but death parts you and me."

Romans 12:10: "Be devoted to one another in love. Honor one another above yourselves."

1 Peter 4:8: "Most important of all, continue to show deep love for each other, for love covers a multitude of sins."

Ephesians 5:21: "Submit to one another out of reverence for Christ." Ephesians 4:32: "Be kind to each other, tenderhearted, forgiving one another, just as God through Christ has forgiven you."

Genesis 2:18–25: "Then the LORD God said, 'It is not good that the man should be alone; I will make him a helper fit for him.' ... So the LORD God caused a deep sleep to fall upon the man, and while he slept, took one of his ribs and closed up its place with flesh. And the rib that the LORD God had taken from the man he made into a woman and brought her to the man."

1 Peter 3:7: "In the same way, you husbands must give honor to your wives. Treat your wife with understanding as you live together. She may be weaker than you are, but she is your equal partner in God's gift of new life. Treat her as you should so your prayers will not be hindered."

DiAnnie wrote;

Good morning my love, how are you this morning? I hope you had a great night. Mine was also great. I was so exhausted last night, that's why I decided to wait until this morning to write you back, so I am messaging back here. Thanks for sharing the story of Jesus with me once again, you make it sound so interesting, and I like that. It is a renewal of my faith, so what can't you become a preacher instead of just writing? I ask again because you are so good, and your presentation of the story of Jesus sounds so simple to me not many preachers can do just as you did.

You make me smile whenever I read with all does names that you called me. You know how to make someone happy I'm here smiling :-) you are a very fun-loving person, and I so appreciate that about you. It makes me love you more and more. You pray for my mom and me each time tells me a lot about your character. I haven't heard about a *one-eyed one-horned flying purple people eater, you silly man. LOL, what's the hell is that? LOL. You will surely kill me with all these jokes. When reading your messages, I laugh so hard, and people would think I'm going crazy. LOL. Sure I agree with you. Sometimes in life, it's not what we know but who we know. That's just the fact about life. I was so happy reading your lovely messages. Have a nice day—regards from me.*

24 April 2019

DiAnnie wrote;

Hi Thomas, first I like to tell you that I'm okay, nothing happened to me. I have been thinking so much about that question you asked me, and honestly, I haven't been feeling right. I talked about this with my mom, and she said something I wasn't happy about. She sounded as if she was behind you. I explained what happened before you asked the question, and she said anyone would have asked me the same thing.

Especially if that person loves me truly, to tell you the truth, I have been angry with the two of you, and since I last wrote you, I haven't talked to Mom as well because I know I told the truth and the two of you do not think I had the right to express myself. I thought things over, and I decided to move to reason as a mature person.

I shouldn't have been angry about this because I now realize if it were me, I would ask as well, if I will be mad at you or Mom, then it's not fair. Mom thinks I'm busy. That's why I haven't written yet, but it's not like I have been that busy. As a child of God, we must forgive, and it this not a big deal to keep things in my heart.

So once again, I have forgiven you and her and hope you can do the same for having you worried about not hearing from me.

You guys must be busy again on the house. The curtains will be another work. If the purple color is cute no need for us to change it to gray, I know, by all means, Mom and I will still have some work to do on the house. You make me laugh Zorro, you told me the clear place you had, and out of a sudden, you're carrying on a huge development on the house.. lol.. so if I weren't coming?

Meaning the house was going to stay that way.. lol I just like you because you say the truth each time. Please stay that way, okay? True love does not look at many material things, but the inside doesn't worry about if your house wasn't heaven. We can still work together and make it better. So let's pray for the best. We will never be broken apart. We can bend but not be broken apart because our bond is more profound than what may come against us. It is more profound than how people see it. We have so much in common, my love. Well, I didn't say you are giving an ultimatum. You're just concerned. Having you here isn't bad either. It's how you would make me feel somehow.

Your sick sense of humor got me laughing and smiling all the time. You just know how to contact me. Right? Sleep well till I hear from you, my love. All my love and prayers and, of course, kisses and hugs to you. Bon Nuit.

Thomas wrote;

Beautiful when you fly from Europe. First of all me say this how are you doing? How are you feeling? How is your mother doing? How is your mother feeling? To my precious Guardian Angel, my delightful, scrumptious treasure from the North country. I have more fun saying those words. As I was saying, when you and your mother fly from Europe, keep in mind you're flying to your home in Arizona. Right? Please let your mother know that for my safety, LOL, I may kidnap Anna and keep her here forever with us for my protection from my beautiful wife. LOL laughing. I believe, honey, you and your mother are just going to love this house that will become a home the moment you step into it. It will then become you and your mother's home as well as our home as a family.

There's so much you do not tell me about yourself for well over a year now. My life is an open book. I will tell you every little detail and every person I contact and why I am coming into contact with them. Because I do not want any doubts in your mind, it should be a sincere, open relationship, especially between a husband and his wife. I'm not sure if you live in an apartment?

Sharing a room with somebody? Renting a room from somebody? How big is it? Etc. etc. etc., and for the first time, you mentioned giving a coworker my telephone number. I would have liked to have known that sooner. Just because I love you, I care about you, and you are my best friend in the whole wide world.

There is no one else but you in my life other than your mother and brother Brian. The only difference between you and I, Brian and your mother, Anna. Is that our communication between one another we know came from God. And should be built on that Christian foundation of honesty, trust, forgiveness, love, consideration, kindness, and all the other good things that go into a relationship, especially a marriage. I love you so much, honey.

You are my girl. So please do not take anything I say offensive, and I pray to God you understand why I am asking a few questions. And it is like putting the cart before the horse at this point. It's no big deal other than I care about you and love you, and I want to be a part of your life no matter where you were or who you are with. Can you understand that? With love for your husband?

Let me suggest another very important reason I should know these things about you that I have a question about for the simple reason that when you and your mother get here. And after a while when your tummy starts to protrude. Family members are going to want to know why? LOL :-) with their toes pointed in the wrong direction, no, let me take that back with the toes pointed in the right direction.

They are going to be full of a lot of questions. And if I do not know the answer to those questions. Well, you understand what I'm saying, right? There's nothing I do not want to know about you; I want to know everything about you. And please take your time and have patience. I do not need to know the answer to these questions yet, just slowly but surely if you would care to volunteer some information to me as very best friends. And as a wife to her husband. There's not much about myself I have not told you about. And if you're in question, I gave you two autobiographies of myself that would know about myself in detail and my relationship with God because you and I both know that our relationship started with God introducing us to each other without a doubt—knowing that his time was just right. And we were the right to man-woman that God chose for each other.

Before we knew it, God knew it. God also knows I needed a guardian angel in my life and all the right ways. Of course, I cannot tell people other than yourself only. And always will be. And let me say this about that. That was in addition. I had no idea how I would rid myself of that dreadful stronghold in the grips that Satan had on me. Until you came along, and it did not take me long to know that you were a guardian angel sent from God.

You may not have understood that at the time. But when it hit me like it sledgehammers in the head. I cried, and I called, and I thank God, and I think God and I love the way we came about in each other's lives. And more shall be revealed, honey. This not only has to do with you and me, but it also plays a part in your mother's life that is very important. And also our children. And everyone's lives that you and I touch.

They are going to know they have just witnessed a miracle. That could have only come from God. And more shall be revealed as we go through this happy destiny called life and the path God has chosen for us. And we have been struggling, sweetheart. And I'm sure your mother as well. When this house is not divided anymore, I will not have to think of you the way I do now, spending so much of my life doing so.

But it is God's time, and it is the right time to do that. It allows me to read a lot of Scripture and continuously study the Bible, as I do daily ever since I met you. God is preparing us for something great.

Believe me. I know this is true, with my unshakeable faith in the love I have for God our Father through Jesus Christ, his only son our Lord, and the Holy Spirit that works through us to help others. If we are of this world, we belong to Satan. If we are of the spiritual world and are of God, we are of heaven and all the blessings that heaven has to offer us here on earth.

We are going to work together as a team. We cannot worry about it at this point. We most certainly can think about it and dream about it, and pray about it. Trust me, honey, and believe in me. I know this with my unshakeable faith for a fact. I will have so much more time after the education God has prepared me for. To be devoted to my wife's family and career.

Finally, and the love you have for me. I will show it to you through the abundance of blessings God will shower us with. You trust me, don't you, honey? Believe me. I know this because the Bible tells me so. Blessings in abundance. Please make sure and let your mother, Anna know that my prayers are with her, and I think her for being your mother. And let your mother know that you came into my life as a guardian angel sent from God because of the daughter you are. You let your mother know that if you have not already, let her know.

I love you so much, honey. Peace and grace of the Lord be with you and your mother through Jesus Christ the Lord's name amen. Xoxox from your Zorro. Have a good day, sweetheart.

Thomas wrote;

Beautiful, all of a sudden, I am Thomas and not my love? LOL laughing, you are still angry, aren't we? And I have forgotten all about that until you just brought it up, my love. Smiling, you're my girl. You are my precious guardian angel, my treasure from the North country. And yes, you're right, as usual, I was concerned about your missing in action. LOL smile. The lack of communication draws the heart further apart. Thank God for Anna. Thank you, Jesus, for Anna. Thank you, DiAnnie, for having a mother like Anna. I can see your mother's knowledge and wisdom and her daughter Annie. Slightly a little more developed in years. Although I'm still in love with my girl, my guardian angel. Because this young lady has made me who I am today. And has brought my soul to the gates of heaven. And this I always pray to God and thank God for you in my life. To become my wife and possibly, create a grandmother in your mother and make her the happiest mother alive. Of course, there will be two happy mothers DiAnnie and Anna. Then there will be 1/3 father even happier for all of these beautiful souls in my life. Sweetheart, one thing if you agree. Whether we have a daughter or son. That their middle name is Zorro. Now, what do you think?

sweetheart scrumptious, my curious little girl. Smiling

: All I know is you are my girl, my wife, and we will be together the rest of our lives. Once again, beautiful, will you marry me? You make me laugh. I'm not going to pour salt on the wound continuously. LOL :-) you funny girl. My beautiful young lovely wife. My precious Guardian Angel, my scrumptious delight, my tasty little morsel beautiful young lady from the North country, the treasure of my life. You're very exquisite, very elegant. And a tasty little morsel. Of whom I would be delighted to entertain the opportunity of pleasing my pallet. And I give great thanks and appreciation and love to the MasterChef, God our Father.

All I can say is thank God that a coworker has my telephone number. That makes me feel a lot better, sweetheart, and your good life could show up at any moment. There are some things we are not just in control of. That's why we pray. By the way, when mistakes off the top of my head when I'm thinking of God, all the time. There is so much to that sermon I want to say to you, and I will. I surprised myself by not knowing how much I knew about the word of God in the Bible until I explained that sermon to you.

Once again, you brought me to some spiritual growth that more was revealed to me. And I thank God, and I think you. No worries, no stress. Thank God for your mother coming to stay with us, LOL :-) to protect me from you. LOL, double smiling and laughing. My God, my wife, DiAnnie, will hang me for hours up in the ceiling until I turn her favorite color purple. Laughing laughing. You make sure and let your mother know that I thanked her profusely. For being on my side and rightfully so with righteous indignation. I just love Anna and a mother-to-son-in-law way. LOL, thank you, Jesus. You be nice to your mother now, and I mean it. She is a precious soul.

I'm so excited about your trip, sweetheart. I'm excited for you. Finally, you and I have been doing all this preparation and running around, although you have been the mastermind behind this. And that's my Marine Corps wife. That is the wife of a sergeant in the United States Marine Corps. As my wife, DiAnnie. And my wife and I are growing and learning to have a love that has no beginning and no end, and there will never be one harsh word between us. Right? Did I say right? LOL smiling and laughing.

About what I was going to say in that sermon, change. It is the thief that they set free and crucified Jesus instead. It was not the name Judas. But it was the name, Barnabas. Only Satan will twist the Bible around and make mistakes to trick us. But if we know the Bible. As Christ told Satan, every time, Christ was tempted. Jesus Christ the Lord would say, "for it is written." Like when Satan was tempting Jesus in the garden for 40 days. The devil said to Jesus one time, "throw yourself down off this temple." The Angels have charge over you. What the devil left out of that verse is, "in all thy ways." And Jesus said every time, it is written. The devil will never know the word of God. Unless we know the word of God, the devil will be able to trick us. There was so much to the greatest story ever told, and I have so much. Like I have mentioned before, I have not even scratched the surface of how much I know of the Bible. And that is all thanks to you that made me realize that. Please let me know, sweetheart, whenever you are ready for another sermon. "The greatest story ever told." I just love you.

I just want to keep my mouth on you. How can you keep your mouth off of me that long? LOL smiling with frustration and concern for where oh where could my little wife be? Where oh where could she be? Was my wife hiding from me? LOL laughing. My wife is going to hang me. Aren't you, sweetheart? LOL, you make me laugh. And then I have to make you laugh. And that's the way we should live our life together. The unfortunate thing about that is what makes me laugh is when you get angry at me.

That's when I start laughing hard. Especially at one time before you hung up the phone on me. I forget what that was about. I remember calling you right back and leaving a message. I think I left several messages. Wanting to know your mother's telephone number so that I could call her, and I ask you to make sure she had an interpreter. Do you remember that beautiful?

You are so angry with me and hung up the phone on me. But maybe laugh is how fast you can talk. Laughing harder. I never knew anybody in my life could say that many words that fast. LOL laughing. I'm laughing now, just thinking about it. I must be sick. LOL, I'm laughing hard when my wife is angry.? There might be something wrong with my brain. LOL, laughing harder. And. Al, your fault honey. See what you do to me.

You are mean mean mean you are a mean Marines wife. Torture your poor husband. Laughing harder. Until he turns your favorite color. "Purple." LOL, no wonder your favorite color is purple. I am going to be seeing a lot of that color and more ways than one. I have the unfortunate feeling. LOL laughing hard. You are so tasty. I will kiss you real slowly and softly and gently, just like I have a stick of cotton candy. Smile with great anticipation, love, and compassion.

Honey, how long can I keep my mouth on you? Smiling now that you finally open your mouth and decided to calm down. Now I am laughing hard. You're right. I am sick, sick, sick, sick. Laughing harder. We are going to have fun together, honey. And we may do a lot of pretending, and I may torment you and to bringing you right to angry. I will be laughing so hard that I will become weak, and you will beat the hell out of me. And for some reason, it makes me laugh harder to thinking about that. I would be having so much fun and laughing so hard I could not even tell your mother. For the simple reason, she would not understand. The unhealthy relationship between her beautiful young daughter and this good-looking Marine has developed.

I love you, honey. I am in love with you. Don't you want to know what size ring I wear? Laughing harder. Not the ring you're going to put around my neck. LOL, that ring is going to get tightened up from slipping over my head around my neck pulled up to the ceiling until I turn purple. Quit this. I'm laughing so hard and ready to fall on the floor.

Good night honey, no worries, no stress. How long are you in your mother going to be in Europe before you come to Arizona? Can you give me some kind of idea? Will you be able to keep me updated from time to time? I just want to know how much time I have left to work on this house. Because my nephew Samuel is supposed to come down in about a week or two weeks, and he will be staying with me for a couple of weeks. To paint and repair the outside of the house, so it looks beautiful for you and your mother. And yes, you are right again. Brian and I are working on the house. And you are right again. This house was most certainly at the clean home that I initially had mentioned to you.

And that's embarrassing. I just pray to God that you and your mother like how this bachelor has fixed this house up?. Like I mentioned to you before, honey, a woman's cleaning is far different than a man's. Just keep in mind that I have thrown, and I'm not kidding. I would estimate about 2 tons of junk. And fixed a lot of things and replaced many things, and I'm still working on them.

And I would assume that it is going to be from Europe to hear? Or are you both going home first? And then flying from your homes to attend? I love you so much, my precious beautiful wife. Xoxox from your Zorro

Thomas wrote;

Beautiful, how are you doing, sweetheart? And how are you feeling? I pray everything is going well. I assume no news is good news. God willing, this is what I pray for. I understand that you are a very busy, beautiful young lady, exasperated and exhausted, and need all the rest you can get whenever you can get it. I would imagine preparing for your trip to your mother may be psychologically and physically wearing on you. Please know that everything is okay. Please, honey, do not worry or stress. And know in your heart that there is a man in Arizona who loves you and cares about your mother. And I do not ignore God our Father through our Lord that we have been put together for the perfect reason. And you always remember that I love you. When I do not hear from you for this long, I want to know that you are okay. And if there's anything you need or anything I can do for you, please do not hesitate to let me know. Because I care, you are my girl.

And if you decide to call me, I would certainly love to hear your voice. I get so many sales calls every day that I do not pick up my phone unless I listen to a voice left on the answering machine. So if you ever call and get the answering machine, please do not ever feel that I am avoiding you for any reason. If I knew it was you for sure calling me, I would undoubtedly pick up immediately. It's just all the sales calls. And they do not leave a message. They just hang up halfway through the recording. But I have to hear the phone ring quite often during the day.

You realize that if anything ever happened to you and I did not hear from you for quite some time. I would have no one to contact the Montréal. And I would plan a trip to

Montréal on the airplane. I do not even know the restaurant you worked at or the name of it.? Or the address for the telephone number. I believe you feel it is none of it—my business. And I could understand that. Although I think we have developed trust, truth, and honesty in a relationship over the last year. At least I do. Anyway, I would feel better if I knew someone you knew to have my phone number to contact me if anything should happen to you. And if I could contact somebody if I did not hear from you within 72 hours, let's say? I'm not sure how you feel about that. It's just a way of me showing you that I care for you. I would never infringe on your privacy. You are my girl. And I'm in love with you. And I always will be. This love I have never experienced in my life, and I have prayed for it. And it is a gift from God you can come into my life as a guardian angel the way you did. And I feel you cannot deny that yourself. I know you love me, honey. Let me put it this way I care about you enough to know that you're okay?

To try and find you. Possibly if you feel only it would be a good idea to give my number to your mother or close friend. If anything should happen to you, they could contact me and let me know that you are okay? I'm not sure how you feel about that? Have a good day, honey. Get some rest, and if you happen to get this message, just send me a sentence saying you were okay.

I would appreciate that. I'm so in love with you and this Love that God has given to both of us. It should be cherished because it is a miraculous gift only through the grace of God that we will be able to experience his love with one another, God willing. There is no way anybody is going to convince me otherwise. Too many miracles between the two of us that most certainly could not be coincidental. Have a good day, honey. Hugs and kisses from your Zorro

Sweetheart, I just did something for fun. So I am going to start compiling our emails. And start a series of a journey of two soulmates from heaven. What do you think? And sweetheart, please, please, please, please do not feel guilty or pressured or anything of that nature. I have way more time studying and writing because that's what I am as a writer.

At this point in your life, you are working very hard physically, and I'm sure it is mentally challenging. I know because every female in my family, including my mother, my aunts, my sister, every female in my family, and extended family that I have known, has always waited tables. My mother did it for years and years. She loved the tips and the hustle because we all love to work hard in our family. I would love nothing better than to have that opportunity again.

Anyway, I found that to be interesting and give me some incentive to characterize our emails and organize them into a series of short novels. As well as our book, ". Soulmates from heaven". And I am intrigued and interested because of you. To write the book. "The greatest story ever told." And of course, I'm working on one called. "Souls to perdition." There is so much to do as far as writing goes. I spend a lot of time watching and listening to theological documentaries. And, of course, sermons from various ministers throughout the world that are renowned—then thinking about us and communicating with you. Believe it or not, sweetheart, I do keep myself very busy as well as brother Brian. LOL smile. Tomorrow we are going to take down some curtains and put up some curtains. And all I would have to do is get area rugs for the few stains on the rugs. And just leave this whole house as-is.

Of course, continuously cleaning. I'm telling you, honey. Early in our relationship, I was bragging to you about how clean I was in my house. What a joke that was. Talking about embarrassing. And I'm not even going to smile over that one. Well, maybe a tiny smile. And LOL. I'm thinking of just putting up the curtains tomorrow, putting your mother's vanity together, and just keep cleaning the windows inside and out. Order some new towels, red and purple. In some areas, rugs. And all the rest of the drapes in this house, I will wait until you and your mother get here, and we can order them together, or you and your mother can order them. I feel you and your mother should do some interior decorating the way you would like the house or the way you would like your home, I should say. It is your mother's home and your home, and of course, it will become my home as soon as you and your mother make it a home. Does that make sense? We are starting with a small family, but most importantly, God has brought us together. We all thank God profusely through Jesus Christ our Lord's name that the Holy Spirit was able to work through all three of us and bring us together in a miraculous gracious way. I'm in love with you, honey. Hugs and kisses from your Zorro

25 April 2019

Thomas wrote;

My Love

Beautiful, do not compare yourselves amongst yourselves. It's unholy and not biblical. You do realize, of course, when we are going to get to know one another? It is something we have never done as of yet. When we are lying in bed with one another, reminiscing each other's past, these are all the questions that will be answered. This ritual has to be done to go out into our families and community and be a witness to others. In doing this, we will know each other's character defects. We will know one another spiritual gifts. There is nothing we will not know about each other. This way, we can face life together honestly. We can sit here and email each other back and forth back and forth. But until we have intimacy between the two of us, we are not going to know one another. And I will love you like the love I have never had before. And you will be satisfied each and every day we are together. And we will be happy and will be one strong force to reckon with. And we are not of this earth.

That is of Satan. If we walk in the spirit and do God's work together, we will receive abundance showers from heaven. Would you please trust me? We are not going to get greedy. We are not going to get into wanting for everything and anything. We have to have faith and trust in the Lord. And to his work. And this takes patient sometimes. Although in our case. If we both honestly look back on the way we have met. And the changes that have been made in each other's lives because of our meeting one another. and be rigorously honest with one another.

In my heart of hearts, I do not think our abundance will be years down the road. I'm saving every penny I get from now on, sweetheart, for your mother and yourself, flight from wherever you are in the world to our home here. And if I do not start saving now. We will be no more than a house divided amongst itself. We have both struggled long enough. The sooner we get together, the better off we will both be. However, I am so excited about your trip, meeting up with your mother, and traveling abroad. Do not let me repeat. I do not want anything to interfere with that. You are going to get an excellent education, traveling abroad. It is hard for me to explain.

Other than when you get back to the United States. Like we did when we disembarked in Morehead city North Carolina. 5000 Marines got on their knees and kissed the pavement. And not one Marine had to say anything to the other. It was automatic. And life seems to flow a little easier. I love you, honey. I'm in love with my girl, your precious Guardian Angel.

I love you so much, and it would be hard for me to live without you. Peace and grace of the Lord be with you and your mother through Jesus Christ the Lord's name amen. Hugs and kisses from your Zorro

26 April 2019

Thomas wrote;

Grace that heals –. Now Maphibishef, the son of Jonathan, and Jonathan, the son of King Saul. Who was fighting a battle on Mount Gilda Bork? In both King Saul and his son Jonathan were killed. Hearing the news, the nurse. Of Maphibishef grabbed him from his crib and dropped him, and broke both of his ankles, trying to escape from the carnage. Maphibishef.

Now it was common practice in 1000 BC. The new king would come in and kill all the family members and extended family of the previous king. Jonathan was a good friend of King David. Even though King Saul tried to kill David, they were like brothers, continuously hunting him like a dog that pursues a rabbit.

David, a 12-year-old boy, With five smooth stones and a sling, the reason David have five smooth stones, he heard Goliath had four brothers, he was going to kill them all. David was a sheepherder and had practice on occasions killing a lion and a bear with his sling. David also played the harp to soothe his sheep herd.

David killed Goliath. Saul the king, jealous of David,

Now King David was remembering his good friend Jonathan one day and said to Ziva. A paper-shuffling bureaucrat. Is there anyone from the house of Saul that I'm showing kindness? Ziva said, indeed,

The only way you can get to heaven is to confess your sins and forsake them through the blood of Jesus Christ, our Lord, who died on the cross for our sins. But if you do not make amends and forsake your sins, you just have a one-way ticket to hell. You make amends to your sins.

You ask others you have wronged if they could please forgive you? Saying I'm sorry is a cheap word. Give that person the opportunity to either ignore you or not dismiss you. You will find in most cases that when you ask others you have wrong to forgive you, they will grant you forgiveness. Sounds simple, your evil ego and Satan who want to soul. I will tell you continuously do not to do it.

Jesus, who was perfect, caught a harlot and was going to stone her to death. Jesus said, "go and sin no more." And she never did.

Confessing your sin over and over and thinking you are forgiven. Without confessing your sin, you must forsake your sin. And not do it anymore.

Forgiveness emotional prison they have built, you become it's the only prisoner. And you live your life cheated of the grace of God.

Forgiveness is a golden key that unlocks the handcuffs of hatred. And opens the door of resentment. Forgiveness, you do not have to associate yourself with that person, you do not have to be their doormat, begins with an act of your conscious will, is not an emotional thing. You do it from the active choice. And once you learn to do that, God will let the poison within your soul escape. And you will feel the amazing grace of God. You can walk out of that emotional hell swimming and the love of God. You can get your strut back. You can swear your shoulders. You can lift your head. You will have a song in your heart that you can sing. The best in your life is yet to be because of God's amazing grace. That will heal you and give you a new beginning.

James 4; 17 – what is sin? To him, that knows it and not do it that is sin. Sin is cancer. Either you get rid of it, or it will get rid of you. Poor atheists spend their lives fighting God, and they do not even know if he exists. Can you imagine the frustration? I'm not bothered by redneck that lives like hell, and he knows it. Be concerned with a man or woman that goes to the house of God. Lives ruthless has a toxic tongue, they talk the talk, but they do not walk the walk. They cover the stench of their sin with their godless lives and there covered with grace. Be very careful here. Grace justifies the sinner. Greasy grace justifies sin.

Grace allows you to confess. Your sins and become a new creature in Christ. The only way you could be saved is by confessing your sins. Granting forgiveness in a person without demanding a change in conduct only makes the grace of God an accomplice to evil.

In the name of the Lord Jesus Christ, Heavenly Father, I ask you to cleanse me from all sins. I want to be restored to God the Father, I want to live like a king's child, I want the amazing grace of God. To heal my wounded soul, to heal my broken family, to remove the stain of sin from my foolish choices. Today I received that, in Jesus Christ the Lord's name amen.

The blessing; may the Lord keep you, and may the Lord make his face shine upon you. May the Lord be gracious unto you and give you his peace. But today, you experience the joy of the grace of God that heals. Do not be manipulated by people, circumstances, but just be obedient to the love of Christ. I give you peace that surpasses all understanding. In Jesus's name, we pray and say amen.

27 April 2019

DiAnnie wrote;

Hi my love, how are you? I hope you're okay, sorry for my delay for the last time. I have been so busy because I have to prepare for my trip and finalize papers to quit my job and travel. Oh yes..lol, you are Thomas, because I was angry! Why don't you think you should be Thomas when you ask your girl such a question? And you think I should be happy to say, my love? To be honest, I'm not hungry right now because I have forgiven you as usual. I just expressed myself in that sense because from your first message, I was angry, but in the end, I realized that you've asked for forgiveness, and I don't think.

I should be angry anymore. Do you think I like it when we do not seem to be on the same path or misunderstanding? No, I always want peace between us. I don't want us to ruin what we have started for all this time for any silly reason. You have forgotten, but I didn't because I was responding to the exact messages you wrote. Well, you think I was a missing action?

No, I was not absent action. I was busy and felt that I would get back to you when I have free time, so here I am writing you back, so Am I missing action? My Zorro thinks I have forgotten him! ..LOL. Do you say you still love me? Why's that? Did you not love me before? For me, I love you all the time until the end of time. No matter what you know, I have a forgiven heart for you. Do you think my mom will always defend you?

So you're afraid of me? Lol, she'll only do that when she thinks you're right, not when you're wrong. I know the mistake I made by writing from my friend's phone on another person's account could not be accepted readily, even if it was in my case. I told my friend about the error, and she said she wishes it didn't bring any issue between you and Thomas. She knows about you. It's the girl.

Do you think if I gave you a broken heart, would I be fine and happy? No, it would be as if I wasted my time and yours or some girl who is like the rest out there. I'm scared to death for us to lose one another. There are so many people, my friends, that I have to quit from because of us, and my mom would be so disappointed in me. There's so much involved apart from the love I have for you. Sure, I'll marry you. I'm not looking for a one-night stand from you. If it's what you want, I would be heartbroken as well! My love, you have done nothing wrong, and no need to ask for forgiveness.

You're forgiven no matter what. If you don't hear from me, it's not that I'm mad at you, I have been so busy till today. I'm sorry for my delay, okay. You're always on my mind, no matter my busy schedule or delay. Thanks for all the excellent bible stories and your sweet messages. We have so much in common to let each other go apart. Never think about that, okay. I'm yours, and you're mine forever. Have an excellent time, my love. I'll get some rest now. All my love and regards to you. Kisses and hugs from your girl and the one that truly loves you.

Thomas wrote;

Beautiful, how are you feeling today? I pray everything is going well and according to plan? And I pray for your mother, Anna, as well. Please let her know my prayers are with her. I can well imagine the both of you and the excitement you both feel about seeing one another and being with one another. You're my girl. You always be my girl. My precious treasure from the North country. And I realize this is very difficult for young ladies. As to not live your life in the rearview mirror. It's easy for me to do as a man. Because that's the way, I live my life. I am not looking in that rearview mirror, knowing that everything is okay right this very moment. Because that's all we have beautiful is the moment. Yesterday was history tomorrow is a mystery today is the present as well it's called a gift. And praying together, most will stay together. It's hard to pray with your significant other when one of the other is angry at the other one. In holy matrimony of marriage, God acknowledges both of you as one or two of you separate that will never be.

We have Christianity number one. And we have all the coincidental miracles I could've only came from God. Anyway, Brian and I have been busy. I am fixing this house. You are not going to believe today. We finally got so much progress done as far as looking back where we started. We are working faster with more efficiency, and it is coming together with great appreciation and love. I want to break out all the new blankets, sheets, towels, bedspreads, comforters, and rugs. I know it is going to blow my mind when I do that. And please do not let me coerce you or make you feel obligated. This is not what I want. I want emotional intimacy between the two of us as a couple. And maybe dreaming about our marriage was looking a little too far forward into the future.

Possibly we should stand back. From one another for a while. And if it's meant to be will come back to us. You know I love you. I'm in love with your soul. I carry you in my heart. And a significant part of the day, you consume my thoughts. However, I have been getting a lot of studying done with the Bible. This time has given me an excellent opportunity to show got my love.

And if we stop the communication, a relationship or friendship will die. Communication is what blood is to the body. If you run out of blood, you're going to die. And I would like to communicate on a gut level feeling with one another, without us getting angry at each other. Keep in mind that constant communication and forgiveness of one another continuously is one of the keys to a great marriage or relationship, as the case may be.

Communication between a husband and wife. And we are not married, and God willing, will be one day. Exactly what we think, how we feel, what we love, what we honor, what you hate, what you fear, what you hope for, what you believe in, what you're committed to, without fear of a long argument.

Sweetheart, have a good day, peace, and grace of the Lord be with you and your mother through Jesus Christ our Lord's name amen. Hugs and kisses from your Zorro

postscript; tomorrow, I will start with Bible sermons. I feel you will enjoy it because I have studied the Bible quite a bit and came up with some great stories today. And they are not stories. It is the accurate word of God. I love you, honey. Take care, have fun, and enjoy life. Please do not feel committed or pressured. These are not my intentions. Suppose you want me to stop communication completely. It will break my heart, but I will do it for you. All you have to do is block your emails from me.

28 April 2019

Thomas wrote;

Beautiful, I precious guardian angel from the North country, Worry means there is something you cannot have your way. And in reality, it's personal distrust. And irritation with God.

Matthew 6; 25-33 –25, therefore I say unto you. Take no thought of your life. What you shall eat or what you shall drink. Not yet your body. What you should put on. Is not life more than meat and the body more than clothing?26; behold the fowls of the air, for this sow not, Neither do they reap nor gather into barns. Yet your heavenly Father feeds them. Are you not better than them? 27; which of you, by taking thought, can add one cubit unto his stature? 28; And why take ye thought for raiment? Consider the lilies of the field, how they grow, they toil not, Neither do they spin. 29; and yet I say unto you That even Solomon in the whole his glory Was not arrayed like one of these. 30; wherefore, if God, so clothes the grass of the field, which today is and tomorrow is, Cast into the oven shall he not clothe you, oh ye of little faith? 31; therefore, take no thought, what shall we eat? Or, what shall we drink? How shall we be clothed? 32;(for all these things the Gentiles seek) For your heavenly Father knoweth That ye need all these things. Thirty-three but seek ye first the kingdom of God and all His righteousness; all these things shall be added to you.

My precious Guardian Angel, this is how I live my life. And I did not fully understand it until I just came across is biblical scriptures. And I thank God for showing me the way, and through his Holy Spirit, more shall be revealed. The things that you are thinking about right this very moment, God has already answered them. So, as usual, no stress, no worry, no fear. Okay? Everything is going to be okay. I ask you once before, Do you trust me? Do you have faith in me? The same unshakable belief that we both have for

God. I trust you. I have faith in you. What you say, you mean. This is why you are the Marine Corps wife of a sergeant of the United States Marine Corps. LOL :-) with great love for my soulmate. And Anna, your mother, who I have great reverence, respect, and passion for. The daughter that only God could have brought into my life to change my evil ways. Peace and grace of the Lord be with you and your mother through Jesus Christ the Lord's name amen. I love you, honey xoxo. You are my girl; I am your Zorro.

29 April 2019

DiAnnie wrote;

Hello honey, how are you today? I'm just anxious that everything gets on course to travel because I'm so impatient right now, and mom is also pressuring me to come over. Still, I must have everything in place before traveling, so it is not intentional even though there is a delay. Honey, I want you to understand that never think that I'm going to stop communicating with you I don't know why you panic about this. Honestly, I have no reason to stop sharing with you because I have a strong feeling for you, and it would break my heart when we don't communicate anymore.

Well, you think God will bless us and inform us that he's going to bless us? He does that with surprises! Miracles do not come with our expectations but when we least expect. He brought us across one another when we least expect and knew we needed each other at this moment in our lives. I love how you talk about the work on the house and all you have to do for both rooms. It makes me want to tell Mom for us to fly out to Arizona, lol. I know we have a few things to do before. It would be nice to get a few pictures of those things you got for the house, you're doing a great job with Brian, and I'm so proud of you guys. Sounds great about the news of meeting the property manager. I'll continue to pray for you for the best things to get in place concerning the property. I wish there weren't those in your family that do not think about themselves. If not, you would not be going through this financial situation, we all have our challenges, but we should know that God is our stronghold in all this and will undoubtedly take away. You make me have so much courage with all your lovely words and the word of God. I go through each and every message you send me because it's not easy ignoring your messages. I know you knew God when you were younger, but what surprises me is meeting your childhood character Zorro, and I didn't know that but started to call you Zorro!

I can't call this a coincidence, but it wouldn't happen if it weren't for God! Thanks so much for the prayers for mom and me. It means so much to us. Sounds nice that Samuel is coming over to help to do some work on your house. I guess he's still struggling with the depression caused by leaving his ex.. he needs someone to have him forget about his past. Do me a favor, don't talk about us to him till we get to Arizona.

The material things that we as humans want are only for our earthly lives. So know that as long you have the assurance that you can make heaven, then you're the wealthiest person alive, okay? Haha, you asked your questions and answered them! Lol, I was saying to myself when I read the first question like what the hell is he asking these and if I love him? Did you want to make me angry once again?

You know I love you very much, and there are no words to describe how much I love you. It is dangerous to tell a man that you love him. It's when he starts to behave silly.. but don't dare try that with me, Zorro.. you will be tied up all the time till you change. Sure, I'm looking forward to Mother's Day. It's a special day for a woman, not just for those who have kids.. lol when mom is here, and I'm saying this, she'll say hey you! You're not yet a mother so let's me enjoy my day!!!! You think you're silly. She's super in it lol also I have some silliness in me as well. So we have the same blood running in our veins, lol. And your sick sense of humor drives me crazy, lol. Enjoy the rest of your time, honey. I am here thinking of the man I love so much!

Thomas wrote;

Beautiful, my precious treasure from the North country, my scrumptious delight, my eloquent cuisine, a tasty little morsel. Smile with compassion love, and holding my wife, smiling again Precious, now think about this one. I have been in business almost all of my life. I know how to start a business. However, I have never been in the restaurant business. I had washed dishes when I was a kid at a very fancy restaurant called the village pub. Before that, I worked at a restaurant here in town called Baw's barbecue. Having always known that everyone needs to eat. I love that name. It is very catchy and could go national and even worldwide, similar to McDonald's.

Annie's, I would not even mention this to anyone. I feel the name is that catchy that someone else might use it. And I would not name its French cuisine. You will limit the audience. There may be people that do not like French people for some reason or do not like French food or do not like the name cuisine may sound too fancy. Personally, God knows how much I love French; otherwise, God would not have put my beautiful DiAnnie in my life. Or her mother, Anna. You ladies are all I think about, and I pray about the guardian angel that you are who has brought me this for spiritually through the Holy Spirit. God in Jesus Christ our Lord. I get so excited and happy every day just thinking about the two of us. And your mother, Anna, is right there in those thoughts.

This is only a suggestion, sweetheart, and I need your opinions. This is only a dream and an idea at this time, and everything could change, and it is all because of you. It is why I am even writing this letter. To the one I love. Now when your mother and yourself get to Arizona. Before we even talk about the restaurant or the name. And sweetheart DiAnnie you are in the restaurant business for a reason. LOL, I am smiling with Holy Spirit thoughts. More shall be revealed.

Realizing, of course, this is only a dream. If you do not have a plan, it cannot become a reality. So this is why we dream. And sometimes, they are God's thoughts. And the way this has come together, it only as came from God. Not mean that you are not your mother. Somebody prayed, somebody up there loves us. Your birthday, my Father's birthday? Our fathers? Zorro? Etc. etc. etc., and blab blah blah. LOL, smiling and dreaming, and thank you, God, for the thoughts.

I cannot stand lawyers; I cannot stand attorneys. Lawyers are only being groomed to become politicians. And I mainly do not like politicians. Lawyers started as a used-car salesmen. I never could stand a used car salesman. So who do I like the most between a used car salesman, a lawyer, or a politician? None of them. Possibly I would be impressed if they were on death row. LOL smiling. Sometimes we have to use them, though. The guy said I dislike lawyers. I happen to know one who has an office in San Francisco, Arizona, who represented me in the mediation. His first name is John, and I get a book that he gave me that he published called the Texas Rangers after I gave him copies of my two books.

First of all, get that name copyrighted so no one else can use it without being sued. And to do that legally, we would need a lawyer. Yuck.

You notice I don't laugh when I talk about lawyers. That's how much I dislike them. If I contacted John only with your permission first, sweetheart, this all has to do with what you think about what I am saying has any validity.? Like I mentioned before, your mother and yourself when you come to Arizona. In our kitchen, start cooking French Putin. I pray I spell that right. I've never had it in my life. It simply looks delightful. You don't mind if I put you to work and your mother as a slave in the kitchen, do you? LOL LOL, now you have me laughing. Can you hang me after dinner, okay? LOL, laughing with a big smile. But I was thinking it is doing some cooking and experimenting with cooking In our kitchen. I should say in your mother's kitchen and yours. Come up with some recipes.

And we have John the lawyer, yuck. Copyright the name, run the idea by him, and see how we can sell the name through a. chain of restaurants nationwide without doing anything other than the name in the recipe. Corporations, corporate leaders, and CEOs would love to invest in our interests and idea. Others have started just like this. We sit home. We orchestrate the ideas relay them to John. He gets in touch with corporations or stock investors who would be interested. And we could be multimillionaires overnight— just an idea. Do not jump up and down and count the pennies we do not have. LOL laughing now I can smile and laugh.

Keep in mind all the monies we should make together. We are going to tithe. 1/10 of whatever we make goes to God. Do I hear an amen? Smiling with joy that the abundance of blessings will come from heaven only if our intentions are honorable. You might run this by your mother, Anna, and see what she thinks. I would not run this by anybody other than that. By the way, beautiful my scrumptious petite tasty French cuisine from the North country.

I have not told Samuel about you and me. The only one that knows about you and me is Brian. You and I are top-secret. I must be honest with you. I did mention to my nephew Christopher today because he was telling me all about the insurance he got for the employees. I said I met a couple in the program and thought about coming to the United States for a few months, but they were concerned about getting medical while they were here. Because in North country it is social throughout the country healthcare.

And Christopher said the same thing every other American says about the taxes in North country. And that's all who knows about you and your mother—just Brian. Oh, I forgot, AT&T employees. And those criminals needed to Here something spiritual. It's miraculous in that I find ways of the Holy Spirit working through me to mention God in a way that the words just come from my mouth, not my head. I love you, honey. You're my girl. Please read this email carefully and let me know what you think. I need to know your feelings. These are only dreams, these are her only dreams, but they will not become a reality unless we dream first

Some guy call me so drunk he could not even talk. All he could do was mumble. It is a gentleman that works for my nephew. Thank God he has a wife and children to keep him home is a full-blown alcoholic, though. Beyond prayer, I believe, is a wet brain. I pray anyway.

Thomas wrote;

Beautiful, Guardian Angel treasure from the North country. I do realize and know for a fact without a doubt with my infinite wisdom, LOL smile. Is that you love me.

Did you feel by those questions of whether you love me? I'm not if you answer them correctly. LOL smiling, honey, I think you are going to be the tattletale wife. LOL laughing. You know you make me laugh hard when you are angry. LOL LOL laughing. And I have a feeling you would be just mad enough not to hesitate to grab the rope and tie me up. And for some reason, the thought of me laughing while you are performing your ritual. I cannot help myself but get a little turned on. This is why I'm not ready to be a preacher as of yet. LOL :-) we are going to have so much fun together. And for the life of me, I think you are going to be the tattletale wife and will not hesitate to tell your mother what I said to make you angry. And I'm going to make you mad in a way that your mother, Anna, will speak to us both, do not drag me into your little games, you children choose to play. LOL laughing and smiling. I just have a feeling it could end when I get tired of being tied up, significantly when the rope slipped around my neck and pulled to the ceiling until it turned purple. LOL laughing again, when am I going to get enough? I'm going to have to pray to God to remove this church, a defect of mine. However, I feel my wife will cure me faster than I can pray. LOL LOL

Please do not ever doubt for a moment without reservation that I know you love me. And I appreciate this beautiful young woman for living this good-looking gentleman. This God-fearing gentleman. Who also realizes that this guardian angel has been sent to me from heaven. Smile with great love. I am the lover of your soul through the grace of God. Jesus Christ, our Lord, went to the cross, and with his blood, we are saved and healed with his stripes. And we confess to Christ our Lord for the forgiveness of our sins.

And we forsake our sins. We have a grace that heals, for we are God-fearing children of God. You have taught me so much, beautiful. You have brought this Marine from the depths of hell to the gates of heaven. And for that, I pray to God for you daily and continuously growing on spiritual lines studying the word of God with righteous indignation. I am proud of you. And I love you.

Tomorrow, Tuesday, Brother Brian and I are going to set up our bedroom and take pictures. I'm excited and anxious. And I feel without a doubt you are going to like what you see. As I have mentioned before, this house will never be home until your mother, and yourself arrive.

Then we will go into your mother's bedroom and set everything up. And I'm interested to see which one is more appealing to you. I have a spiritual feeling that both bedrooms are going to be luxurious. Most certainly, anyone who enters into your mother's home and our home will know without a doubt. Those two extraordinary ladies reside here. With the Holy Spirit and the spiritual feeling, others will be in awe. Similar to entering the Sistine Chapel in Rome and seeing Michelangelo's works for the first time. Get the feeling as the hair on your arms stand up, and you know you are in the presence of the Holy Spirit. And there is more to do as I have mentioned before there is. Nothing more. Charming than a ladies touch. You are a mother. You have taken care of your mother, and for that, I am proud of you. You are Praying for two mothers to enter this humble abode, smiling with great appreciation and love. Peace and grace of the Lord be with you and your mother to Jesus Christ the Lord's name amen. I love you, honey hugs and kisses from your Zorro

PostScript; Income property and zoned commercial. It's just a thought right now we are thinking of putting it in a store. And possibly some kind of restaurant. I do believe a restaurant is French cuisine that your mother and yourself could operate. Everybody needs to eat. And it will drive hundreds of miles to eat the delicious French dishes your mother and yourself can prepare. This is only a dream right now. But it can be. Done. What do you think, sweetheart?

I just have a feeling that a little French restaurant that your mother and yourself could run. And only stay open possibly during the summer months and on weekends. Let me explain. Everybody in the San Francisco Bay Area needs to drive to the pacific ocean to the beaches.

There are only three roads, highways, but they are small and lead to the sea where we live. I never make it a point of going anywhere on the weekends on these highways. There are that many cars and people. Have you ever eaten at Dionne's French cuisine restaurant? And if you happen to say no, I have never eaten there. You are not the Who's Who of fine French cuisine. LOL, :-) :-) big. And You and your mother Anna, I'm sure you can come up with the original name for the restaurant. Keep in mind, sweetheart, these are only dreams right now, although they are obtainable. And this is only one of thousands and thousands of opportunities here. And they're always looking for a tax write-off or something to buy or shop. I can go on and on about this.

And that is a total tourist trap of art studios. And no good places to eat. There's nowhere to eat that I can think of that I could rave about being unique. This is only one opportunity, honey of thousands.

30 April 2019

DiAnnie wrote;

How is my Zorro doing? I hope your day is going great. Mine was busy as usual, but I think I do not have to complain or talk about it each time. It's all part of life. The more a person is determined to fight, the more things get easier. Being a hard-working person is something that has been a part of my life. My parents, especially my mom, made me a self-sufficient person. I know there's more left to achieve in life. I'm never overconfident because life is about hard work. How was work on the house yesterday? It seems like you guys had the busiest day yesterday! It is fun seeing men at work, lol. I realize you were in and out of the house writing to me and paying attention to those working, lol.

Sure, I believe what you say.. we're sure made for one another. If not, we wouldn't have flown so freely till today. There's so much connection between our families and us, and it can not be debated that we are not connected. It's all God's! Not us. It's only a blind person spiritually that wouldn't see things as we see them. I'm excited each time when I hear from you as well. It's always fun reading all your messages and those jokes make my day each time. You have a lot of great qualities! A fun guy steals the heart of a lady easily than someone who does not have any sense of humor. Have you observed that before? Anyway, it's a lady's secret.. lol.

I'm very appreciative. You're such a lovely person and one in a kind. I appreciate the love you have for me. I can not explain how much I love you, the love that we share is beyond human comprehension, and we can only be thankful for God bringing us together. Oh yeah, I wait eagerly for Mother's Day to show my mom how much I love her. I thank God for such a great mother she is to me. I pray each time for God's direction for this. I know God will work things out according to His plan. Keep me updated I'll continue to pray about this till everything falls in place.

Well, I do not worry like before. No one wants to worry, but when inevitable setbacks arise, it's not easy bearing it. God does not like when we worry. Our faith in Him is tested when we do, so you're right better to leave things in God's hands, and He will direct everything according to His will, mind you, it is easier said than done.. lol. Well, the questions you asked whether I loved you or not weren't going to be answered because I thought like it was repetition, and I know you were trying to pull my leg.. lol and you know what?

When you ever ask that you'll be tied up, sometimes I ask myself, why would you want to tie your Zorro, but then this Zorro has a sick sense of humor, and I just tied him up to heal that sick sense of humor, lol. Wow, your explanation of the location of where we'll live and the property not being far from the ocean and the idea of having a restaurant and you bringing that name up tells me you have a lot of ideas for a business. The proposed name is already driving me crazy lol it's a great combination. Do you remember you brought up the picture of me teaching French classes?

All these are great ideas, but when we come we will see how best we can arrange the pictures but believe me all these ideas are beautiful! Oh no, my love, you're okay. You didn't pressure me to bring these lovely ideas out. You're only thinking about the future and our survival. When we have children, there should be income coming in. I love those dreams. In the end, you're a farsighted individual, and I'm so proud of you! Annie's wow, it's one copy! And it'll drive Arizona crazy, lol. You're the most brilliant guy I ever know, honey. Haha ☺ I was wondering why are we going to kill everybody?

Then I just read the correction not to kill everybody but tell everyone lol I'm laughing so hard. You make me laugh so hard. Tu est mon Zorro! Thanks for all the sweet messages. My love, you always bring a smile to me.

I am looking forward to hearing from you. All my love and regards and sweet kisses to you.😘 ♥ ♥.

Thomas wrote;

Beautiful, Guardian Angel scrumptious delight God's treasure from the North country. I love adding and mixing these words up. I love the word treasure, Guardian Angel, and North country, but most importantly, I love the phrase, God. And all these add up to DiAnnie, my girl. Sweetheart, I have hundreds of ideas for businesses. God willing, you will never work for anybody again only unless you care for yourself. I feel you would always be happier working for yourself, helping others, and being blessed abundantly from heaven. Then to be a slave and work for someone else. The only reason I say that is because you had mentioned to me that you felt like a slave from your work. Those things stick in my mind. And the last thing on earth is my guardian angel feeling like she is a slave.

Thank God was spiritual discernment knowing the difference between right and wrong sometimes. LOL smile that's why my guardian angel DiAnnie reminds me from time to time that I do not always see the difference between right and wrong. LOL laughing hard but truthfully. Can you imagine us having this conversation if we had just met for the first time?

It was interesting, and I cannot say I did not have fun because I was on a journey with my girl. You're right there with me. And that's what kept me from pulling over and askinG Rick to go and buy me a candy bar while I drove off and left him there. LOL smile

Another biblical scripture and I'm glad the Holy Spirit working through me thought of that name for the restaurant pretty cool. I like it. So you think it's in the title? It came from God. Thank him. I'm not that smart, beautiful.

I just use the brains God gave me. And I know about working hard. I'm doing something 24 seven, usually taking up most of your time reading what I'm thinking about. LOL, smile, and our children are going to know more than we will. Have to go right now, right back later. Love you

Thomas wrote;

Beautiful, delicious guardian angel residing temporarily on this earth as a treasure in the North country. Computer all the software companies Yahoo Google every computer industry or software industry you can imagine is within a 40. mile radius from where we live. And of course, they are building mansions all around us, and I mean huge. We are right in the middle as well as the movie stars and singers in all the sports athletes. And I do not say this to impress you or to pressure you. I'm only honest.

Sweetheart, They are building this huge, and I do mean colossal mansion that overlooks the ocean and overlooks the beautiful valley leading up to our home. Like 40 horse stalls. It is so big that I can even comprehend or begin to tell you what is there, just what I have heard. Although driving up stage Road one the little One Mile Rd. going from the little town of San Gregorio, Arizona, a shortcut to half-moon bay Arizona you can get a glimpse of it. And they have been building on this estate for one year now and still building. It turns out. They have a young son, teenager, or in his mid-20s. They found him hanging from a tree with the needle stuck in his arm three days ago. I'm not saying the money contributed, and I do not know anything about the details—just small-town gossip. I will keep you informed on the truth.

Over the last year, sweetheart, you and I know for fact money could have never bought our love. We love each other freely, and we have that no one faith that God brought us together to experience the love that has no beginning and no ending that either of us has not known as of yet. More is being revealed to us through this love as we are both experiencing.

Please, honey, let me know what you think of the pictures in our bedroom? Our bedroom is far larger than the images portray. Brian and I are not photographers. LOL, smile by any stretch of the imagination. Double LOL and a big smile. Brother Brian's toenails were getting so long that I saw him sitting on the ground the other day scratching behind his ears with his toenails. LOL, smile only kidding, I think.

About the email as I ended abruptly. And this is in the Bible. Let us portray a scenario I'm not saying you specifically when I say this, okay? Let me talk about a guy named Bob. He will be the fictitious character in this short story. Bob had an excellent idea for the name of a restaurant that he wanted to run and operate. Bob has been a waiter in a restaurant for quite some time and is a hard worker. Giving notice and quitting his job and moving on to a dream that just came to him. Bob thought of this great name called "Bob's burgers" for fast food type restaurant and a drive-through.

He could get his many people in and out as possible because it was in a good location. And Bob even thought about what he was going to prepare and serve for. this restaurant and how he was going to run it. Then, suddenly, something came up in Bob's life and changed his destiny and his fate in another direction. So Bob let it go and continue living his life. Then a friend of Bob's named Earl they were talking one day. And it seemed her role wanted to start a fast-food restaurant and had the same idea Bob did. Now Bob knew that if he told Earl about him having the same idea. And never told Earl anything about his vision. And did not offer any information to Earl to help him start his own business. That is similar to the ninth commandment in the eighth commandment. The eighth commandment, "thou shalt not steal," the ninth commandment "shalt not bear false witness against thy neighbor." and especially the 10th commandment. "Thou shalt not covet thy neighbor's wife man goods or anything of the neighbors."

Withholding information from others When you know for a fact they can use it to be beneficial to them is a sin. I know this from personal experience, sweetheart I put this one to the test. It's been a few years back. I always have great ideas, and they are not my ideas. They are God's ideas, and I thank God for these ideas that work through the Holy Spirit to help others.

Let me put it in short form, "as my dad used to say" "if you do good things, good things will happen. If you do bad things, bad things will happen". It's that simple. But you know me, Mr. blabbermouth. LOL smile sometimes I forget who I am, or should I say I forget who I have my mouth talking to. My beautiful scrumptious lovely gorgeous precious delightful delectable exquisitely elegant to the pallet. My scrumptious guardian angel from the North country I treasure so vastly that I have not yet experienced it, and I give great compliments and prayer and love to the chef, "God our father."

I may not keep my mouth off you this evening. I'm so excited about this whole house. The bar over the bed, I feel I should make that disappear before you, and your mother should arrive. LOL :-) because it is the perfect location to loop the rope through and pull me to the ceiling and have me blend in with the bedroom decor, Purple. LOL, smiling, laughing hard, big smile. And the concrete block under the bed. LOL, a smile you could tie that around my ankle and drag me out into the septic tank and push me in. LOL smiling. See, I give you more great ideas. And I'm not sure if I will be thankful for these ideas that I am planting in your sweet little mind.

I'm going to take a break, honey, and lay down for a while. I certainly wish we were together to lay here with me or with good legs together. Let us put it that way. You realize over the last year. I have been crucifying my old self. To make a life with a guardian angel I have never met, but spiritually I know.? Because God loves you, and God loves me, and God loved your mother, and that's our family. Brian is the Butler, the gofer, the dishwasher, the housecleaner, the house mouse, the redheaded stepchild that we will beat occasionally. The slave that's the word I was looking for. LOL, a smile.

I'm only kidding God. Realizing none of this work would be accomplished if it were not for Brian. Of course, with my adult supervision, this dream is becoming a reality.

Now I'm just thinking, sweetheart. Do not get angry with me, please. It's only a suggestion. If you even for a minute get mad, it will keep me from being honest with you. And I never want to be dishonest with you. Now that being said and I pray till you agree. We met about I put it personally 15 January 2018. Your birthday is my dad's birthday. And God chose the time when it was just right for two of God's elect to be brought together for a very special reason.

The ideas and the blessings and abundance will come from God so rapidly we are both not going to be able to believe it, working, thinking about me, me thinking about you. You know what beautiful forget what I said above, and I should erase it. If I had any brains, I would. It was the joy of living your life and the joy of us getting to know one another. This is what this is all about. I'm trying to out-think God. Very very dangerous. Please pray for me and have your mother pray for my period.

The above paragraph is none of my business. LOL, being tied up and hanging from the bedroom bar dragged out into the yard with the block of concrete tied around my leg. First of all, my wife DiAnnie is preparing me a great big jar of greemie grimy golfer guts, mutilated monkey meat, saturated chicken feet, making a delicious pate, oh I almost forgot the tremendous big Glass of all-purpose porpoise puss, with crushed ice and umbrella with a straw. Of course. LOL smiling anyway, honey, pay no attention to me. If I said anything to have offended you once again, can you please forgive me? When I say, can you please forgive me? I'm usually guilty of doing or saying something wrong—a small smile. I love you, honey, peace, and grace of the Lord be with you and your mother to Jesus Christ the Lord's name amen, and please tell Anna my prayers are with her, and I pray for her happiness and safety. And look forward to the time, God willing, when Anna should arrive in Arizona. Hugs and kisses from your Zorro

Thomas wrote;

Beautiful, How are you feeling today, sweetheart? Should I ask you whether you love me or not, depending on whether you get the right answer? LOL LOL, smile laughing. One thing you do is make me laugh, sweetheart. I know how to make you tie me up. LOL, smile, smile. Do not be the tattletale wife and squealed to your mother on me. LOL smiling. I will make it look like it's all your fault. I would tell Anna. Anna, do you know what DiAnnie did? And she will say what? And I will say to her while I was taking a nice Jacuzzi enjoying myself and relaxing. Annie pushed my head underwater and would not let me up for air. And then she dared to do it again. Finally, I threatened DiAnnie and told her that I would tell her mother, Anna, about her behavior. LOL :-) have a good day. Sweetheart, tie me up pulled the noose around my neck up and down a few times, untying me, and let's make love. Romantically passionately, I'm going to love you as you have never been loved because I have never loved a whim going to love you. I keep getting sidetracked. I have these romantic dreams getting huge. And I'm still not sure if it's the right thing to give it to you at once. I have to quit talking like this. I'm getting huge just thinking about the two of us together.

And since I have never experienced this a little before, only God knows. I certainly believe we do not. Anyway, those pictures, sweetheart. I just jumped out of the shower and was soaking wet. I'm not sure if I shaved close enough. I still work out every day for two or three hours, getting better at walking. My arm is getting huge, my legs are getting muscular, and I pray. I have to start fasting more often in prayer. I pray a lot and thank God for a lot, but fasting makes all the difference in the world. I love you, honey, I love you,

I love you, honey. I pray to God you are getting rest. I feel you are a. workaholic, similar to how I am now in a different way. And this is why we are so much alike. There was a time when I spent the greater my assets became, although I missed the most important thing in life that was free. Love. The million-dollar love of God. Reading these words, I praise you for taking the time.

You may not realize it. Thomas occasionally lacks the sensitivity of my girl DiAnnie. So if I say something and there are possibly two different interpretations for the meaning. And one makes you angry or upset. I met the other one. LOL, smile not too funny old time. and I mentioned to you repeatedly on occasion.

That because I am a man, I am going to hurt your feelings. And once again, please do not hesitate to let me know when I do, for it is only then that I can change and become a. better person, and the one that you have made me, and for that, I thank God for you in my life, and I am very proud of you. And I praise you for continuously forgiving me. Once again, I would like to have that opportunity, God willing, to praise you publicly when we are together and in public.

Simply by stating God's love has no beginning, God's love has no end, and my wife DiAnnie and I are learning to tap into that love, and so far, we have experienced heaven on earth together. Just that statement, sweetheart, people stop their conversations whatever they are doing, and it is the silence of God. Everyone that hears that statement listens attentively without reservation.

Time is like spokes through a keyhole. Less than a vapor, according to the Bible. God's gift to us is his life. What we do with his life is our gift to God. And I thank God for you in my life, my precious Guardian Angel. With unshakable faith is no doubt in my mind that through God's grace, you have been a miracle and a guardian angel sent into my life. And there are times from time to time. I forget that. And start talking to you like you are just a mortal. Instead of a child of God. I do not pray as often as I would like to. Although sending you emails as I do continuously having got on my mind and thanking him profusely for such a beautiful young Guardian Angel that has crossed my path. This is why when we first met, and you sent that long email, I knew in my heart at that very moment. That you were a guardian angel. I remember saying to God. "God, are you kidding me"? "as I looked up into the heavens."You know the intelligent wisdom of an angel. Created a little higher than men.

Without the warm, gentle romantic intimacy of touch. Without the warm, soft romantic whispers of communication, love with your wife is nothing more than domestic rape. love is the grace from God between a man and a woman. There's far more to God's love than a man just wanting love with his wife. ladies want spiritual intimacy. They want a man that will pray with them regularly.

Matthew 18; 19 –Again, I Say unto you.If two of you shall agree on earth. As touching anything that they shall ask, It shall be done for them of my Father which is in heaven. every husband and wife as a God-given gift to pray for their children for their jobs for the business and God will give it unto them. But they must ask first through prayer. The thing I know will work with the unshakable faith in God and Jesus Christ our

Lord is the power of prayer. This, my beautiful Guardian Angel, is missing between the two of us from a direct spiritual standpoint.

I asked for you and your mother's prayers quite often. And the power of prayer, God knows our thoughts are words what we do and fail to do. There is nothing he does not know about us. But that awesome powerful Holy Spirit working through a husband and wife together is the most awesome prayer that any two people can pray together with love for God. I would love just to hold your hands bow our heads, and let us pray together.

Please, honey, as the love I have for you and our small family and as the Godhead of the family, I love this family as Jesus Christ our Lord loves the church, and the positive power of love, let me say this prayer for us please four blessings in abundance in the security.

I realize you are reading these words, and this means we are saying the prayer together. God out Father with all power of heaven and earth before you and in Jesus Christ our Lord's name, my wife DiAnnie would like to pray this prayer together, let me communicate the power of Jesus Christ with my wife, from this day forward in my words and my action let me communicate the love of Jesus Christ to my wife to my wife's mother Anna and to our children from this day forward Christ is Lord of my life and Lord of my home and Lord of my marriage.

May the Lord bless our family with the Lord and keep our family, make the Lord's light shine upon our family, and may the Lord be gracious unto our family, and may the Holy Spirit give this family strength to obey the word of God. That our family may live in our home that these be the days of heaven on earth, may peace rule our hearts and minds. And that our children and our children's children may know the joy of the Lord That makes them rich and with no sorrow. this my wife DiAnnie and I pray with her mother Anna through Jesus Christ the Lord's name amen

God's love revealed through this romantic dimension of love

To be continued…

CHAPTER 6

Romantic Love, God's Love

You know you're in love when the hardest thing to do is say goodbye. If you love someone, tell them because hearts are often broken by words left unspoken. Alter your attitude, and you can alter your life. I pray from my heart, with love, that the forgiveness I ask is God's will. I am the light; he who follows me will never be in darkness...I Love You, Jesus Christ!

Ephesian 3:20, Concentrate on the first sentence. *"The will of God will never take you where the Grace of God will not protect you."* Something Goodwill happens to you today. Something that you have been waiting to hear. That is my prayer for you today.

For the souls who never thought that God could or would work in our lives, those who pray together stay together. I'm a Christian, and only through the Grace of God am I blessed for that.

Perfection is a set-up for disappointment. This is not the Garden of Eden; everything happens for a reason; giving and receiving is a two-way street. Proverbs 6:16-19, "There are six things the LORD hates, seven that are detestable to him. Haughty eyes, a lying tongue, hands that shed innocent blood, a heart that devises wicked schemes, feet that are quick to rush into evil, a false witness who pours out lies, and a man who stirs up dissension; among brothers."

From every human being, there rises a light that reaches straight to heaven, and when two souls that are destined to find each other together, their streams of light flowed together, and a single brighter light goes forth from there. United being. You were born together, and together you shall be forever.

That is God...he talks to us through the Holy Spirit. It is not how much you know but what you can do that count. God can do for us what we cannot do for ourselves.

I've brought souls through hell with me. God's not done with me yet. I've got a past reckoning to make amends to all those unfortunate souls I've brought through hell with me, and I feel that I have the destiny to rectify. Revelation 3:3, *"Remember, therefore, what you have received and heard; obey it, and repent. But if you do not wake up, I will come like a thief, and you will not know at what time I will come to you."*

FACT-ladies think with both sides of their brain. Over time women have learned to develop that intuitive intelligence as a survival tactic to protect their children and themselves. In our younger years, the male and a female are likely to be controlling and egotistical and not understand the true foundation of a relationship. In our younger years, women seem always to keep a scorecard on every negative thing that a man has done to hurt their relationship. On the other hand, a man looks at the past with an immature way of looking at all the fun things that happened in a relationship.

We must always remain faithful and trust one another with an unshakable faith in God, pray together that we will stay together. I store my riches in heaven.

In my eyes, she is the only woman in the world. This is if we are equally yoked through Grace. "And you shall be together even in the silent memory of God. Honor yourself. When you hold yourself high with integrity and self- respect and never compromise your values, you can trust each other. It is the basis for everything else that defines your life and your marriage. Honor each other. Do not hesitate to see more in each other than what is presented at face value. Look deep. People tend to live up to our expectations of them.

Listen to each other. What you give your attention to grows. It does not matter if it is a plant, a bank account, your marriage, or your children. Look at the solution and not at the problem. When you focus on the solution, ideas and opportunities will present themselves in unusual and magical ways. This is the most little-known and most influential commandment of all, surrender your will to God.

What chance will you take that there is no God? If you believe that only a six-foot hole awaits you at the end, now that would be depression.

We create our destiny; if that is what you believe, that is where you are going. What a grim thought, not a joyous life to look forward to. 1 million years from now your soul will be one of two places, "heaven or hell". And the brevity of life we have your on this earth our choices will determine our eternal destiny.

Will you take the chance that you have no faith in God, Jesus, the Holy Spirit, the Bible, Angels, Saints, the Prophets, Heaven, The Pit of Hell, Judgement, Miracles, Eternity, Christianity, Sins of the Flesh, or Lucifer? It is the year 2021, the year of our Lord Jesus Christ. Not the Dalai Lama, not Mohammed, not Bugs Bunny, or the tooth fairy. The agnostics, atheists, secular humanists, anti-Semitism, when they acknowledge the date of their birth or any other date. They are referring to the year of our Lord. Hypocrites at their finest.

I am just driving along with God as my copilot, picking up lost souls one at a time, sometimes consecutively. God willing, this is what I pray. When we are gifted with grace and understand where we came from, who we have become, and comprehend and understand our spiritual purpose, this is due to the total surrender of our will to God.

And God willing, we will help others to lighten their loads every chance we have. I write from the heart and soul, letting the spirit of God flow through me because it brings me joy to my undiscovered dreams. I humble myself before God and give Him thanks for my appreciation of understanding, "Let there be few spaces in our togetherness and let the winds of the heavens dance between us. Love one another but make not a burden of love: It is quiet when the spirit moves you; it will be well worth the adventure if you decide to venture into the dream one day.

Two just meetings are barely touching the father to spirit concurrently. Is this a miracle, happy, joyous, and free? Or is it cunning, powerful, and baffling? I pray because Jesus wept. You want we should be one with God with each other, and can you feel my precious spirit, spending eternity with never-ending growth is of biblical proportion, go with that woman intuition and know that it's for real. Together we will never want; as long as we pray together, we will stay together.

And growing together in love with you we have never experienced. Beyond my comprehension, I'm not sure what love is, not sure if you have ever known love before until the word you put down our they have a love of the Holy Spirit behind them? Fifteen years have been looking for you and praying for you, and only God knew before we did.

Touching each other, two spirits greeting, trying to carry it further, you are one, and I am another. We should be one with God with each other You can feel my sweet spirit; will you likely have always wanted to be loved and know love come and spend eternity with me? are you inspired through holy love? We have not even talked on the telephone or video chat, and then I'm curious about the spiritual love that is why?

Your convenience and consensual spirit have to work for you to feel that only God should desire and love the Holy Spirit and Jesus Christ.

You can feel my presence of spirit, only lacking the knowing and courage. Are you willing and feeling that infinite powerful love growing while we're here? The whole world is turning; we should be one fulfilling our gracious love together; waiting is a waste of life because you're worth it. Why are you worth it?

Because my path is leading to heaven and reading prophecy, Jesus Christ will come; after Israel became a nation in 1948, God endowed man with threescore and ten years of life. This is explained in Jesus Christ's parable of the fig tree. God will come like a thief in the night we know not when the first time Jesus came as a lamb this time he was becoming a roaring lion looking at society there will be plenty of firewood for the lake of fire.

We are miracles only from the grace of God's love for us, and 97% of the people do not even turn a page in the Bible or know God. I know one thing if and when you decide that we get together, I will love you like no other, and we will know love together and what happens and what happens in our sensual sexual love is between God yourself and I, and it will be all good. You're a lovely lady with lots of insight. Do know that I can teach you, and growing together, you can teach me.

The key to love is trust. Though dark doubts lay in hollow thoughts, they must shine brightly on were thoughts with a reassuring confidence that supports fear with faith. Understanding, the ability to comprehend not only the unspoken word but these unspoken gestures, the little things that may be too much by themselves.

Love is friendship that has caught fire. It is quite understanding, confidence, sharing, and forgiving. It is loyalty through formal and inopportune times. It settles for nothing less than perfection and makes allowances for human weaknesses. Love is content with the present, hopes for the future, and does not brood over the past. It is a day in, day out, a chronicle of irritations, problems, compromises, minor disappointments, significant victories, and working toward a common goal. If you have love in your life, it can make up for many things you lack. If you do not have it, no matter what else there is, it is not enough.

The key to love is inside us all, it takes time and patience to unlock all the mysteries that will take you to your destinations and demands much work, but the rewards are more than worth the effort. May the gracious Lord watch over you as you grow in love? May He bless your home with peace that surpasses understanding? May he crown your work with success and fulfillment? May you always be thankful for every blessing, grand and small. To love and be loved is the greatest joy on this earth. If you are rooted in love, every season brings new growth.

Matthew 6:20-21. *"Store up riches… in heaven… for your heart will always be where your riches are."* I refuse to have a detrimental second, I thoroughly insist on enjoying life, and I do not take myself too seriously. I try not to let people, places, or things, including myself, rent space in my head. No drama. God has me right where I need to be.

Forgiveness, to accept each other's faults and pardon mistakes Without forgetting, remembering what you learn from them. Sharing, facing your trusty fortunes, as well as the damage, together. Both conquering problems and forever searching for ways to create your happiness and giving, without thought of return but with the hope of love and a sincere smile! And by giving in, but never giving up. Respect, realizing that you are two separate people with different personalities, that you do not belong to each other, but that you belong and share a mutual bond with God.

Thou shall lighten up and often laugh, especially at yourself.

What I expect in my best friend is a soulmate that believes in God and Jesus, the Bible, Saints, Angels, Prophets, Miracles, Prayer, Faith, Heaven and Hell, and Judgment. The person I care about who is willing to surrender their will to God and pray together unconditionally will stay together. Two souls must work together and financially be not a burden to the other but an asset.

This is not an independent relationship; it is helping, caring, loving nurturing, trusting, and this integrity will give all relationships the best. Two souls are to come together as one; the bond must be God's and beyond our comprehension.

I am having devoted my life to God and service. Although I remained open, and I know I cannot be selfish, I need a soulmate that will bond tightly with me and make us both as one, like a hand in glove. When it works, it is advantageous to the moment, but it takes away from that moment if it does not work. I feel you will have to convince me, in some miraculous grace from

God, and with the knowledge and wisdom that can only come from God. Us getting together is just short of being a colossal miracle, in my mind's eye.

My love for God, Jesus Christ, and the Holy Spirit satisfies my being. At the time, I have no clue what the next five minutes will be like; I'm not there yet. There is something of Biblical proportion on the horizon, please, God gave you a brain to use.

We are talking about our soul's destination for eternity. Help others and pray hard; God did not stutter; pray hard. Please, time is short; time is like parachuting off the edge of a dime laying flat.

Spiritually, a woman and a man should be equally yoked. When we learn to share, each of us becomes a Spirit in that new world.

Always broke, although mostly helping the lesser than thou. Live on faith, and it is unshakeable for years, as God has provided without flaw.

Have powerful dreams and goals—for yourself, each other, and the marriage. It would help if you had dreams to keep you genuinely alive and vital. They allow you to create passion; for life and each other.

Say "Thank you" every day. Every day, find a way to show appreciation to people you love and people who give you service. This also includes clerks, salespeople, wait staff, people who hold doors open, people who let you in traffic, etc. "Thank you" is a universal currency that pays BIG dividends.

Say "I Love You" to each other at least once a day! This is another way to say, "Thank you." Use both phrases. They multiply each other by at least ten! Do little things for each other, and you multiply the effect by one hundred! Never go to bed angry with each other because talking it out will save you time, energy, and mistakes the next day.

At the end of this journey, God willing, fall on my face at the feet of God and give thanks and praise to God. Through Jesus Christ our Lord's name, God's only begotten Son, born of the Virgin Mary, begotten not made, of the Holy Spirit.

No one owns anything; we came into this world with nothing, leaving the same way. And knowing the fact that I am a Christian and my faith is unshakable, I have a happy, joyous, and free life devoted to God and service. We are only caretakers of the land, the short time that we are here. The faith and all my riches are stored in heaven and not of this earth or the materialistic world.

Pray to God to send me lost souls. God willing, I can learn and help one at a time. There are times they come all day long or call consecutively. They have many visitors, have an open-door policy, and never lock my door.

The best way to determine what God wants for you in your relationship life is to seek Him. Pray to God for wisdom concerning your marriage. The only way to determine if you're making the right choice is by aligning yourself with the One who created you. Only then can you understand what God wants for you. No one else can tell you what is best for you than God through the power of the Holy Spirit.

Love knows no age; While people who date only people much younger or older than them owe no one an explanation, it may be helpful to understand the underlying reason.

"Then he (Boaz) said, 'May you be blessed of the LORD, my daughter. You have shown your last kindness to be better than the first by not going after young men, whether poor or rich" (Ruth 3:10). In searching the Bible for documented marriages, we don't find any that can sway us in an accurate direction or give us an idea of what God may be leading us to.

The only warning regarding age in marriage is to avoid marrying someone young for lustful purposes and avoid marrying someone older for money.

Follow this love as it blossoms

Continued with passion, romance
Premeditated murder, rape, and drama

Printed in the United States
by Baker & Taylor Publisher Services